ON

Britaines Ile
and tru pourfile.

warke   34

LITERARY LONDON

LITERARY LONDON

Andrew Davies

ST. MARTIN'S PRESS
NEW YORK

Library of Congress Cataloging-in-Publication Data

Davies, Andrew.
       Literary London.

       Includes index.
       1. Literary landmarks—England—London.   2. Walking—
England—London.   3. Authors, English—Homes and haunts
—England—London.   4. English literature—England—London—
History and criticism.   5. London (England)—Description.   6. London
(England)—Intellectual life.   I. Title.
PR110.L6D38   1989   914.21'04858   88-30601
ISBN 0-312-02600-5

First published in Great Britain by Macmillan London Limited.

First U.S. Edition

10 9 8 7 6 5 4 3 2 1

Endpapers: Detail from a seventeenth-century panorama of the City of London by Wenceslas Hollar, reproduced by permission of the Museum of London.

'To the Reader'

And I wish the reader also to take notice, that in writing of it [this book] I have made myself a recreation of a recreation; and that it might prove so to him, and not read dull and tediously, I have in several places mixed, not any scurrility, but some innocent, harmless mirth, of which, if thou be a severe, sour-complexioned man, then I here disallow thee to be a competent judge . . . .

IZAAK WALTON, *The Compleat Angler*, 5th edition (1676)

Contents

Acknowledgments

Many thanks to my adult education classes at Friday Hill House in Chingford and particularly to my London University Extra-Mural class at Brentwood which I have been taking for the last five years. They have certainly kept me on my toes! I have also much enjoyed taking people on walks around London three or four times a week, notably the groups from Friday Hill House, Brentwood and the Town and Around Club.

Thanks, too, to Adam Sisman for commissioning this book and for being such an enthusiastic editor; and to Fred Martin and Fran Hazelton for being such inspirations. As always, the support of my parents has been unstinting.

My biggest debts are to Ann Rossiter, who read through the early drafts of *Literary London* and who proceeded to criticise, alter, cut out, approve and improve. I am very grateful to her, and to my wife Jean, who did all this, too, as well as having the additional burden of living with this book as it was being researched and written. This book is for her.

February 1988   ANDREW DAVIES

Introduction

In his autobiography *Memory Hold-the-Door* (1940), John Buchan recalls his first visit to London at the end of the nineteenth century and the way in which the capital slowly wove a spell around him: 'Behind all the dirt and gloom there was a wonderful cosiness, and every street corner was peopled by ghosts from literature and history.' The aim of this book is to try to put some flesh on Buchan's ghosts.

When I first began to research the topic of literary London I quickly built up piles of file cards, full of detailed information and quotations but lacking in human interest. First drafts of chapters were little more than a rather boring catalogue of names and addresses, conveying nothing of the atmosphere or excitement which such a subject needs and deserves. I then came across a lecture given by Robert Graves (printed in *The Crane Bag*, 1969) in which he declared that 'The craft of writing good English is based on a single principle: never to lose the reader's attention'. Whereupon I decided that library research needed to be combined with some 'street reconnaissance' – a mixture of walks and talks familiar to those who attend my London history classes. I hope therefore that *Literary London* will be enjoyed both by the person who wants to go out and explore London on foot and by the armchair reader.

I realised, too, that I would have to concentrate on the centre of London in order to do justice to what is an almost inexhaustible subject. I have therefore focused on what is normally known as 'inner London', with the addition of Hampstead and Highgate, without which no book on literary London would be complete.

The next question, of course, was who to put in and who to leave out? There were the obvious choices, such as Pepys, Dickens and Orwell, yet I was determined to include not only novelists and poets but also journalists, diarists, librarians and historians. I also decided not to stick to any arbitrary 'Great

Tradition', and thus readers will find Edgar Wallace, P. G. Wodehouse and C. S. Forester alongside Byron, Keats and Milton. Clearly a book of this size can only be a selection from the mountain of available material, concentrating in any case on British writers. Foreign visitors and observers deserve a volume to themselves. However, I think that a glance at the index does show that quite a number of writers have been covered here, always bearing in mind that I was writing a book to be read and not compiling a catalogue. Selection was also necessary when dealing with the lives of the writers themselves. Boswell in his biography of Samuel Johnson lists the doctor's sixteen London residences, and Charles Dickens during the course of his life had about twenty London addresses. Few will be interested in them all, and I have therefore concentrated mostly on those which are still standing – for example, Johnson's House in Gough Square and Dickens House in Doughty Street.

The chapters are written in order to suggest the 'feel' of each area, emphasising its social history. There is a mixture of fact and fiction, although both are clearly identified. Some writers appear in several sections. Although each chapter is entirely self-contained, I have tried not to repeat any stories or major pieces of information. This means that before anyone feels disappointed that a story about, say, Pepys is not in the Tower Hill section he should first look at the index. To give an example: Kenneth Grahame, creator of *The Wind in the Willows*, worked for many years at the Bank of England, and his career there is dealt with in 'Around the Bank'; he lived in Kensington and began the book there, covered in the 'Kensington' chapter; the book itself is mentioned in the pages on the Thames in 'Coming and Going'. Most books on London offer neither notes nor a reading list, an omission which may not matter to the general reader but irritates the critic, the academic or anyone wanting to do more research on a subject. I have included a short essay on further reading together with notes which detail sources and the material that I have used. Often it is clear in the text where a particular quotation comes from. I hope this will please everyone!

One final paragraph. Researching, writing and talking about this book has given me enormous pleasure. I love books, and my home is crammed with them. But books are not the be-all and end-all. Karl Marx once wrote that 'books are my slaves, they must do as I will'. When his wife Jane died, Thomas Carlyle wrote that 'I have no book a thousandth-part so beautiful as thou'. Crabby and irritable Carlyle may often have been, but he was right: some things in life are more important than books.

Around the Bank

Ever since the Roman historian Tacitus, writing in AD 60, described London as being 'filled with traders', the City and commerce have been inseparably linked. The Bank of England, the Royal Exchange, the Stock Exchange – the 'square mile' is the heart of the financial world. One or two writers, whose business skills matched their writing talents, might well have made pots of money if they had forsaken the writing-desk for the counting-house. One name which springs to mind is that of Charles Dickens, the first author to demand and receive royalties rather than to sell his copyright for a lump sum as was then the convention.[1] Anthony Trollope was another man of letters with a decidedly businesslike manner, most obviously seen in his autobiography where he carefully noted down the sums gained from each of his books, totalling in all £68,959 17s 5d.[2] Often, however, the literary mind has tended to dismiss all talk and thought of money as rather unseemly. A. A. Milne, for example, in the introduction to his dramatised version of Kenneth Grahame's *The Wind in the Willows* muses on the wonder of Grahame's having worked for the Bank of England: 'Reading these delicately lovely visions of childhood, you might have wondered that he could be mixed up with anything so unlovely as a Bank; and it may be presumed at the Bank an equal surprise was felt that such a responsible official could be mixed up with beauty.

Be that as it may, several writers have indeed been mixed up with the City. Charles Lamb was employed by the East India Company in Leadenhall Street between 1792 and 1825 even though, in his own words, he had 'an incapacity for business'.[3] John Stuart Mill was a later employee at the same institution. Kenneth Grahame joined the Bank of England as a clerk in 1879, becoming Secretary of the Bank between 1898 and 1908. Another City clerk of the same vintage was Arthur Henry Sarsfield Ward, who later, under the pseudonym Sax Rohmer, alerted the reading public to the existence of Dr Fu Manchu and the 'Yellow Peril' threatening to spread out of Limehouse. P. G. Wodehouse worked at the London branch of the Hong Kong and Shanghai Bank in Lombard Street between 1900 and 1902. He used to run to work all the way from his lodgings in Chelsea, worried about losing his Christmas bonus if he was late too often: 'One of the great sights in the City in the years 1901–2 was me rounding into the straight with my coat-tails flying and my feet going pitter pitter pat and just making it across the threshold while thousands cheered. It kept me in superb condition, and gave me a rare appetite for the daily roll and butter.'[4] It is more difficult to imagine T. S. Eliot sprinting to Lloyds in Lombard Street where he was employed from 1917 until 1925. Ian Fleming spent six years in the City in the 1930s.

What did this mixed bunch think of their experiences in the City? Charles Lamb confessed to ambivalent feelings. In his essay 'The Superannuated Man' he dwells on the youthful shock of taking up his position: 'Melancholy was the transition at fourteen from the abundant playtime, and the frequently intervening vacations of schooldays to the eight, nine, and sometimes ten hours a-day attendance at the counting-house.' The annual week's holiday disappeared all too soon: 'Before I had a taste of it, it was vanished.' At the end of the essay Lamb emphasises the pleasures of retirement: 'I am now as if I had never been other than my own master.' However, in a letter to a friend he recommends all would-be writers lacking independent means to find additional employment: 'Trust not to the public: you may hang, starve, drown yourself, for anything that worthy personage cares. I bless every star that Providence, not seeing good to make me independent, has seen it next good to settle me on the stable foundation of Leadenhall.'[5] Whilst with the East India Company, Lamb did find the time to write, with his sister Mary, *Tales from Shakespeare* for children.

John Stuart Mill was quite content working in the City and accumulating the knowledge which formed the foundation of his philosophical and political essays. Kenneth Grahame was also happy in the City, although he nearly ended his life here when one day at the Bank of England he was shot at by a madman. Fortunately both shots missed.[6] Sax Rohmer spent all his time writing short stories and subsequently receiving a mass of rejections; he papered one wall in his bedroom with the slips of paper.[7] P. G. Wodehouse was another clerk writing away hard in his spare time, although he did manage to publish some eighty pieces during his career at the Hong Kong and Shanghai Bank. This was just as well since he confessed to having no idea how the bank worked at all. The final straw came during a spell in the cash department when he opened a new ledger and wrote out a short story on its first page. He then lost his nerve and tore out the page. Unknowing, the head cashier later confronted the head stationer and accused him of supplying defective materials:

'Somebody must have cut out the page,' he said.

'Absurd!' said the head cashier. 'Nobody but an imbecile would cut out the front page of a ledger.'

'Then,' said the stationer, coming right back at him, 'you must have an imbecile in your department. Have you?'

The head cashier started. This opened up a new line of thought.

'Why, yes,' he admitted, for he was a fair-minded man. 'There is P. G. Wodehouse.'

'Weak in the head, is he, this Wodehouse?'

'Very, so I have always thought.'

'Then send for him and question him narrowly,' said the stationer.

This was done. They got me under the lights and grilled me, and I had to come clean. It was immediately after this that I found myself at liberty to embark on the life literary.[8]

Wodehouse later made use of his experiences when writing *Psmith in the City* (1910) in which neither Mike Jackson nor Psmith is enamoured of 'the cold unfriendliness' of his surroundings at the New Asiatic Bank.

Another writer who found it difficult to comprehend what was going on around him in his City work was Ian Fleming: 'I never could understand what was meant by a sixty-fourth of a point.'[9]

By contrast T. S. Eliot seems to have fitted in well, and each day his smart and well-dressed figure could have been seen routinely making its way to and from Moorgate Tube station. However, in *The Waste Land* Eliot conveys a picture of City clerks unwillingly travelling to work:

> *Unreal City,*
> *Under the brown fog of a winter dawn,*
> *A crowd flowed over London Bridge, so many,*
> *I had not thought death had undone so many.*
> *Sighs, short and infrequent, were exhaled,*
> *And each man fixed his eyes before his feet.*
> *Flowed up the hill and down King William Street,*
> *To where Saint Mary Woolnoth kept the hours*
> *With a dead sound on the final stroke of nine.*

Another author who had connections with the City, albeit unhappy ones, was Charles Dickens, who as a very young man fell in love with Maria Beadnell. Her father worked for a small bank at 2 Lombard Street, and the Beadnell family lived next door. Dickens often came here to see Maria: 'I told her there was no woman in the world, and there were very few men, who could ever imagine how much [I loved her].'[10] The father prevented the relationship from coming to anything, arguing that the young Charles had very few prospects. Many years later Maria contacted the now world-famous author. Her letters to him prompted a revival of his old feelings, and Dickens put much of Maria in the portrayal of Dora in *David Copperfield*. Sadly, when he met her she turned out to be a 'grotesque revival', 'tossing her head with a caricature of her girlish manner'. Further attempts on Maria's part to see Dickens were met by evasions and half-truths from the writer, and she finally passed out of his life. Posterity does not record what Maria thought of the middle-aged Dickens or of their reunion.

The most famous of the fictional clerks is Mr Pooter, created by George and Weedon Grossmith in *The Diary of a Nobody*, first published in *Punch* and then in book form in 1892. Mr Pooter fastidiously travels down from Holloway by bus each morning, is thoroughly conscientious and quails whenever his senior, Mr Perkupp, asks to see him. One of the finest scenes in the book comes when Mr Pooter and his wife Carrie are asked to a ball at the Mansion House. For a start there is an accident ·with the invitation: 'May 4. Carrie's mother returned the Lord Mayor's invitation, which was sent to her to look at, with apologies for having upset a glass of port over it. I was too angry to say anything.' They then find that their ironmonger, Mr Farmerson, is also there at the Mansion House, which rather takes the edge off the occasion. The Pooters slip and fall when dancing, and the final ignominy comes when the *Blackfriars Bi-weekly News* fails to announce that Mr and Mrs Charles Pooter had been present at the ball.

One hundred years on from Mr Pooter's self-important but charming activities, the City is dominated by huge and impersonal institutions such as the Bank of England, the massive NatWest Tower and the new, shining Stock Exchange. Literary associations are rather few and far between. Fortunately there are still some old alleys and backstreets which remind us of the City once familiar to Daniel Defoe, who had his own business, seemingly as a 'middleman', just off Cornhill. Defoe would often have walked beside the Monument in Fish Street Hill, built as a memorial to the Great Fire of September 1666 which had started nearby in Pudding Lane. Although caused by carelessness in a baker's shop, popular prejudice ascribed the outbreak of the Fire to the devious machinations of the Catholics. Until the early nineteenth century the Monument carried an inscription that referred to 'Papist frenzy', which explains why Alexander Pope, born nearby in Plough Court in 1688 and brought up as a Catholic, wrote: '. . . London's column, pointing at the skies, / Like a tall bully, lifts the head and lies'.[11]

Inside the Monument is a spiral staircase of 311 steps, always a challenge to the fit and the foolhardy. In Dickens's *Martin Chuzzlewit* (1843–4), Tom Pinch sees a couple pay a shilling for the dubious pleasure of enduring the steep climb. The doorman opens a dark little door:

> When the gentleman and lady passed out of view, he shut it again, and came slowly back to his chair and laughed.
>
> 'They don't know what a-many steps there is!' he said. 'It's worth twice the money to stop here. Oh, my eye!'

Foremost amongst the City's delights are of course the Wren churches, and in particular one should visit St Margaret Pattens and St James Garlickhythe. St Margaret Pattens gets its name from the pattens or shoes made with a wooden sole mounted on an iron ring which were produced nearby – an example can be seen inside the church on the south wall. The interior also contains an hour-glass which timed sermons and a Beadle's Pew complete with 'Punishment Bench' that immediately summons up an image of Dickens's Mr Bumble. In the Middle Ages, St James Garlickhythe stood near the stalls which sold garlic, a substance used to disguise the taste of food often not as fresh as it might have been. The Vintners' Hall is close by in Upper Thames Street, on the same site as it has been for over 500 years. Geoffrey Chaucer's father was a vintner, and Chaucer himself was born in this neighbourhood in the early 1340s. The gateway to the church was a gift from the Vintners' Company and depicts clusters of grapes. The interior, recently redecorated, is one of the finest in London. A cupboard holds the mummified body found many years ago and irreverently known as 'Jimmy Garlick'. A pretty little spot called Whittington's Garden sits in front of St Michael Paternoster Royal, the church which Dick Whittington attended and where he was buried in March 1423. A plaque in College Hill marks the site of his house, and a modern stained-glass window inside the church shows Dick and his cat, a legend much used in popular literature.

Another little City church is St Andrew Undershaft, so called because it once stood underneath the maypole usually erected nearby. Now, however, it is in the shadow of a very different structure, the new Lloyd's building in Leadenhall Street; as the critics put it, in 300 years Lloyd's has progressed from a coffee-house to a coffee-percolator.[12] Inside St Andrew Undershaft is an effigy of John Stow, who was buried here in 1605. The inscription on his tomb records that 'He exercised the most careful accuracy in searching ancient monuments, English annals and records of the City of London. He wrote excellently and deserved well of both his own and subsequent ages.' Born in 1525, Stow was the first proper historian of London, and his *Survey of London and Westminster*, first published in 1598, is often drawn upon by historians. Stow's effigy was erected by his wife, and every year on a day near to the anniversary of his death on 5 April the Lord Mayor replaces the quill pen in its hand.

Other City churches with literary links include St Dunstan in the East, wrecked during the Second World War but now transformed into one of London's most pleasant and unusual gardens with benches instead of pews. In April 1668, Samuel Pepys was returning home late after an evening spent frolicking with Mrs Knipp when he was nearly mugged near St Dunstan's by 'two rogues with clubs'; he was forced to make a detour in order to reach his house on Tower Hill. A few hundred yards away is St Magnus the Martyr, the church which once stood right beside old London Bridge – the bridge's two replacements have been built a little way to the west. In contrast to St Dunstan's, the atmosphere of the high-church St Magnus is thick with incense and the walls are full of monuments. Until recently a different kind of smell was also apparent – Billingsgate Fish-market was just down the road. In *The Waste Land* T. S. Eliot refers to this vicinity:

> *Where fishmen lounge at noon: where the walls*
> *Of Magnus Martyr hold*
> *Inexplicable splendour of Ionian white and gold.*

In his notes to this poem Eliot claims that 'The interior of St Magnus Martyr is to my mind one of the finest among Wren's interiors'. In 1926 it was planned to sell off some of the City churches, including St Magnus the Martyr. Eliot and some friends led a protest march through the City singing 'Onward, Christian Soldiers' and other hymns.[13] Their campaign was successful. Buried at St Magnus is Miles Coverdale, rector for several years in the 1560s and famous for being the first man to translate the Bible into English, which he published in 1535.

Two other City churches stand on ancient sites, St Peter and St Michael in Cornhill, and both have tiny but charming gardens to their rear. It was behind St Peter's that Bradley Headstone declared his love for Lizzie Hexham in Dickens's *Our Mutual Friend*. At the back of St Michael's is the churchyard which would have been known to the poet Thomas Gray, who was born nearby in Cornhill in November 1716. The plaque on the site of the house shows the head of the poet and also the line 'The curfew tolls the knell of parting day'. Although Gray did not like London and his elegy was written in a country churchyard, on Sundays when the traffic is absent it is just about possible to imagine oneself in the country when standing in St Michael's garden.

Other City survivals with literary connections include the George and Vulture inn where Mr Pickwick stayed with Sam Weller after leaving Mrs Bardell's. It was also here that Sam wrote his valentine to Mary. On the south side of Cornhill at number 32 stands the Cornhill Insurance Company, but once it was the site of the publishers Smith, Elder & Co. The bottom right-hand panel of the fine insurance company door reveals, to anyone who doesn't mind grubbing around the pavement, Thackeray meeting the Brontë sisters at Smith, Elder & Co. The Brontë sisters first came here in 1848 to meet George Smith. He was expecting to be introduced to a gentleman called 'Currer Bell', Charlotte's pseudonym, but quickly recovered from the initial shock.[14]

Much in the City has fallen victim to bombs and bulldozers. Particularly missed is the Boar's Head tavern which once stood in Eastcheap and was run, according to Shakespeare, by Mistress Quickly and frequented by Falstaff and his gang. It was here that Falstaff regaled Prince Hal with his exploits on Gadshill when he saw off an ever-growing number of travellers, dallied with Doll Tearsheet, and revelled with Bardolph and the rest of his drinking companions. The Boar's Head was burnt down in the Great Fire, then rebuilt, but demolished again for good when the new approach roads to London Bridge were being constructed in the early nineteenth century. In 1820 the American writer Washington Irving, creator of Rip Van Winkle, had gone in search of the Boar's Head and of Falstaff who 'has bequeathed a never-failing inheritance of jolly laughter, to make mankind merrier and better to the latest posterity'.[15] He found only a boar's head carved in stone and in a neighbouring public house a goblet and tobacco-box which had once belonged to the old tavern:

> Alas! how sadly is the scene changed since the roaring days of Falstaff and old Stowe! The madcap roister has given place to the plodding tradesman; the clattering of pots and the sound of 'harpe and sawtrie', to the din of carts and the accursed dinging of the dustman's bell; and no song is heard, save, haply, the strain of some siren from Billingsgate, chanting the eulogy of deceased mackerel.

Now even Billingsgate has been shifted elsewhere and the cart and the dustman's bell replaced by the infinitely worse thunder of road traffic. Surely here, if only to provide a welcome relief from the mercenary considerations which animate life in the City, there should stand a statue of Falstaff, one of London's most memorable and enduring literary figures.

Bloomsbury

God help the writer about literary London who does not include a substantial section on the Bloomsbury Group, that collection of writers, artists and intellectuals at work during the first half of the twentieth century which has already provoked more than a thousand books and theses. Never mind that their houses have now been colonised by the administrative offices of London University or that Bloomsbury's few residential places today are mainly occupied by students; the familiar names of Woolf, Bell, Strachey and Keynes have to be here in this chapter. Nevertheless, there is rather more to this district in the way of literary associations than the Bloomsbury Group, notably the British Museum, Dickens House, London University and Bloomsbury's squares.

For centuries the village of Bloomsbury lay well outside the City of London and was favoured above all for its good clean air. The historian John Strype wrote in 1720 that 'this place by physicians is esteemed the most healthful of any in London'.[1] Several aristocratic families were attracted both on this account and because its open spaces offered ample room for them to build massive mansions in what was effectively the countryside. By the end of the seventeenth century both Southampton (later Bedford) House and Montagu House stood in the fields of Bloomsbury. To the north these fields were much frequented by duellists. One particular duel gave rise to the name of the 'Field of the Forty Footsteps'. Apparently two brothers fell in love with the same girl and decided to fight over her as she sat watching on a nearby bank. Both fell in the struggle, but it is said that the marks of their footsteps, forty each, were supposed to have been indelibly left behind. The young Robert Southey, a future Poet Laureate and friend of Wordsworth, came looking for these footsteps at the end of the eighteenth century and claimed to have found them three-quarters of a mile north of Montagu House and 500 yards east of Tottenham Court Road:

> The steps are of the size of a large human foot, about three inches deep, and lie nearly from north-east to south-west. We counted only seventy-six; but we were not exact in counting. The place where one or both the brothers are supposed to have fallen is still bare of grass. The labourer also showed us the bank where (the tradition is) the wretched woman sat to see the combat.[2]

Within thirty years of Southey's visit the northward development of Bloomsbury had covered the 'Field of Forty Footsteps' with buildings, although the gardens in Gordon Square and Tavistock Square survive to this day.

One other substantial building stood here in the fields during the eighteenth century. This was the Foundling Hospital established by a Captain Thomas Coram, a retired sea-captain who was horrified to see so many babies and children abandoned by their parents in the London streets. Its full name was 'The Hospital for the Maintenance and Education of Exposed and Deserted Young Children'. It was granted a royal charter in 1739, and the hospital's buildings here in Bloomsbury were completed in 1752. Both the musician Handel and the painter Hogarth were heavily involved in this charity. In the eighteenth century the nameless children who were looked after here were called after famous Englishmen in the past. Thus there were several William Shakespeares and John Miltons.[3]

In the nineteenth century Charles Dickens helped popularise the work of the Foundling Hospital with a long article in his magazine *Household Words*. It also figures in the story 'No Thoroughfare' written with his friend and fellow-novelist Wilkie Collins for Christmas 1867. Tattycoram in *Little Dorrit*, as her name suggests, was a foundling child. In 1926 the hospital moved away to Redhill and then to Berkhamsted, until it was closed down in 1954. Some of the Bloomsbury buildings have survived, and at 40 Brunswick Square is the Coram Foundation which still deals with children's welfare. Although this building dates only from 1936, it contains in its Court Room an excellent reconstruction of the original eighteenth-century Court Room. The Coram Foundation is open to the public. This building also possesses several of Hogarth's paintings as well as Handel's copy of *Messiah* and Thomas Coram's first edition of Samuel Pepys's *Memoires Relating to the State of the Royal Navy* (1690). A statue of Thomas Coram stands outside 40 Brunswick Square, while his tomb is now in St Andrew's, Holborn. In 1926 a campaign led by Mrs Trevelyan, the wife of the historian G. M. Trevelyan, saved the space where the hospital was once situated from being built over, and it is today a children's playground forbidden to adults unless accompanied by a child.[4]

At the same time that the children were being received into the Foundling Hospital, Montagu House was also experiencing an influx of newcomers, but in this case they were books. The catalyst for the transformation of this mansion into the British Museum came with the death of Sir Hans Sloane in 1753 at the age of ninety-two. Born in Ireland, Sloane spent several years in Jamaica as the governor's doctor before coming to London where he became extremely successful, his patients including Pepys and Queen Anne. In 1695 he bought himself number 3 (and later number 4, too) Bloomsbury Place, his town home for forty-seven years. As well as owning the manor of Chelsea and becoming President of the Royal College of Physicians, Sloane amassed a huge private collection of books, manuscripts and oddities, amounting in all to 79,595 objects. It was a craze that Jonathan Swift was to satirise in *Gulliver's Travels* (1726); Gulliver leaves Brobdingnag with a bizarre store: four wasp-stings 'like joiners' tacks'; breeches made out of a mouse's skin; and 'a corn that I had cut off with my own hand from a Maid of Honour's toe; it was about the bigness of a Kentish pippin, I got it hollowed into a cup and set in silver'.

Sloane himself valued it at £80,000, but the sceptical Horace Walpole remarked 'so would anybody who loves hippopotamuses, sharks with one ear and spiders as big as geese'.[5] In his will Sloane left his collection to the nation, on condition that a sum of £20,000 was paid to his daughters. After much debate a state lottery was held in order to raise the necessary money. In fact over £300,000 was raised by this means – enough to buy Sloane's collection, the Cottonian Library put together by the Cotton family, the Oxford manuscripts of Sir Robert Harley (1st Earl of Oxford and once a patron of Daniel Defoe and Jonathan Swift) and Montagu House as well. The British Museum Act of 1753 established the legal framework for its administration.

At first only ticket-holders were allowed in; not until 1879 was unrestricted access permitted. By the 1820s the museum had far outgrown its existing premises, and Robert Smirke built the imposing building which we see today, having pulled down what remained of old Montagu House. The British Museum houses the British Library. Its wonderful domed Reading Room was designed by Sir Anthony Panizzi, the Principal Librarian, whose bust stands over the entrance, and completed in 1857. On the morning of its opening on 2 May 1857 readers were treated to breakfast at the desks and the women readers were also given bouquets.[6] How much longer readers at the British Library will be able to enjoy the pleasures of working here remains a contentious issue. New and much larger British Library buildings are rising inexorably on a site close to St Pancras railway station, and the projected move there is generating much controversy as professor attacks professor (in print) over the merits or otherwise of the migration from Bloomsbury.

How best to describe the experience of entering the Reading Room? Leave it to Adam Appleby in David Lodge's *The British Museum Is Falling Down* (1965):

> He passed through the narrow vaginal passage, and entered the huge womb of the Reading Room. Across the floor, dispersed along the radiating desks, scholars curled, foetus-like, over their books, little buds of intellectual life thrown off by some gigantic act of generation performed upon that nest of knowledge, those inexhaustible ovaries of learning, the concentric inner rings of the catalogue shelves.

The Library is legally obliged to hold a copy of every book published in English, although some material was lost in the Second World War. The Reading Room is open to anyone who can obtain a reader's pass, having proved themselves to be a serious researcher. Some have assumed names for this purpose – Lenin became 'Jacob Richter' and sat at L13.[7] The range and variety of the Reading Room's past occupants knows no bounds,

from Karl Marx at seat O7 trying to change the world to George
Eliot, Robert Browning, Oscar Wilde, Thomas Hardy and Gandhi.
George Bernard Shaw wrote five novels here as well as his first
play, *Widowers' Houses*, while H. G. Wells came to the Reading
Room because it was comfortable and saved on lighting back in
his dingy rooms. The lexicographer Eric Partridge sat at K1 for
over forty years. George Gissing in *New Grub Street* (1891) called it
'the valley of the shadow of books', while Hesketh Pearson in his
biography of Shaw remarked that it catered for everyone from
'earnest seekers to heavy sleepers'.[8] At the end of the nineteenth
century some readers apparently tried to bathe in the cloak-
rooms: George Gissing in his semi-autobiographical *The Private
Papers of Henry Ryecroft* records that the authorities had to put up a
notice which stated 'These basins are intended for casual ablu-
tions only'.

To obtain a book one has simply to consult the catalogue, hand
in the order form, sit back and wait. Nevertheless, scholarship has
its strenuous moments. W. B. Yeats lived not far away in the
charming Woburn Walk from 1895 to 1919, and in his *The Trembling of the Veil* writes that he 'spent my days at the British
Museum, and must, I think, have been very delicate, for I
remember often putting off hour after hour consulting some
necessary book because I shrank from lifting the heavy volumes
of the catalogue'. Virginia Woolf seems to have been made of
hardier stuff: in her *A Room of One's Own* she managed to obtain
'an avalanche of books sliding down on to the desk in front of
me'. Sherlock Holmes came to the Reading Room in 'The Adventure of Wisteria Lodge' to consult Eckermann's *Voodooism and the
Negroid Religions* (not listed in the current catalogues!). There
were so many political exiles studying at the British Museum that
the police detailed an inspector to come here and watch their
movements.[9] Such surveillance did not prevent Lenin from paying a graceful tribute to the Reading Room: 'It's a remarkable
institution: a lot can be learned from them, especially that excep-
tional enquiry department. . . . And how comfortable and easy it
is to work at the Museum. . . . I will say this: for those sources of
information in all languages which I need at the shortest notice,
you can't even think of a better place to work in than the British
Museum library.'[10]

The British Library is not, however, the only major library in
Bloomsbury. On the west side of Gordon Square is to be found Dr

Williams's Library, a vast collection of books on nonconformity and all aspects of religion. It has been here since 1890. Amongst its holdings are 2400 volumes bequeathed by George Henry Lewes and his lover George Eliot, many with annotations by their former owners.[11] There are also the manuscripts of the seventeenth-century poet George Herbert.

By the end of the eighteenth century, although some of the aristocracy had abandoned Bloomsbury for residences further west, the district was still much patronised by the wealthy and respectable and parts of it were called 'Judge-Land'.[12] One attraction was doubtless Nicholas Hawksmoor's church of St George, completed in 1730 with a fine portico and a statue of George I surmounting the spire. One judge who had cause to rue his stay in Bloomsbury was the Lord Chief Justice, Lord Mansfield, who lived in the north-east corner of Bloomsbury Square. In 1780 his home was attacked by the Gordon Rioters and razed to the ground, a loss which included his fine library. Dickens portrays the conflagration in *Barnaby Rudge*:

> . . . they then began to demolish it with great fury, and setting fire to it in several parts, involved in a common ruin the whole of the costly furniture, the plate and jewels, a beautiful gallery of pictures, the rarest collection of manuscripts ever possessed by any one private person in the world, and, worse than all, because nothing could replace this loss, the great Law Library, on almost every page of which were notes in the judge's own hand, of inestimable value – being the results of the study and experience of his whole life.

Lord Mansfield's most important judgement had been delivered eight years before in the Somerset case, declaring that slaves could not be taken from England by force – a step on the way towards the abolition of slavery.

A later occupant of Bloomsbury Square was Isaac D'Israeli, who lived at number 6 from 1817 until 1825 while working on the later volumes of his *Curiosities of Literature*. His son Benjamin, who was then a boy, knew the area well, perhaps better than his father: 'In London my father's only amusement was to ramble about among the booksellers' shops; and if ever he went into a club, it was only to go into the library.'[13] Close to Bloomsbury Square was solid, respectable Russell Square, where Thackeray's Osborne and Sedley families live in *Vanity Fair*, and there was also the smart late-eighteenth-century Bedford Square. Nearby is Keppel Street where Anthony Trollope was born in 1815. His father was an unsuccessful barrister with a volatile temper who mistakenly thought his fortune lay in farming, so that soon after Anthony's birth he leased a farm in Harrow. He quickly went bankrupt, forcing his wife Frances to support the family from her own writing. She managed this by producing over forty books after the age of fifty. She wrote novels and commentaries on other countries' habits and customs, as well as bringing up a large family, most members of which seemed to suffer from chronic ill-health. How did she manage all this? As her son Anthony later wrote, 'She was at her table at four in the morning, and had finished her work before the world had begun to be aroused' – a discipline which makes Trollope's own punctual start of 5.30 a.m. seem rather laggardly.[14]

Charles Dickens spent part of his youth reading in the British Museum, in between taking acting lessons and learning to be a parliamentary shorthand reporter. On his marriage to Catherine Hogarth in March 1837 he moved into 48 Doughty Street. This charming terrace of houses had been built in about 1801 and was then in a private road patrolled by uniformed commissionaires. Here Dickens wrote much of *Pickwick Papers*, all of *Oliver Twist* and *Nicholas Nickleby* and part of *Barnaby Rudge*. Like most writers he was acutely conscious of distracting noise and complained irritably about the bells of St Paul's: 'I can hardly hear my own ideas, as they come into my head.' Nevertheless his brother-in-law recalls an occasion when Dickens worked away on the monthly portion of *Oliver Twist* whilst taking part in a conversation surrounding him:

> In a few minutes he returned, manuscript in hand, and while he was pleasantly discoursing he employed himself in carrying to a corner of the room a little table, at which he seated himself and recommenced his writing. We, at his bidding, went on talking our 'little nothings'; he, every now and then, (the feather of his pen still moving rapidly from side to side), put in a cheerful interlude. It was interesting to watch, upon the sly, the mind and the muscles working (or, if you please, playing) in company as new thoughts were being dropped upon the paper. And to note the working brow, the set of mouth, with

the tongue tightly pressed against the closed lips, as was his habit.[15]

It was here at 48 Doughty Street that his beloved sister-in-law Mary died in his arms. He wrote the epitaph for Mary's tombstone in Kensal Green Cemetery: 'Young, beautiful, and good, God in His mercy numbered her among his angels at the early age of seventeen.' She lives on in the rather insipid and impossibly good characters of Florence in *Dombey and Son*, Little Dorrit, Rose Maylie in *Oliver Twist* and Little Nell in *The Old Curiosity Shop*. It was from 48 Doughty Street that Dickens set off to see William Makepeace Thackeray, who then lived nearby at 13 Coram Street, offering him the chance to illustrate *Pickwick Papers*. Thackeray declined and instead began a novel-writing career of his own. Since 1925, 48 Doughty Street has been the Dickens House museum, exhibiting many of the items from Dickens's life, such as an iron grille from the Marshalsea prison in Southwark where his family was once incarcerated and a desk on which he worked when a clerk at Gray's Inn. It is a charming place to visit, not least because it shows how a typical Victorian household lived. When in season red geraniums, the author's favourite flower, decorate the window-boxes.

In late 1839, Dickens and his family moved to Marylebone, but in 1851 he returned to Bloomsbury, and Tavistock House on the east side of Tavistock Square became his home. This building has long since been demolished and replaced by the characterless offices of the British Medical Association. It was whilst at Tavistock House that Dickens threw himself into amateur theatricals, with fateful results. In August 1857 he was rehearsing Wilkie Collins's melodrama *The Frozen Deep* when he first met and then fell in love with a young actress called Ellen Ternan. He later separated from his wife Catherine.

Dickens also involved himself in the support of the recently opened Hospital for Sick Children in Great Ormond Street, which had been founded in 1851. He gave public readings of *A Christmas Carol* to raise money for the hospital and described it in *Our Mutual Friend* as 'a place where there are none but children; a place set up on purpose for children; where the good doctors and nurses pass their lives with children, talk to none but children, touch none but children, comfort and cure none but children'. The hospital has often been rebuilt. It continued to receive the royalties from the play *Peter Pan* by the generous wish of its author, J. M. Barrie, although these were due to expire in 1987.

Near neighbours of the Dickens family were the Morrises. In 1865, William, his wife Janey and their two daughters moved into 26 Queen Square.[16] Their spacious Queen Anne house enjoyed a wonderful view of the Hampstead heights because the north side of the square had still to be built. As with Dickens, Morris was not happily married and he threw himself into an enormously wide range of projects, perhaps as a consolation. He set up a workshop, turning the scullery into a dye-house. He also published several volumes of verse, including *The Earthly Paradise*, the work by which he was best known to the Victorian public and the reason why he was offered the Poet Laureateship after Tennyson's death. The first volume of the poem opens with a vision of London as it might be:

> *Forget six counties overhung with smoke,*
> *Forget the snorting steam and piston stroke,*
> *Forget the spreading of the hideous town,*
> *Think rather of the pack-horse on the down,*
> *And dream of London, small, and white and clean.*

Morris lectured nearby at the Working Man's College which had been situated at 45 Great Ormond Street since 1857. In later years he was friendly with the college principal, Thomas Hughes, better known as the author of *Tom Brown's Schooldays*. Other tutors here were to include the poet Dante Gabriel Rossetti, the critic John Ruskin, the novelist E. M. Forster and the historian G. M. Trevelyan. In 1906 the Working Man's College moved to Crowndale Road in Camden where it remains.

Near to the homes of both Morris and Dickens was one of Victorian England's most important literary institutions, the circulating library run by Mr Charles Mudie. From 1852, Mudie's was based at the corner of Museum Street and New Oxford Street, and its strength came from the fact that there were very few libraries then in existence. Members paid a subscription entitling them to borrow volumes from the stock of nearly a million books. Mudie did much to influence the inordinate length of so many Victorian novels by insisting that they should come in three volumes so that his public of 25,000 subscribers could feel that they were indeed getting value for their money. He also operated a stringent form of censorship, leading the Irish novelist George

Moore to attack Mudie's in 1885 in an article entitled 'Literature at Nurse, or Circulating Morals'. Not until the 1890s did the one-volume six-shilling novel begin to displace the three-decker. The spread of the public library system in the early twentieth century brought Mudie's to an end.[17]

Another major institution located in Bloomsbury is London University and some of its colleges. University College in Gower Street, for example, was founded in 1828, and one of its sponsors was the political philosopher Jeremy Bentham. His clothed skeleton is kept in a cupboard at the college and is displayed on request. The college is housed in a splendid building designed by the architect of the National Gallery, William Wilkins. On the west side of Gordon Square is the University Church of Christ the King, a large mid-Victorian building which Sir John Betjeman described as a 'cathedral': 'Everywhere vistas, everywhere dignity, and above all mystery – Gordon Square church is solemn and suited to the mystery of religion. It is built for worship not for lectures.'[18]

Also to be found in this vicinity are the Slade School of Art, attached to University College, the Warburg Institute with its fine library, and Birkbeck College in Malet Street which generally deals with 'mature' students. The Victorian playwright Arthur Wing Pinero was an early student, whilst Stephen Potter was one of Birkbeck's lecturers in the 1930s. Potter's most lasting claim to fame is *The Theory and Practice of Gamesmanship* (1947), which he defined as 'the art of winning games without actually cheating'. He followed this book with *Lifemanship*, *One-Upmanship* and *Supermanship*.

The most imposing London University building is undoubtedly Senate House, which was erected in the 1930s and contains the University's administrative headquarters. During the Second World War it was the home of the newly established Ministry of Information. Not surprisingly, the Ministry is described several times in print, since it employed a collection of writers to boost morale. No one portrays it favourably. In Evelyn Waugh's novel about the 'Phoney War' period, *Put Out More Flags* (1942), it is depicted as 'that great mass of masonry'. Waugh describes the Ministry as a shambles in which all kinds of miscellaneous literary oddballs drift in and out of the Senate House. Ambrose Seal obtains a post as 'the sole representative of Atheism in the religious department'. Dorothy L. Sayers was scathing, too: '. . . as the place is packed with everybody's wives and nephews and all the real jobs seem to have been handed over to other departments, it's as good a spot as any to intern the nation's troublemakers.'[19] For George Orwell, however, the Ministry and Senate House took on a more sinister aspect, and it can be recognised in *1984* as 'MinTruth':

> The Ministry of Truth – Minitrue, in Newspeak – was startlingly different from any other object in sight. It was an enormous pyramidal structure of glittering white concrete, soaring up, terrace after terrace, 300 metres into the air. From where Winston stood it was just possible to read, picked out on its white face in elegant lettering, the three slogans of the Party:

> WAR IS PEACE
> FREEDOM IS SLAVERY
> IGNORANCE IS STRENGTH

London University has always been distinguished by its relatively progressive attitude towards women. In 1878, University College became the country's first higher co-educational institution, and that year the University itself began to award degrees to women on the same terms as men. Bloomsbury was even then no stranger to feminist thought. In 1792, for example, Mary Wollstonecraft was living in Store Street when she wrote *A Vindication of the Rights of Woman*, regarded as one of the earliest and most significant feminist books. In it Wollstonecraft argues against 'the divine rights of husbands', for women's education, and for women MPs: 'I really think that women ought to have representatives, instead of being arbitrarily governed without having any direct share allowed them in the deliberations of government.' *A Vindication* was a success when it was published but did prompt some shameful abuse of its author – Horace Walpole called her 'a hyena in petticoats'.[20] This emphasis on the equality of the sexes is certainly a feature of 'the Bloomsbury Group' in which personal relationships disregarded the secondary issue of gender. Woe betide anyone who suggested that a Bloomsbury woman's tasks were confined to the kitchen sink. Virginia Woolf in *A Room of One's Own* (1929) argued that women, too, needed time and space for themselves: '. . . a latch on the door means the power to think for oneself.'

Why has Bloomsbury proved attractive to writers for so long? In Jane Austen's *Emma* (1814), Isabella Knightley lives in

Brunswick Square and considers it 'so very superior to other parts of London'; 'I should be unwilling to live in any other part of the town; – there is hardly any other that I could be satisfied to have my children in: – but we are so remarkably airy!' Although the Bloomsbury of the early twentieth century was by then a part of central London and therefore rather more crowded and dirty than in Jane Austen's day, it still possessed attractive squares and gardens as well as being close to the British Museum. In 1904, Vanessa Bell and Virginia Stephen moved to 46 Gordon Square and gradually their friends and acquaintances followed them into Bloomsbury. Lytton Strachey lived at 51 Gordon Square from 1909 to 1932, and his study *Eminent Victorians* (1918) exhibited the Bloomsbury dislike for many 'Victorian values'. John Maynard Keynes was to live at 46 Gordon Square from 1922, E. M. Forster at 29 Brunswick Square from 1929 to 1939.

Virginia Stephen married Leonard Woolf in 1912 and the couple moved to Hogarth House in Richmond where, five years later, they began the Hogarth Press. In 1924 both the press and its proprietors returned to Bloomsbury and a house at 52 Tavistock Square. Over the next fifteen years Virginia Woolf produced several novels and literary studies – *To the Lighthouse*, *The Waves*, *The Years*, *A Room of One's Own*, *Orlando* – but her work which above all concerns London is *Mrs Dalloway*. The novel follows the lives, both internal and external, of a number of characters on a single day in Westminster, St James's Park, Green Park, Bond Street, Regent's Park, Harley Street and Victoria Street as they go about their everyday activities: thinking, talking, remembering, hoping, fearing. Tragically, the disturbed Septimus Warren Smith throws himself to his death from a Bloomsbury window. Virginia Woolf's own suicide occurred in 1940.

The Hogarth Press and the Woolfs had moved to 37 Mecklenburgh Square in 1939. In the next year it was badly damaged in a bombing raid. The press's former home at 52 Tavistock Square was also demolished, and the critic John Lehmann, who once worked for the Hogarth Press, has left a sad description of the ruins waiting for redevelopment after the war: '. . . for many years the rooms where the Woolfs had entertained so many of the great literary figures of their time, lay open, like a smashed jaw, to the view of the public, while rain and smoke slowly disfigured the paintings which had adorned with such fresh elegance and gaiety of colour their hospitable walls.'[21]

There was, however, more to literary Bloomsbury than Virginia Woolf and her friends. Another famous writer who lived here and struggled at first to make her name was Dorothy L. Sayers. After the First World War she moved into a flat at 44 Mecklenburgh Square, which was then a rather rough district. In a short story called 'The Vindictive Story of the Footsteps That Ran' she referred to Bloomsbury as a place 'where people are always laying one another out' and 'drunks and wife-beatings are pretty common' – rather a different view of Bloomsbury from that associated with the aesthetic Woolfs. By the summer of 1921, Sayers's financial problems were mounting and she determined to write a novel which would sell. She invented the character of Lord Peter Wimsey and wrote the first Wimsey novel, *Whose Body?*, in three months.[22] Sayers succeeded in her aim. Late in 1921 she moved around the corner to 24 Great James Street. This was to be her home for over twenty years, and here she wrote the rest of the Wimsey novels. Although Lord Peter himself resides in Piccadilly, his future wife Harriet Vane lived at 100 Doughty Street.

A further important literary figure who knew Bloomsbury well was T. S. Eliot. His *Poems* was published by the Hogarth Press in 1919. Although Eliot lived in Kensington, he worked in Bloomsbury as an editor for the publishers Faber & Faber at 24 Russell Square from 1925 until 1965. A steady stream of authors and would-be poets climbed the steps of this building, eager for Eliot's advice. Unfortunately so did Eliot's first wife Vivienne, from whom he had separated. She used to waylay him on the stairs at 24 Russell Square and also turn up at lectures wearing a placard on her back which read 'I am the wife he abandoned'.[23] Like so many other buildings in Bloomsbury, 24 Russell Square now belongs to London University, and we should be grateful that so much of the area's elegance has been preserved from the inroads of commerce. The writers and artists and their friends seem to have left, although several publishers remain. The area now wears a sedate, rather institutional air and is full of scholars eager to study what was once created in Bloomsbury's houses and squares.

Chelsea

In 1914 a heated debate took place in Chelsea Town Hall over a motion proposed by a Councillor Wright that 'the artist who painted the first mural panel on the left-hand side of the hall be requested to substitute another figure in the place of the one representing Oscar Wilde, and in the event of his being unable or unwilling to do so, that the panel be removed'. Councillor Wright went on to assert that 'our Town Hall was not erected for the exhibition of criminals'.[1]

The object of Councillor Wright's displeasure was the figure of Oscar Wilde in the 'Literature' painting on the wall, which had recently been put up along with three other panels depicting Chelsea's links with History, Science and Art, at a cost of £200 each. Other writers in the Literature panel included Jonathan Swift, George Eliot, Thomas Carlyle and Charles Kingsley. During the debate in 1914 another councillor pointed out that George Eliot had lived for years in open adultery, and as for Henry VIII in the History painting . . . ! The motion to remove the Literature panel was in fact passed overwhelmingly, but the outbreak of the First World War led the council to concern themselves with more serious matters. Thus Oscar Wilde remains to this day in the Town Hall along with the other Chelsea worthies. The building itself now houses the Chelsea Library, but the council chamber can be seen by request – a splendid room it is, too.

This controversy over the representation of Wilde in a painting may be seen as a struggle between two aspects of Chelsea itself, for it was home to the wealthy and opulent who were above all 'respectable' as well as to the Bohemian and artistic community which has ever been less concerned with custom and convention. Wilde of course belonged to the latter group and helped to establish a longstanding reputation for nonconformity. E. M. Forster in *Howard's End* (1910) refers to 'long-haired Chelsea', and Bertie Wooster prattles on about coming to Chelsea for 'sandwiches and absinthe in the old studio'. In more recent years it has been the 'punks' arrayed along the King's Road, charging American tourists £1 for the privilege of photographing them in their finery, who have maintained Chelsea's reputation for idiosyncrasy.

Chelsea's association with literary figures who have flouted authority goes back to Sir Thomas More, the polymath lawyer, statesman and writer who appears in the 'Science' panel at the Town Hall.[2] By the time he came to live in Chelsea in about 1520, More had already published a Latin version of his *Utopia* (from the Greek word meaning 'no where'), which discusses England as it is and as it might be – although the book was not published in English until 1551, over fifteen years after his death. In those days Chelsea was a small fishermen's village several miles to the west of London, but More appreciated its rural seclusion and built himself a house in what is now Beaufort Street. He threw himself into local life, singing in the choir of Chelsea Old Church, which was only a few hundred yards away from his home. Later he built a chapel there which miraculously survived the devastation of the rest of the church during a bombing raid in April 1941. His domestic life was often held up as exemplary, whilst his official career also prospered with his appointment as Lord Chancellor by Henry VIII in 1529. Such good fortune was not to last long. Disagreement with Henry over his divorce from Catherine of Aragon and his self-appointment as the head of the Church led to More being summoned to Lambeth Palace and then imprisoned in the Tower of London. He was executed on Tower Hill in July 1535. More's body is thought to have been buried at Chelsea Old Church. Although his house later passed to the 1st Duke of Beaufort and was then demolished in the eighteenth century, there is still much to remind us of More. The seminary on the site of More's house has a mosaic of him on one of the outer walls, and there are statues of him in Astell Street and outside the church facing the noisy Embankment. The garden to the west of Chelsea Old Church is named after Margaret Roper, More's favourite daughter, and it formed part of her marriage settlement. Her husband William Roper was himself the first biographer of More. Finally, the Catholic Church of the Holy Redeemer in Cheyne Row has More's coat of arms over the entrance.

One other building in Chelsea connected with More is Crosby Hall, the great hall of which was erected in 1466 for a wealthy wool merchant called Sir John Crosby. It originally stood beside Bishopsgate in the City and was where More once stayed in 1523. On Crosby's death the Hall passed to the Duke of Gloucester, later to be Richard III. Shakespeare in *Richard III* inaccurately – the playwright was never one to let the facts spoil a good story or speech – places several important events here: Richard hears of Henry Tudor's uprising:

> *Away towards Salisbury! While we reason here*
> *A royal battle might be won and lost.*
> *Some one take order Buckingham be brought*
> *To Salisbury; the rest march on with me.*

It was a march which was to end at Bosworth in defeat and death for Richard and the coming of the Tudor dynasty.

Over the years Crosby Hall served a variety of functions, being a post office, a grocer's warehouse, a Presbyterian meeting-house and a restaurant. In 1910 it was taken down piece by piece and re-erected here in Chelsea. Crosby Hall is now run by the British Federation of University Women, who allow visitors to see the magnificent scissor-beam roof and oriel window of the great hall. On the wall opposite the reconstructed musicians' gallery is a copy of Holbein's famous painting 'The Family of Sir Thomas More'.[3]

Henry VIII often came to visit More in Chelsea. One of his more callous acts was that despite the death of More he still could not resist building himself a manor house only a little way from More's former home. Throughout its existence this manor house was surrounded by fields and market gardens, and when Sir Hans Sloane bought it in 1712 the King's Road was still a narrow path. On his death Sloane wanted the manor house to be turned into a museum, but in fact the house was pulled down in 1756 and the collection transferred to Montagu House, which is now the British Museum. Nevertheless the memory of Sloane lives on in

Chelsea, not least in the Chelsea Physic Garden, which he saved from closure and where his statue still stands in this four-acre oasis of peace and quiet. His elaborate tomb is in the churchyard of Chelsea Old Church, while the chained books inside – the only ones in a London church – were his gift. His name of course survives in the several streets and squares of Chelsea.[4] Another reminder of rural Chelsea is provided by Chelsea Farmers Market, which was opened on the north side of the King's Road in 1983 to commemorate the three hundredth anniversary of the first market garden here.

Sloane's enthusiasm for collecting seems to have been catching. In 1695 his valet, James Salter, opened a coffee-house near the church which included a 'Knackatory' full of unusual objects, one of which was a stuffed alligator that swung from the ceiling. Known as 'Don Saltero's', the establishment moved to 18 Cheyne Walk where it became a meeting-place for such literary notables as Addison, Steele and Swift. It closed down in 1867.[5]

Although nothing remains of the manor house or of Don Saltero's, another Chelsea institution from that period remains, namely the Chelsea Hospital, whose pensioners are frequently to be seen negotiating the traffic or sitting at café tables refighting the Battle of Waterloo for the benefit of tourists. 'The Hospital of Maymed Soldiers' first began to admit army pensioners from 1689, and Sir Christopher Wren's buildings have survived largely intact, including the chapel and dining-hall.[6] Diarist John Evelyn was consulted over the plans and he was later appointed the treasurer at a salary of £300 a year. The little burial-ground to the east contains the body of Dr Charles Burney, who was the organist at the chapel between 1783 and 1814 and wrote a monumental four-volume *History of Music*. The father of novelist Fanny Burney, he was also a friend of Samuel Johnson: 'I love Burney. . . . I much question if there is in the world such another man for the mind, intelligence and manner, as Dr Burney.' A tour conducted by one of the Chelsea Pensioners with their fund of anecdotes is an experience to savour; it is easy to understand why Thomas Hardy came here on several occasions in the 1870s in order to talk to the veterans of Waterloo and the Napoleonic Wars, gathering the material which he drew upon later in his long verse drama *The Dynasts* (1904–8).[7]

To the rear of the Chelsea Hospital are the gardens which host the annual Chelsea Flower Show each May. Called the Ranelagh

Gardens, they are a reminder of the eighteenth-century pleasure garden which was opened here in 1742 in the grounds of Lord Ranelagh's house. Ranelagh was the most magnificent of such resorts and it offered a Chinese House, a Venetian Temple, a Rotunda and a pavilion in the middle of the lake; it was also the most expensive at *2s 6d*.

Diarist and letter-writer Horace Walpole, who had as a boy lived with his father Sir Robert Walpole close to the Chelsea Hospital, gives some idea of Ranelagh's delights when he came here in 1749 for a masquerade:

> . . . nothing in a fairy tale ever surpassed it. . . . When you entered, you found the whole garden filled with masks and spread with tents, which remained all night very commodely. In one quarter, was a May-pole dressed with garlands, and people dancing round it to a tabor and pipe and rustic music, all masqued, as were all the various bands of music that were disposed in different parts of the garden; some like huntsmen with French horns, some like peasants, and a troop of harlequins and scaramouches in the little open temple on the mount. On the canal was a sort of gondola, adorned with flags and streamers, and filled with music, rowing about. All round the outside of the amphitheatre were shops, filled with Dresden china, japan etc., and all the shop-keepers in mask. The amphitheatre was illuminated; and in the middle was a circular bower, composed of all kinds of firs in tubs, from twenty to thirty feet high: under them orange-trees, with small lamps in each orange, and below them all sorts of the finest auriculas in pots; and festoons of natural flowers hanging from tree to tree. Between the arches too were firs, and smaller ones in the balconies above. There were booths for tea and wine, gaming-tables and dancing, and about two thousands persons. In short, it pleased me more than anything I ever saw.[8]

Samuel Johnson was another visitor who praised Ranelagh: 'When I first entered Ranelagh, it gave me an expansion and gay sensation to my mind such as I never experienced anywhere else.' Laurence Sterne was lionised at Ranelagh after the success of *Tristram Shandy* in 1759. Some observers of Ranelagh viewed it with more cynicism as a matrimonial cattle-show. Oliver Goldsmith in *The Vicar of Wakefield* referred to Ranelagh as a market for wives, and the historian Edward Gibbon in similar vein thought it 'certainly the best market we have in England'. In 1803 the gardens were closed, and nothing remains other than the name.

Another local landmark was the Chelsea Bunhouse, which had been started by a Mr and Mrs Hand in the early eighteenth century and was much patronised by royalty. Like Don Saltero's, it, too, possessed a museum. On Good Fridays huge crowds besieged the Bunhouse, clamouring for buns. It closed in 1839, and its only legacy is our Bunhouse Place.[9] One writer who visited it but who found that his penny bun was stale was Jonathan Swift, who lived in Church Street in 1711, having been attracted here by Chelsea's healthy air. In an entry in his *Journal to Stella* Swift remarks that 'we are mowing already and making hay and it smells so sweet as we walk through the flowering meads', although Swift then goes on to spoil his pastoral by referring to the 'perfect drabs' of 'haymaking nymphs'. Swift used to walk into London – he once measured it as 5748 steps from Chelsea Old Church to Pall Mall – but he was not happy with his accommodation: 'one silly room with confounded coarse sheets and an awkward bed'. His residence was pulled down in 1910 when Crosby Hall was moved to Chelsea.

Swift was certainly not the only writer of his day who lived in Chelsea. The Duchess of Monmouth, widow of the duke who had been defeated many years before at the battle of Sedgemoor, lived in Monmouth House and once employed John Gay as her secretary. After her death the house was occupied by Sir John Fielding, the half-brother of novelist Henry, and later by the Scottish writer Tobias Smollett, who moved here in 1750 because he hoped that Chelsea's clean air would help his sick daughter. Originally a surgeon's mate, by this time Smollett was already the author of *The Adventures of Roderick Random* and whilst at Chelsea he published *The Adventures of Peregrine Pickle*. Neither book was successful, and Smollett's six years here were marked by constant financial worry, although this did not prevent him keeping open house for his friends every Sunday. Smollett's best-known novel, *Humphry Clinker*, was issued in 1771, several years after he had left Chelsea, but it contains a number of Chelsea scenes, including one set in Ranelagh Gardens. A plaque in Lawrence Street marks the site of his residence.

Even in the early nineteenth century Chelsea with its population

of less than 10,000 inhabitants was barely a town and there were
fields between it and London. In Dickens's *The Old Curiosity Shop*
the Chelsea school attended by Miss Sophia Wackles was still in
1840 ringed by countryside. The prospect of peace and quiet was
what attracted Thomas Carlyle. While house-hunting in Cheyne
Row he wrote to his wife Jane that the road ran out on to the
shore of the river:

> . . . a broad highway with huge shady trees, boats lying
> moored, and a smell of shipping and tar. Battersea Bridge (of
> wood) a few yards off; the broad river with white-trowsered,
> white-shirted Cockneys dashing by like arrows in their long
> canoes of boats; beyond the green beautiful knolls of Surrey
> with their villages – on the whole a most artificial green-
> painted, yet lively, fresh, almost opera-looking business, such
> as you can fancy. Chelsea is a singular heterogeneous kind of
> spot, very dirty and confused in some places, quite beautiful in
> others, abounding in antiquities and the traces of great men –
> Sir Thomas More, Steele, Smollett, etc.[10]

Jane was worried about the damp and the possible bugs, but to
no avail. They moved into 24 Cheyne Row in June 1834, paying
a rent of £35 per annum. Here Carlyle wrote most of his biographies and histories, including the three-volume *The French
Revolution* in 1837 that made his name and where he inveighs
against 'Dryasdust' historians. Even if little read today, Carlyle's
writings earned him a substantial Victorian reputation and the
local nickname 'The Sage of Chelsea'. In his own lifetime Oakeley
Square was changed to Carlyle Square.

This was not always, or even often, a happy marriage. Neither
Thomas nor Jane was an easy person – someone once said that it
was as well that they had married each other, thus making only
two rather than four people unhappy. Thomas Carlyle was visited
here in Chelsea by Charles Dickens, who dedicated *Hard Times* to
him, and also by Tennyson when the two men were forced by
Jane to smoke their pipes in the kitchen. Every afternoon
Thomas Carlyle went for a walk to St James's Park. He did not
find the house as quiet as he had hoped. Complaining of the
noise of adjacent pianos, he had himself built a supposedly
soundproof study up on the roof. Not only did Carlyle object to
the workforce – 'men of all types, Irish hodmen and upwards, for
real mendacity of hand, for drunkenness, greediness, mutinous

nomadism, and anarchic malfeasance throughout, exceeded all experience or conception'[11] – but he also discovered audible 'evils he knew not of' in the lower rooms, such as railway whistles.

Jane Carlyle's letters give a vivid picture of a well-off Victorian household, dealing with recalcitrant servants, putting iron bars on the windows after a burglary, and fussing over her pet dog Nero. Even the formidable Thomas seems to have welcomed the dog's affection: '. . . when he [Carlyle] comes down gloomy in the morning, or comes in wearied from his walk, the infatuated little beast dances round him on its hind legs as I ought to do and can't; and he feels flattered and surprised by such unwonted capers to his honour and glory.'[12] Jane died at Cheyne Row (then number 5, but today number 24) in 1866, a blow which Thomas said 'shattered my whole existence into immeasurable ruin'. He wrote little more other than the *Reminiscences*, published after his death. He died here in February 1881 in the first-floor room. The house has been virtually untouched since that date and is now run by the National Trust. Open to visitors between April and October, it is well worth a visit. A statue of Carlyle stands at the end of Cheyne Row facing the Thames.

The friend who had suggested to the Carlyles that they might like to move to Chelsea was the journalist and critic Leigh Hunt, himself a resident at 22 Upper Cheyne Row in a charming little house which has survived. Whereas Carlyle demanded absolute silence when he was working, Hunt with a household full of seven children had to make do as best he could. Whilst here he did manage to produce *The Town* (1848), a guidebook which still conjures up the atmosphere of mid-nineteenth-century London. He is generally thought to have been the basis for the character of Skimpole in Dickens's *Bleak House*. Hunt moved away from Chelsea to Kensington. Beneath Hunt's bust in Kensal Green Cemetery are his own lines: 'Write me as one that loves his fellow men.'

Whereas Thomas Carlyle lived in Chelsea for over forty-five years, another of his near neighbours, also a writer and philosopher, found Chelsea much less hospitable. In September 1849, after the failure of the revolutions of 1848, Karl Marx and his family came to live at 4 Anderson Street, just off the King's Road. With no money or income the Marxes were soon badly in debt and after six months they were evicted. Marx's wife, Jenny, described in a letter to a friend what happened:

> We had to leave the house the next day. It was cold, rainy and dull. My husband looked for accommodation for us. When he mentioned the four children nobody would take us in. Finally a friend helped us, we paid our rent and I hastily sold all my beds to pay the chemist, the baker, the butcher and the milk-men who, alarmed at the sight of the sequestration, suddenly besieged me with their bills. The beds which we had sold were taken out and put on a cart. What was happening? It was well after sunset. We were contravening English law. The landlord rushed up to us with two constables, maintaining that there might be some of his belongings among the things, and that we wanted to make away abroad. In less than five minutes there were two or three hundred persons loitering around our door – the whole Chelsea mob. The beds were brought in again – they could not be delivered to the buyer until after sunrise next day. When we had sold all our possessions we were in a position to pay what we owed to the last farthing. I went with my little darlings to the two small rooms we are now occupying in the German Hotel, 1, Leicester St., Leicester Square. There for £5 a week we were given a human reception.[13]

During the first decades of the nineteenth century Chelsea's population began to increase rapidly and the ecclesiastical authorities decided that another church was needed to supplement that of Chelsea Old Church. Very different in size from its ancient and more intimate predecessor, St Luke's was completed in 1824 and its spire remains a local landmark. Literary associations have included the Reverend Kingsley, whose son Charles was to write several novels including *The Water-Babies* and also to become Professor of History at Cambridge. St Luke's saw the marriage in 1836 of Charles Dickens to Catherine Hogarth.

When the manor house was pulled down in 1753 it was replaced by Cheyne Walk, a very fashionable street much favoured by Victorian writers and intellectuals. Elizabeth Stevenson was born at 93 Cheyne Walk in 1810. After her mother's death and her clergyman father's remarriage, the young girl was brought up by an aunt in Cheshire. In 1832 she married the Reverend William Gaskell of Manchester and began to write novels as Mrs

Gaskell. Her *North and South* is about a young woman who moves from the rural south of England to the industrial north, and the very different world she encounters there. Another woman novelist was connected with Cheyne Walk, if only for a tragically short time. At the age of sixty-one George Eliot married a banker called J. W. Cross, twenty-one years her junior, and moved into 4 Cheyne Walk. Three weeks later she caught a chill at a concert and died. Further down Cheyne Walk to the west is the lovely Queen's House, now 16 Cheyne Walk. Dante Gabriel Rossetti lived here between 1862 and 1882, for a part of the time with the poet Algernon Swinburne. Novelist George Meredith stuck it out for just one night, and then left, objecting to Rossetti's style of living – he used to hold wild parties which upset his neighbours.[14] Nevertheless he still appears in the 'Art' panel at the old Town Hall, and a bust commemorates him on the Embankment opposite the house.

Two years after Rossetti moved out, Chelsea was to witness yet another thoroughly unconventional figure striding through its streets, oblivious to the normal dictates of society. In the summer of 1884, Oscar Wilde bought 16 (now 34) Tite Street with his wife Constance. Tite Street was known as an artists' quarter. The artist James Whistler had had the White House especially built for him, and the eminent painter John Singer Sargent lived at 31 Tite Street where he painted portraits of the actress Ellen Terry, another Chelsea resident, and of the author Henry James. The long studio windows of the Tite Street houses are still visible. At first the Wildes got on well and they had two sons. Gradually, however, his homosexual tendencies began to emerge, and in March 1893 the increasingly successful playwright, author of *Lady Windermere's Fan* and the banned *Salome*, took rooms at the Savoy Hotel. There were still family gatherings, as in September 1894 when the Wildes went to Worthing for a holiday – the three weeks there were responsible for *The Importance of Being Earnest*.[15] By then his friendship with Lord Alfred Douglas had already set in train the events which led to Wilde's arrest in room 53 of the Cadogan Hotel in Sloane Street for sodomy. One of Sir John Betjeman's best poems, 'The Arrest of Oscar Wilde at the Cadogan Hotel', shows Wilde being implored by his friends to escape to the Continent. He delays, and two plainclothes policemen arrive:

> '*Mr Woilde, we 'ave come for tew take yew*
> *Where felons and criminals dwell:*
> *We must ask yew tew leave with us quoietly*
> *For this* is *the Cadogan Hotel.*'

The poem ends with Oscar Wilde being helped into a hansom cab. The Cadogan Hotel is still there, and both its architecture and style have changed little from what they were a hundred years ago. After Wilde's arrest crowds gathered outside his house in Tite Street, actually breaking in and rifling through the rooms – as in Marx's case, too, an example of the Chelsea mob at its worst. The house was eventually sold in order to pay off Wilde's debts. After his release from Reading Gaol in 1897, Wilde lived in France where he died in 1900 at the age of forty-six.

In the last hundred years Chelsea has been something of a literary haven and it is impossible to include everyone. But to pick out some of the most famous and interesting – if Oscar Wilde had walked west from Tite Street, he would have come to 6 Victoria (now Netherton) Grove where Arnold Bennett lived from 1891 until he moved to 75 Cadogan Square in 1923.[16] Or Wilde might have strolled along the Chelsea Embankment, built in the 1870s and which, although it lopped off part of the Physic Garden, was praised by E. M. Forster in *Howard's End* (1910) as 'something continental' and 'an open space used rightly'. Here Margaret Schlegel meets Henry Wilcox once again, an encounter which leads to their fateful marriage. If Wilde had walked east, he might have visited Bram Stoker who lived at 18 St Leonard's Terrace. Stoker was the author of *Dracula*, published in 1897 whilst he was living here. Wilde might have gone to the new Court Theatre opened in Sloane Square in 1888. Several plays by John Galsworthy and Somerset Maugham, both Chelsea residents, were performed here. In fact it was the production at the Court of Maugham's *Lady Frederick* in October 1907 which made Maugham's name: within a year he had four plays running concurrently in the West End.[17] Shaw's works were often put on at the Court. In *The Unbearable Bassington* (1912) by Saki there is a satirical scene in which a first-night audience gathers at the Straw Exchange Theatre ostensibly to see a new play by 'Sherard Blaw, the dramatist who had discovered himself, and who had given so ungrudgingly of his discovery to the world'. The High Society is there to see, to be seen, and above all to make itself heard: 'Like sheep that feed greedily before the coming of a storm, the star-ling-voices seemed impelled to extra effort by the knowledge of four imminent intervals of acting during which they would be hushed into constrained silence.' Renamed the Royal Court Theatre, it staged the first performance of John Osborne's *Look Back in Anger* on 8 May 1956 – a fact which is now enshrined in every guidebook to the area.

Not every young writer hammering away at the typewriter in Chelsea is guaranteed success. The young P. G. Wodehouse moved into Markham Square – which he called 'a dismal back-water' – in 1900, hurrying each morning to the Hong Kong and Shanghai Bank in the City and returning home each evening to write short stories. At first he met only with 'a blizzard of rejection slips', but by September 1902 moderate success encouraged him to give up his job.[18] He then moved briefly to 23 Walpole Street, Chelsea, before leaving London altogether. At the other end of his career was Henry James, who moved into 21 Carlyle Mansions, Cheyne Walk, in 1913. He toyed with an autobiography but failed to finish it by the time of his death three years later. There is a memorial to him in Chelsea Old Church where he had often worshipped and where his funeral service was held. Carlyle Mansions seems to have exercised a fascination for many writers. T. S. Eliot lived here after the Second World War, as did Ian Fleming. In 1952, Fleming was tapping away on a gold-plated typewriter, revising the first James Bond novel, *Casino Royale*, with Eliot living below on the second floor – a wonderfully unlikely juxtaposition.[19]

Other names come crowding in: Dylan Thomas in Manresa Road during the Second World War, treating his wife Caitlin with typical disrespect; the young John Betjeman living with his parents in Church Street, desperately homesick for Highgate; the Sitwells at 2 Carlyle Square; A. A. Milne at 13 Mallord Street in the 1920s and 1930s, where he wrote *Winnie-the-Pooh* in 1926 and *Toad of Toad Hall* in 1929. The pleasures which Chelsea offers in abundance, from the Royal Avenue and the charming squares to Chelsea Hospital and the Physic Garden, will never cease to attract writers and literary figures, although only the most successful will be able to afford to buy property here.

Clerkenwell
and Smithfield

Set back a little way off Clerkenwell Road, in the south section of what remains of St John's Square, is the medieval St John's Gate. Built in 1504, it still bestrides the road which until recently had cars zooming underneath. In the last few months, however, bollards have closed it off to all except pedestrians and cyclists. This is an excellent development for the walker, because to stand beneath the Gate is to be at the very heart of much of London's literary history. Here might walk the shades of Shakespeare, Hogarth, Johnson, Goldsmith and Garrick, all of whom were closely connected with this gatehouse. Few other spots in London can conjure up such a wealth of memories.

St John's Gate was originally part of the Priory of St John, unceremoniously closed down by Henry VIII during the Reformation in the 1530s. The last prior is thought to have died of a broken heart. Most of the priory buildings were demolished – but not, thankfully, the Gate, which instead was used as the offices of the Master of the Revels, whose duties included theatre censorship. This post was largely filled by noblemen wishing to receive a salary for not too much work. Every play acted in Tudor and Stuart times was supposed to pass through the office of the Master of the Revels for authorisation, a fee naturally being charged for each production. A certain amount of political and religious censorship was imposed, and it is therefore highly probable that William Shakespeare came to St John's Gate to argue with the Master of the Revels over passages in his work.

In the eighteenth century the Gate was in part a coffee-house run by Richard Hogarth, ex-schoolmaster, failed author, and father of William the artist who was born nearby in Bartholomew Close in November 1697. The young William must have known the Gate well, and no doubt the conversation at the coffee-house stimulated in him that passionate curiosity about London life and people which appears so clearly in his paintings and engravings. Hogarth first made his name with a painting of a scene from John Gay's *The Beggar's Opera* of 1728, and throughout his career his strong sense of narrative or storytelling was demonstrated in his sequences of paintings such as 'A Harlot's Progress', 'A Rake's Progress', 'Industry and Idleness' and the 'Election' series. He was also friendly with, and much admired by, Henry Fielding. The critic William Hazlitt ranked Hogarth second only to Shakespeare as a comic author: 'The wonderful knowledge which he possessed of human life and manners, is only to be surpassed (if it can be) by the power of invention with which he has combined and contrasted his materials in the most ludicrous and varied points of view, and by the mastery of execution with which he has embodied and made tangible the very thoughts and passing movements of the mind.'[1]

Later in the eighteenth century St John's Gate housed the editorial offices of the *Gentleman's Magazine*, a publication run by Edward Cave and the first time that the word 'magazine' was used in the sense familiar to us today. Cave was a harsh taskmaster but he did succeed in building up the circulation to the then remarkable figure of 15,000 copies a month, largely because he possessed an eye for spotting talent. Oliver Goldsmith was one of the contributors who came to the Gate to hand in his work. Another was the young Samuel Johnson, whose labours here provided his only source of remuneration during his early years in London. Johnson was always a lazy man; like so many authors he would find any and every excuse to put off setting pen to paper! He did, however, hit upon a method for making sure he met his deadlines, as recalled by his first biographer, John Hawkins: 'His practice was to shut himself up in a room assigned to him at St John's Gate, to which he would not suffer any one to approach, except the compositor or Cave's boy for matter, which, as fast as he composed it, he tumbled out at the door.'[2] One visitor who was welcome at the Gate was the young David Garrick, who is known to have entertained his friends with little dramatic sketches. The Gate can therefore claim to have been the venue for the début of the eighteenth century's greatest actor, renowned for his playing of the leading parts in Shakespeare's works.

Today the Gate is back in the hands of the Order of St John, which was refounded in the Victorian period and whose best-known offspring is the St John Ambulance Brigade. The Order was originally established at the end of the eleventh century in order to guard the pilgrims on their way to the Holy Land. It was an international body, and the British section built its head-quarters here in Clerkenwell in the 1140s. The Knights of St John owned land all over the country – seen, for example, in the name of St John's Wood in north London – but unlike the Knights Templars they were more than just a military body since they also provided medical care for the pilgrims. In the Middle Ages Clerkenwell lay outside the boundaries of the City, and there was thus plenty of room for the Order to build its priory there. To the north of the priory was a well around which the parish clerks staged medieval mystery plays, hence the name 'Clerks' Well' and then Clerkenwell.[3] The well itself was covered over in the nineteenth century but rediscovered by workmen in 1924 and is still visible from the pavement in Farringdon Lane. To the south of the Priory of St John were the fields described by William Fitzstephen, a clerk to Thomas à Becket, in his *Chronicle* of 1174: 'A smooth field where every Friday there is a celebrated rendezvous of fine horses to be sold, and in another quarter are placed vendibles of the peasant, swine with their deep flanks, and cows and oxen of immense bulk.' From 'smooth field' comes Smithfield, and in Fitzstephen's description can also be detected the origins of the famous Smithfield market.[4]

The English Knights of St John would have returned periodically to their Clerkenwell base, witnessing the myriad activities which took place on the fringes of their land, much of which sprang from another religious institution founded in Smithfield. In the early twelfth century a former court jester turned man of God called Rahere decided to embark on a pilgrimage to Rome. Whilst on his way there he contracted malaria and seemed certain to die – until, that is, he saw a vision of St Bartholomew, the patron saint of healing, who told him that he would recover if, on his return to London, he established a church and a hospital. Rahere was true to his word, and in 1123 he founded the church which we know today as St Bartholomew the Great and also St Bartholomew's Hospital, better known as Bart's.[5] Over 850 years later, notwithstanding plagues, fires and wars, both remain on the same sites. Rahere's effigy can be seen inside the church, which, with its wonderful Norman atmosphere, offers one of the unmissable experiences of London. It is the oldest parish church in the capital. The church inside the hospital is St Bartholomew the Less; Inigo Jones, architect and theatrical designer, was christened here in 1573, although the building was largely rebuilt in 1823.

For the purposes of the literary enthusiast, however, it is the third of Rahere's creations which is of most importance. Bartholomew Fair was first held in 1133 as a means of raising money for the church through the tolls charged on goods sold. One commodity in which Bartholomew Fair specialised was the sale of cloth, as is indicated by the street leading off West Smithfield to the east which is called Cloth Fair. For centuries the fair was a rowdy and vigorous annual event which began on 24 August, St Bartholomew's Day, and naturally enough attracted writers and observers.[6] The best description of it is in Ben Jonson's comedy *Bartholomew Fair*, first performed at the Hope theatre in 1614. Jonson clearly knew the fair well and he peopled his play with the mixed assortment of types who flocked to its pleasures. There is Ursula the 'juicy and wholesome' pig woman who so overflows her chair that it needs to be 'let out o' the sides for me, that my hips might play', and Joan Trask the gingerbread-seller. A pickpocket roams through the crowds, as do the country bumpkin Bartholomew Cokes and the Puritan, Zeal-of-the-Land Busy. The latter proclaims that 'Thou are the seat of the Beast, O Smithfield . . . Idolatry peepeth out on every side of thee'. Busy knocks over the little biscuit figures of the gingerbread woman because they are an 'idolatrous grove of images', and he finally ends up in the stocks.

Another visitor to Bartholomew Fair, inevitably, was Samuel Pepys. He noted the 'Marey Andrey' play he saw – the forerunner of Mr Punch – and also 'monkeys dancing on the ropes . . . such dirty sport that I was not pleased with it'. Pepys went into some of the booths, peering at the Bearded Lady before being shown up by the Learned Horse which picked out Pepys as the spectator most liking a pretty wench in a corner!

Apart from the priories of St John and St Bartholomew the Great, two other religious houses had also been founded in Clerkenwell and Smithfield during the Middle Ages. There was the Nunnery of St Mary which stood to the north of Clerkenwell Green, and the Priory of Charterhouse, established in 1371 on the site of what had been a plague-pit during the Black Death over twenty years before. Thomas More spent four years here as a novice before deciding to re-enter the world. These religious establishments were not universally popular. In 1381 during the Peasants' Revolt the Priory of St John was razed to the ground, principally because its then prior, Sir Robert Hales – nicknamed Hobbe the Robber – was also the government's chief tax-collector. Fortunately the Norman crypt was left intact, as the regular guided visits over the Order of St John's buildings disclose.[7] Many of the peasants camped out around Clerkenwell Green during this episode in English history celebrated by a later writer connected with Clerkenwell, William Morris, in his long poem *A Dream of John Ball*. The leader of the revolt, Wat Tyler, is thought to have taken sanctuary in the church of St Bartholomew the Great, but to no avail as he was dragged out by William Walworth and beheaded in Smithfield.

All four religious houses were closed down during the 1530s and their buildings largely destroyed. By the sixteenth century the growth of London's population meant that parts of the area were starting to become inhabited, although not always by the respectable and powerful. Turnmill Street in particular, then known as Turnbull Street, was a Tudor 'red light' district. In *Henry IV, Part 2* Falstaff reports to Bardolph how fond Justice Shallow is of glorifying his supposed youthful exploits here: 'Lord! Lord! how subject we old men are to this vice of lying! This same starved justice hath done nothing but prate to me of the wildness of his youth and the feats he hath done about Turnbull Street, and every third word a lie. . . .'

Appropriately enough there was also a theatre in Clerkenwell at this time, to the north of the Green in roughly today's Woodbridge Street. Converted from its former use as an inn some time in the winter of 1604–5, it is supposed to have been the place where the young Shakespeare earned a few groats by holding people's horses. As Shakespeare was already a well-respected and middle-aged man by the time the Red Bull opened, one detects another of London's hoary myths. What is certain, however, is that the Red Bull was notorious both for the bawdy flavour of its stage plays and for the unruliness of its audience; as one con-temporary observer complained: '. . . the Benches, the tiles, the laths, the stones, Oranges, Apples, Nuts, flew about most liberally and . . . there were mechanicks of all professions who fell everyone to his own trade, and dissolved a house in an instant, and made a ruine of a stately Fabrick.'[8] Some of the first actresses to appear on the stage in England performed at the Red Bull – until 1660 this was not legal. The Red Bull closed down in 1642.

Apart from the streets around the Fleet river – where today's Farringdon Road now runs – and the Red Bull, Clerkenwell was a fashionable seventeenth-century address. Several members of the nobility lived in the neighbourhood, one of whom, Margaret Duchess of Newcastle, was among the first British women writers. She lived in Newcastle House in Clerkenwell Close which had been built out of the ruins of the Nunnery of St Mary. Rather cruelly known as 'Mad Madge', she published her *Poems* in 1662 and also several plays.[9] Pepys was often scathing about her works, but she did write perhaps the first ever conservative Utopia, *The Blazing World* (1668), a book which was clearly a reaction to her own and her husband's experiences during the recent Civil War when they had been forced to flee to France. The inhabitants of the Blazing World are shown to be believers in a divine government, and when they come to Earth armed with a fleet and flaming fireballs they chase away Oliver Cromwell and set up Charles II as 'the Head Monarch of all this World'. A feminist touch is provided when she attacks a society in which 'all heroick Actions, publick Imployments, powerfull Governments' are kept from women. After her death in 1673 the Duchess's body lay in state for several months at Newcastle House. Demolished in 1793, the only reminder of Newcastle House now is in the name Newcastle Row.

Two other writers of widely differing character who lived around Clerkenwell Green from the 1650s were Izaak Walton and Ned Ward. Walton retired here from his linen-draper's busi-ness and published in 1653 *The Compleat Angler*, a book which is still something of a bible to all fishermen. Ned Ward owned a pub on Clerkenwell Green whilst at the same time writing his sala-cious London guidebook *The London Spy* which first appeared in

1698, but which he then frequently revised. Today Ward is a neglected figure and yet it is well worth searching secondhand bookshops for a copy of his intemperate, rude but always revealing account of London life and manners at the turn of the seventeenth century. A third resident near Clerkenwell Green at this time was Thomas Britton, known as 'the musical small-coal man'. A coalman by trade, Britton turned his little home in Jerusalem Passage at the top of the Green into a weekly concert-room from 1678. Handel was reputedly one of the musicians who subsequently performed here. On his death in 1714, Britton was buried at St James's Church, Clerkenwell. A small green plaque now records the whereabouts of his home, and nearby Britton Street is also named after him.[10]

It is difficult to keep Samuel Pepys out of the literary history of any part of London, and sure enough he was familiar with Clerkenwell in the 1660s. Typically, he attended the church of St James not out of piety but in order to observe the local beauty, Miss Frances Butler. His diary entries during 1664 detail the story:

> Lord's Day – Walked out with my boy through the City over Moorfields and thence to Clerkenwell Church, and there, as I wished, sat next pew to the fair Butler, who indeed is a most perfect beauty still; and one I do very much admire myself, for my choice of her, for a beauty, having the best lower part of her face that I ever saw all days of my life. . . . So away back to Clerkenwell church, thinking to have got sight of la belle Boteler again, but failed; and so after church walked all over the fields home; and there my wife was angry with me for not coming home and for gadding abroad to look after beauties, she told me plainly; so I made all peace, and to supper.

Miss Butler's church has been rebuilt since Pepys's time out remains on the same site. Apart from visiting Bartholomew Fair on several occasions, Pepys also went to the Horse Fair at Smithfield in 1668, paying £50 for 'a fine pair of black horses' for his new carriage. He haunted Little Britain, too, because of its numerous bookshops.

Eight years after Pepys's death in 1703, the first copies of the *Spectator* were printed in Little Britain. Its first two editors were Richard Steele and Joseph Addison, both of whom had been educated nearby at Charterhouse School which had grown out of the dissolved monastery in 1611. Another famous Carthusian literary 'old boy', this time in the nineteenth century, was William Makepeace Thackeray, who was here in the 1820s and who referred to it in *Vanity Fair* as 'The Slaughterhouse', influenced no doubt by the fight he once had with an older boy and during which his nose was broken. In his later novels *Pendennis* and *The Newcomes* several of the characters attend this school. In 1872 it moved to Godalming in Surrey. The buildings are now in part occupied by Bart's Hospital but also by pensioners – back in 1611 Thomas Sutton had originally founded a hospital for eighty poor gentlemen and a free school for forty boys.[11] Despite extensive damage in May 1941 to the Charterhouse, the Master's Residence facing Charterhouse Square dates from 1716 and the visitor entering the cloistered calm of the Master's Court does so under a fifteenth-century arch. Charterhouse is open by arrangement to visitors on Wednesday afternoons – an opportunity not to be missed.

In the eighteenth century Clerkenwell was renowned for its skilled craftsmen who made clocks, watches and jewellery as well as being printers, engravers and bookbinders. Less happily it also contained a notorious gaol called the Cold Bath Fields Prison which stood on the site of what is today Mount Pleasant post office on Farringdon Road. Built in 1794 its harsh regime often necessitated the calling in of troops in order to quell the rioting inmates. Coleridge, in his poem of 1799 called 'The Devil's Thoughts', mentions the Cold Bath Fields Prison:

> *As he went through the Cold-Bath Fields he saw*
> *A solitary cell;*
> *And the Devil was pleased, for it gave him a hint*
> *For improving his prisons in hell.*[12]

The prison was closed down in 1877 to make way for the new Rosebery Avenue.

Throughout the eighteenth century Bartholomew Fair was still being held for ten days starting on 24 August, but by the end of that century it had lost its former fashionable air. William Wordsworth visited it in 1802 with his friend Charles Lamb and was not impressed, as *The Prelude* makes abundantly clear:

> *. . . what a hell*
> *For eyes and ears! what anarchy and din*
> *Barbarian and infernal! 'tis a dream,*

Monstrous in colour, motion, shape, sight, sound . . .
All out-o'-th'-way, far-fetch'd, perverted things,
All freaks of Nature, all Promethean thoughts
Of man; his dulness, madness, and their feats,
All jumbled up together to make up
This Parliament of Monsters. . . .

Under increasing pressure from the authorities, who distrusted its general rowdiness, Bartholomew Fair was held for the last time in 1855. A few years later another ancient Smithfield activity came to an end when the cattle-market was shut down. As late as 1853 over one and a half million sheep and a quarter of a million cattle were still sold at Smithfield each year, with the inevitable result that the neighbourhood was usually dirty and squalid. Pip in *Great Expectations* calls it 'a shameful place', and in his earlier novel *Oliver Twist* Dickens gives a lengthy description:

It was market morning. The ground was covered, nearly ankle-deep with filth and mire; a thick stream perpetually rising from the reeking bodies of the cattle, and mingling with the fog, which seemed to rest upon the chimney tops, hung heavily above ... the hideous and discordant din that resounded from every corner of the market; and the unwashed, squalid and dirty figures constantly running to and fro, and bursting in and out of the throng rendered it a stunning and bewildering scene, which quite confounded the senses.

In 1868 the present covered market was constructed, complete with decorative ironwork.

By the early nineteenth century Clerkenwell and Smithfield had become notorious slum areas, especially around the Fleet river. Rookeries and tenements sprang up all over as the population of Clerkenwell alone trebled between 1800 and 1860. A journalist writing in the *Illustrated London News* of 22 May 1847 declared that 'In Clerkenwell broods the darkness of utter ignorance. In its lanes and alleys the lowest debauch – the coarsest enjoyment – the most infuriate passions – the most unrestrained vice – roar and riot.'[13] Several streets, such as Cock Lane, were famed for their brothels and seedy taverns. Saffron Hill was London's criminal quarter, and it is here that Dickens locates Fagin's den in *Oliver Twist*. Young Oliver received his first disastrous lessons in pickpocketing from the Artful Dodger on

Clerkenwell Green. The Dodger and Charley Bates steal Mr Brownlow's handkerchief, but when he turns around he fastens the blame on Oliver, who is finally captured after a chase through the streets of Clerkenwell.

The Green itself established a reputation as a radical meeting-place, a somewhat daring location in view of the fact that the imposing building at the bottom was the Middlesex Sessions House (now a conference centre run by the Freemasons). One of the first British radicals, John Wilkes, had been born only a hundred yards away in St John's Square in 1764. Wilkes was not only a politician who fought for the freedom of the press but also the author of the notorious pornographic treatise *Essay on Woman*. The journalist and writer William Cobbett, who hated London and depicted it as 'The Great Wen', was another who spoke on Clerkenwell Green, condemning the Corn Laws in 1826.

In 1887 a contingent of protesting marchers led by the writers George Bernard Shaw, William Morris and Annie Besant set off from Clerkenwell Green on their way to Trafalgar Square. There they were attacked by mounted police, and the incident became known as 'Bloody Sunday'. Other observers of a rather different political hue visited the Green to confirm their suspicions: George Gissing came in the late 1880s whilst researching his novel *The Nether World* (1889). He wrote to a friend: 'Last Sunday evening I spent on Clerkenwell Green – a great assembly place for radical meetings and the like. A more disheartening scene is difficult to imagine – the vulgar blatant scoundrels!'[14] Much of the rather bleak *The Nether World* is set in Clerkenwell.

One reason for Clerkenwell Green's radical reputation was the existence at number 37 of the London Patriotic Club, a progressive working-men's club set up in 1872 by John Stuart Mill and several others, including the old Chartist and founder of the *Reynolds News* which bore his name, George Reynolds. Housed in the oldest building in Clerkenwell, which had originally been built in 1738 as a Welsh charity school, the London Patriotic Club, unlike so many others of its type, was open to women. In 1892 the Club moved out and William Morris put up the essential guarantee of £50 which enabled the Twentieth Century Press, this country's first socialist printing press, to move into 37 Clerkenwell Green.[15] The press published the weekly newspaper, *Justice*, and several of Morris's socialist pamphlets. Many of the Twentieth Century Press's publications were illustrated by

Morris's long-time collaborator Walter Crane, probably best known for the coloured picture-books which he produced for children. It was to the Twentieth Century Press on Clerkenwell Green that Lenin came for eighteen months between 1902 and 1903 when he was editing the Bolshevik paper *Iskra*. Seventeen issues were run off on these presses. Since 1933 the building has been the home of the Marx Memorial Library, an organisation which holds thousands of books and pamphlets on the history of the labour movement both in Britain and abroad. Visitors are able to see the 'Lenin Room'. In 1963 the building was threatened with demolition, but a campaign led by John Betjeman and others persuaded the Greater London Council to grant a preservation order in 1966.

The drabness and gloom of late-nineteenth-century Clerkenwell were familiar not just to George Gissing but also to the future Poet Laureate, Robert Bridges, who was the casualty physician at Bart's Hospital between 1877 and 1879. In one year Bridges worked out that he saw 30,940 patients, spending an average of one and a half minutes on each case.[16] In 1881 a severe attack of pneumonia brought his medical career to an end. Poet Laureate from 1913 until his death in 1930, Bridges refused to write poetry to order and consequently was dubbed 'The Silent Laureate'. Several successors might profitably have followed his example.

One of the best novels about Clerkenwell was written just after the First World War by Arnold Bennett, whose excellent *Riceyman Steps* was published in 1923 and centres on a secondhand bookshop run by the miserly Henry Earlforward. Bennett's Riceyman Steps is today's Gwynne Place, and Riceyman Square is Granville Square, tucked away off King's Cross Road – a thoroughfare which Bennett portrays as 'a hell of noise and dust and dirt, with the County of London tram-cars, and motor-lorries and heavy horse-drawn vans sweeping north and south in a vast clangour of iron thudding and grating on iron and granite, beneath the bedroom windows of a defenceless populace'. Bennett spent much time exploring the area, and his firsthand research evokes a picture of sad, seedy but not unsympathetic Clerkenwell, a 'great metropolitan industrial district'.[17]

Today Arnold Bennett would need to write a very different novel. In the last few years the 'discovery' of Clerkenwell has led to its consequent move 'up market'. The *Guardian* newspaper is now in Farringdon Road, wine-bars and bistros ring Clerkenwell Green, and a house in the Georgian Sekforde Street will set the buyer back over £300,000. Despite these changes the area still retains its own unique flavour, helped in large measure by the Italian community who enliven the neighbourhood with their shops and festivals.

Coming and Going

During one of his frequent disputes with the City of London in the early seventeenth century, James I – poet and author of a pamphlet attacking the new craze for smoking – threatened to move his court away to Oxford, thereby diminishing the capital's importance. After he had finished his ranting and raving, one of his opponents replied: 'Sire, there will always be one consolation for the merchants of London: your majesty cannot take the Thames along with you.'[1]

From Ice Age to Nuclear Age the Thames has always been with us, the river which Kipling wrote 'has known everything' and which was called 'liquid history' by Samuel Johnson and 'Old Father Thames' by Alexander Pope. It was the Thames that accounted for London's very existence and for its eventual emergence as the country's capital city. The Roman historian Tacitus wrote that London was 'filled with traders and a celebrated centre of commerce', most of which was conveyed to the city via the river. Today, nearly 2000 years on, despite the high value of riverside property, several walks enable the pedestrian to stroll along beside it, combining a little bit of exercise with a visit to one of the attractive riverside pubs such as the Dove in Hammersmith, the Anchor on Bankside or the Angel and the Mayflower in Rotherhithe.

Not surprisingly, such an immutable feature of London's life plays a major part in literary London. The Thames has provided work for fictional characters such as Gaffer Hexham in Dickens's *Our Mutual Friend* who rowed between Southwark Bridge and London Bridge fishing out corpses. Flesh-and-blood figures employed on the riverside have included Geoffrey Chaucer, once the controller of the Wool Quay 600 years ago, John Taylor the seventeenth-century boatman and 'Water Poet', and the former warehouseman Joseph Conrad. The Thames has proved rewarding, too, for more nefarious activities, appreciated by the smugglers in Arthur Morrison's excellent novel *The Hole in the Wall* (1902) and by Dr Fu Manchu – 'the Thames is his highway' remarks our hero Nayland Smith in the first Fu Manchu book, *The Mystery of Dr Fu Manchu* (1913). Finally, the Thames has often been a source of inspiration. The biographer John Aubrey in his *Lives of Eminent Persons*, written in the seventeenth century, describes Sir Walter Ralegh's Durham House, where the Adelphi Terrace now stands to the south of the Strand: 'I well remember his study, which was on a little turret that looked into and over the Thames, and had the prospect which is as pleasant, perhaps, as any in the world, and which not only refreshes the eye-sight, but cheers the spirit (and to speak my mind) I believe enlarges an ingenious man's thoughts.'

Of course the Thames was also a nuisance; it had to be crossed, and by the time of the Emperor Claudius' visit to this country in AD 43 some kind of wooden bridge had been erected. Not until Norman times was a more permanent stone bridge built, designed by a churchman called Peter de Colechurch who began work in 1176. He had in fact died by the time it was completed in 1209, but his masterpiece survived for over 650 years – a feat indeed when compared with the state of our M25 motorway after only a few months. Paid for in part by a tax on wool, London Bridge was regarded as a medieval wonder of the world, being much admired by foreign visitors. There was a chapel in the middle, dedicated to Thomas à Becket, a drawbridge and also a gate at the southern end known as 'Traitor's Gate' on which the heads and other bits and pieces of executed traitors would be placed as a savage warning to all those entering the City. In 1566, J. J. Scaliger recorded: 'In London there were ever many heads on the bridge . . . I have seen there, as it were masts of ships and at the top of them quarters of men's corpses.'[2] Thirty years later another foreign visitor counted over thirty heads on the gate. Sir Thomas More's head was spiked there in 1535, but his devoted daughter Margaret bribed the keeper to drop it into a boat late one night as she was rowed underneath. It was then buried at Canterbury.

The nineteen arches of the bridge rested on starlings or 'feet' which obstructed the flow of the river, creating an effect like a miniature Niagara Falls; hence the old maxim that London Bridge was made for wise men to go over and fools to go under. Fifty watermen a year were drowned whilst shooting these rapids. Perhaps the best description of such an escapade is in George Borrow's *Lavengro*, which although published in 1851 refers to this old London Bridge:

> As I stood upon the bridge, gazing into the jaws of the pool, a small boat shot suddenly through the arch beneath my feet. There were three persons in it; an oarsman in the middle, whilst a man and woman sat at the stern. I shall never forget the thrill of horror which went through me at this sudden apparition. What! – a boat – a small boat – passing beneath that arch into yonder roaring gulf! Yes, yes, down through that awful water-way, with more than the swiftness of an arrow, shot the boat, or skiff, right into the jaws of the pool. A monstrous breaker curls over the prow – there is no hope; the boat is swamped, and all drowned in that strangling vortex. No! the boat, which appeared to have the buoyancy of a feather, skipped over the threatening horror, and the next moment was out of danger, the boatman, a true boatman of Cockaigne, that – elevating one of his sculls in sign of triumph, the man halloing, and the woman, a true Englishwoman that – of a certain class – waving her shawl.

For many years the Thames was full of fish. William Fitz-stephen in his biography of Thomas à Becket, written in 1183, referred to it as 'teeming with fish', and another observer in 1586 listed the variety to be found there, ending: 'What should I speake of the fat and sweet salmons, dailie taken in this streame. . . .'[3] But, as London grew, more and more muck and rubbish was deposited in the river, reducing it to a stagnant crawl. This meant that during particularly severe winters – about twice each century on average – the Thames froze over, prompting Londoners to call it 'Freezeland Street' and to hold 'frost fairs'. That of 1683–4 was fully documented by the diarist John Evelyn, who called it a 'carnival on water'.[4] Booths, stalls, taverns sprang up as well as what Evelyn coyly calls 'lewder places'. Bull-running, football matches and even a foxhunt took place on the ice before the thaw began in February 1684. In some years the Thames only partially froze. James Boswell stood on London Bridge in January 1763 and viewed 'with a pleasing horror the rude and terrible appearance of the river, partly froze up, partly covered with enormous shoals of floating ice which often crashed against each other'.[5] In Virginia Woolf's novel *Orlando* (1928) there is a fine description of the chaos following the sudden thaw of a frost fair:

> All was riot and confusion. The river was strewn with icebergs. Some of these were as broad as a bowling green and as high as a house; others no bigger than a man's hat, but most fantastically twisted. Now would come down a whole convoy of ice blocks sinking everything that stood in their way. Now, eddying and swirling like a tortured serpent, the river would seem to be hurtling itself between the fragments and tossing them from bank to bank, so that they could be heard smashing against the piers and pillars. But what was the most awful and inspiring of terror was the sight of the human creatures who had been trapped in the night and now paced their twisting and precarious islands in the utmost agony of spirit. Whether they jumped into the flood or stayed on the ice their doom was certain. Sometimes quite a cluster of these poor creatures would come down together, some on their knees, others suckling their babies. One old man seemed to be reading aloud from a holy book. At other times, and his fate perhaps was the most dreadful, a solitary wretch would stride down his narrow tenement alone. As they swept out to sea, some could be heard crying vainly for help, making wild promises to amend their ways, confessing their sins and vowing altars and wealth if God would hear their prayers. Others were so dazed with terror that they sat immovable and silent, looking steadfastly before them.

One group of people not happy with the frost fairs were the Thames watermen, who lost out on their fares, although in 1813–14 they dug channels in the ice, put up makeshift bridges and then charged tolls for people to get across. The importance of the Thames is demonstrated by the fact that the London historian John Stow estimated in 1598 that the river contained '2,000 wherrys and other sortes of boates', and in the next century it is thought that there were up to 40,000 watermen plying their trade. Like our taxi-drivers, both good and bad were told about the watermen. They were noted for their foul language; Boswell in his life of Samuel Johnson tells of the occasion when a waterman swore at Johnson, who then replied in kind and with interest. Not all the watermen knew their way; Pepys notes an unfortunate incident in September 1665 when being rowed to Chatham late at night: '. . . it growing dark, we were put to great difficultys, our simple yet confident waterman not knowing a step of the way; and we found ourselfs to go backward and forward, which, in that dark night and a wild place, did vex us mightily.' But step forward John Taylor, the seventeenth-century champion of watermen like himself who was also a prolific writer. He puts their case, beset as they were by slander and competition on dry land:

> *All sorts of men work all the means they can*
> *To make a 'Thief' of every Waterman;*
> *And as it were in one consent they join*
> *To trot by land i' th' dirt, and save their coin. . . .*
> *Against the ground, we stand and knock our heels*
> *Whilst all our profit runs away on wheels.*[6]

One activity restricted to watermen survives today, namely the race for Doggett's Coat and Badge, rowed by 'Six Young Watermen' from London Bridge to Chelsea – a distance of four and a half miles. Doggett had been the co-manager of Drury Lane Theatre and also an ardent Hanoverian, and in his will of 1721 he left a sum of money for the holding of this race which was to commemorate the accession of George I.

On one issue the Thames watermen were solidly united with the City merchants – that there should be no more bridges over the Thames. The watermen feared the loss of trade, the City the loss of tolls paid on London Bridge. For centuries these powerful vested interests defeated all proposals, until in 1739 work finally began on Westminster Bridge, the second bridge over the Thames, which was completed in 1750. Like London Bridge, Westminster Bridge is full of literary interest. Henry Fielding called it 'the bridge of fools' because it was paid for by a state lottery. James Boswell was here on 10 May 1763:

At the bottom of the Haymarket I picked up a strong, jolly

young damsel, and taking her under the arm I conducted her to Westminster Bridge, and then in armour [i.e., wearing a contraceptive] complete did I engage her upon this noble edifice. The whim of doing it there with the Thames rolling below us amused me much. Yet after the brutish appetite was sated, I could not but despise myself for being so closely united with such a low wretch.

It was on this bridge, too, that the poet George Crabbe waited to hear the results of his appeal to the politician Edmund Burke. Crabbe had come up to London from Suffolk in 1780, armed only with £5 and the fierce determination to be a writer. For more than a year he struggled in vain, his experiences told in his *Journal to Mira* (later his wife): 'It's the vilest thing in the world to have but one coat. My only one has happened with a mischance, and how to manage it is some difficulty. A confounded store's modish ornament caught its elbow, and rent it half-way.' In 1781 he wrote a letter and handed it in to Burke's Westminster home, having decided that if his appeal was unsuccessful he would drown himself in the Thames.[7] It was not, and from that year, with the patronage of Burke, George Crabbe began to establish himself as a successful poet. In 1783, Crabbe's lengthy poem *The Village* was published with the encouragement of Samuel Johnson. It is a moving work which depicts a changing rural world not in a romantic haze but with great realism. Crabbe's tale of Peter Grimes in *The Borough* (1810) formed the basis of an opera by Benjamin Britten.

One of Crabbe's later friends was William Wordsworth and he, too, once dawdled on Westminster Bridge, on the morning of 3 September 1803. It was an interlude which produced one of the best-known sonnets of all, part of which simply has to be quoted in any account of literary London:

> *Earth has not anything to show more fair:*
> *Dull would he be of soul who could pass by*
> *A sight so touching in its majesty:*
> *The City now doth, like a garment, wear*
> *The beauty of the morning; silent, bare,*
> *Ships, towers, domes, theatres, and temples lie*
> *Open unto the fields and to the sky;*
> *All bright and glittering in the smokeless air.*

When Wordsworth looked from Westminster Bridge east

towards the City he would have seen a third bridge across the Thames, Blackfriars Bridge. Soon after he wrote his sonnet, several more were constructed, such as Waterloo Bridge – the poet Thomas Hood's 'Bridge of Sighs' – and Southwark Bridge where John Chivery proposed to Dickens's Little Dorrit. Further upstream were the Lambeth, Vauxhall, Chelsea and Albert bridges – so many of them in fact that Rudyard Kipling was able to write a fine poem called 'Twenty Bridges from Tower to Kew', which unfortunately is too long to quote here in full as it needs and deserves. Even old London Bridge was replaced in the 1830s, although 'Nancy's steps' where Nancy told all to Rose Maylie in *Oliver Twist* can still be seen on the south side near Southwark Cathedral. John Rennie's new bridge was built slightly to the west of where the old bridge stood. Its five stone arches meant that with only four piles in its way the Thames flowed much faster, and hence the absence since the early nineteenth century of frost fairs.

However, the Thames was still comparatively stagnant, so much so that the year 1858 was termed the year of 'The Great Stink' because of the particularly foul odours emitted by the mass of accumulated rubbish. Parliament was sufficiently stirred to authorise the construction of the Embankment, built by London's Chief Engineer, Sir Joseph Bazalgette. The Thames was narrowed, sewers installed and the thirty-seven acres reclaimed from the river turned into the pleasant Embankment Gardens. These gardens are well kept and offer a charming stroll, during which one can see the statues of several literary figures. A memorial to Sir Arthur Sullivan has been placed opposite the Savoy Theatre which he and his colleague W. S. Gilbert made famous. One of the largest statues in these gardens is of Robert Burns, which is somewhat incongruous since Burns never once came to London. This was not, however, an omission which prevented him giving emphatic advice to his brother in 1790: 'London swarms with worthless wretches who prey on their fellow creatures' thoughtlessness and inexperience. Be cautious in forming connections with comrades and companions.'[8]

Throughout the nineteenth century the Thames was a busy working river, especially after the opening of the docks. The London Dock, the East India Dock, the West India Dock and St Katharine's Dock transformed East London and brought wealth to many if not always to the dockworkers themselves. Joseph

Conrad recalled of the year 1878, when he was still a seaman and nearly twenty years away from his first published novel, that the Pool, just below London Bridge, was where 'the vessels moored stem and stern in the very strength of the tide formed one solid mass like an island covered with a forest of gaunt, leafless trees'.[9]

There are several similarities between three writers – Arthur Morrison, W. W. Jacobs and H. M. Tomlinson – who were all born in the East End in the nineteenth century, quite apart from the fact that today the work of all three is unjustly neglected. Much of their writing depicts the Thames and riverside life. Morrison was born in Poplar in 1863, and his Thames masterpiece is *The Hole in the Wall* (1902), which tells the story of a young boy growing up with his uncle who runs a shady pub on the Wapping waterfront. W. W. Jacobs was also born in 1863 but in Wapping where his father was the manager of the South Devon Wharf. As a boy Jacobs knew every inch of the riverside and, although the first sixteen years of his working life were spent as a clerk in the Savings Bank in the City, he managed to establish himself as a full-time writer after 1899 and many of his stories recount the onshore activities of off-duty sailors, usually related by the figure of 'the Night Watchman'. Just as the versatile Morrison also wrote detective fiction featuring Martin Hewitt, the only serious rival to Sherlock Holmes, Jacobs was also responsible for a number of ghost stories, among them the classic 'The Monkey's Paw'. The third member of this group of local writers, H. M. Tomlinson, was born in Poplar in 1873. His father was a foreman at the West India Dock. Like Jacobs, Tomlinson spent the early years of his life drudging away as a clerk in the City at six shillings a week. He eventually managed to break away and became a journalist. His first book, *The Sea and the Jungle* (1912), recounts his experiences on a trip to Brazil and the Amazon where he had been sent on an assignment by his magazine. Several of his books such as *Gallion's Reach*, *London River* and *Below London* portray Thames life in invigorating style.

Apart from being a source of wealth and employment in the nineteenth century, the Thames was naturally used by pleasure-seekers, sometimes strenuously so as when Lord Byron once swam three miles downstream to London Bridge. Less energetic were the boating expeditions enjoyed by William Morris in 1880 and 1881 when he travelled from Hammersmith to his other home, Kelmscott Manor, in Gloucestershire, trips which formed

the basis of several idyllic chapters in *News from Nowhere*.[10]
Another writer who often boated up and down the river was
Jerome K. Jerome. In his autobiography Jerome tells how he
returned from his honeymoon and decided to write a history-
book called 'The Story of the Thames'. Fortunately his editor
threw out all the slabs of history, retaining what we now know as
Three Men in a Boat.[11] When out punting Jerome might well have
bumped into another Thames devotee, Kenneth Grahame,
whose passionate love of the river is clear from Ratty's eulogy in
The Wind in the Willows (1908): 'It's brother and sister to me, and
aunts, and company, and food and drink, and (naturally) wash-
ing. It's my world, and I don't want any other. What it hasn't got
is not worth having, and what it doesn't know is not worth
knowing. Lord! the times we've had together!'

By the first decades of the nineteenth century, with the introduction of the steamboat and the number of bridges enabling
people to cross the river with ease, the Thames watermen died
out and the railway became the most important form of transport. Huge new railway stations were built in London, necessitat-
ing the clearance of thousands of homes and the eviction of those
living in them. Countryside became transformed into suburb – a
process famously described by Charles Dickens in *Dombey and Son*
when the railway passes through Camden, the once semi-rural
neighbourhood where he had passed much of his youth. The
private companies had their own London mainline stations, each
with a very different character. As E. M. Forster wrote in
Howard's End: '. . . he is a chilly Londoner who does not endow
his stations with some personality, and extend to them, however
shyly, the emotions of fear and love.' No one could possibly
confuse St Pancras with Victoria or Waterloo with Liverpool
Street, even if the destruction of Euston station in the 1960s
despite the protests of Sir John Betjeman ('To compare with
Euston, there is nothing')[12] and others has meant that one of the
main stations is now like any other modern building in its dull
utilitarianism.

The railway stations, like the Thames, offered jobs to some who
became writers. Jerome K. Jerome was for many years a clerk at
Euston, earning £26 a year. *Three Men in a Boat* includes a scene in
which the three men and Montmorency the dog arrive at Waterloo and there undergo an ordeal familiar to railway travellers the
world over:

We got to Waterloo at eleven, and asked where the 11.5 started from. Of course nobody knew; nobody at Waterloo ever does know where a train is going to start from, or where a train when it does start is going to, or anything about it. The porter who took our things thought it would go from number two platform, while another porter, with whom he discussed the question, had heard a rumour that it would go from number one. The station-master, on the other hand, was convinced it would start from the local. To put an end to the matter we went upstairs and asked the traffic superintendent, and he told us that he had just met a man, who said he had seen it at number three platform. We went to number three platform, but the authorities there said that they rather thought that train was the Southampton express, or else the Windsor loop. But they were sure it wasn't the Kingston train, though why they were sure it wasn't they couldn't say.

And on it went. They finally reach Kingston by slipping half a crown to an engine-driver and begging him to take them there.

If Jerome did manage to work at a London station, another famous literary figure tried and failed. Karl Marx applied for a job as a clerk with the Great Western Railway at Paddington. He was turned down because of his abominable handwriting![13]

Railway stations are inevitably associated with comings and goings. Sometimes they mark the beginning of adventures, as when Jules Verne's Phileas Fogg leaves from Charing Cross to go around the world in eighty days, or Holmes and Watson hot on the trail of another case visit the country – for instance, in one of the best stories, 'The Adventure of the Speckled Band', they set out from Waterloo for Stoke Moran. P. G. Wodehouse's Lord Emsworth and friends depart from Paddington on their way to the dream world of Blandings Castle, and it is at Victoria Station that the baby is left in the handbag so crucial to the denouement of Wilde's *The Importance of Being Earnest*. As for 'real life', Noël Coward first met Gertrude Lawrence in a train which had left Euston,[14] while the stammering schoolboy Somerset Maugham was pushed to the back of a queue at Victoria by an impatient crowd as he vainly tried to buy a ticket but was unable to get out his words.[15] Sometimes the departures are tinged with relief – Dylan Thomas used to leave from Paddington bound for his parents in Wales in order to recover after a few weeks' debauchery in London[16] – but often with sadness: it was at St Pancras that Vera Brittain said what proved to be a final farewell to her fiancé Roland Leighton in 1915, as she later recalled in her *Testament of Youth*. Some fictional characters, such as Keith Waterhouse's Billy Liar, try but never make it to London by train.

Several writers could have been found hard at work on their rail journeys. Trollope, for instance, took a tablet with him on his trips on which he scribbled away in pencil, his wife copying out his work afterwards.[17] He also made use of the train in at least one of his novels: in *The Prime Minister* the crooked Lopez travels to Willesden where he proceeds to throw himself under the Euston–Inverness express train – a similar death to that which met Mr Carker in Dickens's *Dombey and Son*. Another worker on the train was Rider Haggard, who bet his brother that he could write a better adventure-story than Robert Louis Stevenson's *Treasure Island* and produced *King Solomon's Mines* in six weeks during which he worked partly in the train between Norwich and London and partly at 69 Gunterstone Road, West Kensington.[18] George Bernard Shaw always claimed that much of his work was done between King's Cross and Hatfield on his way home by train to Ayot St Lawrence.

One businessman with cause to bless the coming of the railway was the second W. H. Smith, who realised the possibilities which now lay open to a literary entrepreneur. As the company's historian has put it:

> The conditions of coach travel had made reading virtually impossible for travellers except while waiting at inns where newspapers and journals were occasionally provided. Now – for first- and second-class passengers (at least in daytime and later by night too) – reading was not only possible: it was almost indispensable to the business man and the educated traveller.[19]

Smith became a partner in the family business in 1846, and after several years' hard bargaining with the different railway companies had by 1862 acquired exclusive rights to establish bookshops at the stations. It was an enormously profitable arrangement. Just over sixty years later, in 1934, the young Allen Lane was returning to London by train after a weekend spent in Devon with Agatha Christie and her husband. He was held up at Exeter station, found nothing suitable to read and thought up the idea of the cheap paperback – and so Penguin paperbacks were born.[20]

From 1863 the overground railway system was complemented by the Underground, originally built in order to link North London's mainline stations. The first section of line was opened between Paddington and Farringdon Street in Clerkenwell. Arnold Bennett in his *Riceyman Steps* provides a graphic description of its construction:

> All Clerkenwell was mad for the line. But when the construction began all Clerkenwell trembled. The earth opened in the most unexpected and undesirable places. Streets had to be barred to horse traffic; pavements resembled switchbacks. Hundreds of houses had to be propped, and along the line of the tunnel itself scores of houses were suddenly vacated lest they should bury their occupants.

William Morris in *News from Nowhere* (1891) scathingly referred to the Underground as 'that vapour bath of hurried and discontented humanity' – a remark more than borne out during the rush hour these days. Nevertheless, the often difficult conditions did not prevent Dylan Thomas from thinking up poems on Tube journeys or Stella Gibbons writing parts of *Cold Comfort Farm* during her journeys on the Northern Line from Swiss Cottage in the early 1930s. One enthusiast for the London Underground was the young John Betjeman, who as a schoolboy often spent every day of the holidays exploring the Tube with a friend: 'Our parents used to give us money and we'd start in the morning and travel up and down all day. . . . It used to be my boast that I'd got out at every station on the Underground.'[21] Later Betjeman was to write a fine poem called 'The Metropolitan Railway'. The Underground also features in the Sherlock Holmes story, 'The Adventure of the Bruce-Partington Plans', when the body of a young man is found on the rails by Aldgate station.

For centuries the river was London's main highway, of vital importance to all who lived in the capital and the source of much literary inspiration. Nowadays, when millions of people use the Tube and railway and the Thames flows somewhat forlornly beneath its many bridges, we must be grateful to those writers who have left accounts of its former splendour and regret the passing of the watermen, the frost fairs and the bustling culture of the docks which finally closed in the 1960s.

Yet new life is coming to the river as wharfs and warehouses are being adapted to offices and homes. Perhaps future writers will scribble away while travelling on the Dockland Light Railway or leave us descriptions of journeys undertaken on the high-speed river-buses which ply a brisk trade. Whatever happens in the years to come, the Thames will remain one of London's greatest assets and a potent image for all who write of meetings and departures.

6

Covent Garden and the Strand

For many lovers of London the Strand has always inspired feelings of deep affection, simply because its hustle and bustle somehow characterise the lively vigour of the metropolis itself. In the eighteenth century Samuel Johnson considered that 'the full tide of human existence is at Charing Cross', and in the nineteenth century it was Charles Lamb who wrote that 'Often, when I have felt a weariness or distaste at home, have I rushed out into the crowded Strand and fed my humour, till the tears have wetted my cheek for unutterable sympathies with the multitudinous moving picture which she never fails to present at all hours, like the scenes of a shifting pantomime'. This century it is T. E. Lawrence who can be found saying that on each joyous homecoming to London he wished to eat the pavement of the Strand.[1]

The Strand gets its name from the strand or shore of the River Thames and it has always been an important thoroughfare. London's earliest maps emphasise that there were in effect two 'Londons' – the City of London and the City of Westminster – joined together by the Strand. To its south, on the riverside, were several large mansions belonging to those members of the nobility self-confident enough to live in neither the City nor Westminster. The Savoy Palace, for example, was owned by John of Gaunt, whose sister-in-law Philippa married Geoffrey

Chaucer, probably at the Savoy Chapel some time in the 1360s. Nothing remains of this palace, although a reminder of its presence comes with the name of 'Savoy' often used in this neighbourhood. Today's Queen's Chapel of the Savoy near Waterloo Bridge was built in 1505 but extensively remodelled in 1864 after a fire. One of its stained-glass windows contains Geoffrey Chaucer's coat of arms. The only legacy of these mansions once on the edge of the river is the seventeenth-century Watergate, probably built by Inigo Jones, which was formerly a part of York House and stands at the southern end of Buckingham Street. It indicates, too, how the width of the Thames was reduced by the construction of the Embankment.

To the north of the Strand in the Middle Ages were fields and gardens owned by the monks of Westminster Abbey who cultivated the land as their 'convent garden'. The surplus food produced by the monks was sold off, and thus began the area's long association with fruit, vegetables and flowers. At the dissolution of the monasteries in the 1530s the land was given first to the Duke of Somerset and then, after his downfall, to the Dukes of Bedford, whose family name is Russell. Several new houses were built on this north side of the Strand, including the Drury House which eventually gave its name to Drury Lane. The poet John Donne lived here for five years from 1612 in a building adjoining Drury House. In his youth Donne had eloped with a young woman called Anne, and the couple were married at the Savoy Chapel.[2] Anne's guardians were furious, pursuing Donne and having him thrown into the Fleet prison. While in captivity Donne was supposed to have written a brief letter to his wife which ended: 'John Donne – Anne Donne – Undone.'[3] Although he was subsequently released from prison and reunited with Anne, the poet's job prospects were decidedly unpromising until an elegy dedicated to Sir Robert Drury's recently deceased daughter – whom John Donne had never met – secured him a patron and a home here.

A few years after Donne left Drury House (which was demolished in the early nineteenth century), the 4th Duke of Bedford began to develop his land. Realising that the growth of London and the drift of the wealthy westwards away from the City might enable him to profit handsomely, the Duke obtained a licence for building which cost him £2000 and stipulated that the houses should be 'fit for the habitacions of Gentlemen and men of ability'. The Duke entrusted much of the work to the theatrical designer and architect Inigo Jones, a man of versatile talents who had already co-operated with Ben Jonson, himself born near Charing Cross in 1572, in presenting thirteen royal masques. Both Jones and Jonson were men of fiercely independent views, and their relationship is sometimes coyly described as 'stormy'. Inigo Jones's travels in Italy had made him familiar with the Palladian style of architecture, and the square or piazza he designed for the Duke in Covent Garden in the 1630s still retains this Continental feel, even though Jones only completed two sides. He also built the church of St Paul whose portico faces out into the square. Thousands of people have passed this building but have never found its entrance, which is in fact best approached from Bedford Street. Originally the altar was to have been at the west end, but the church authorities objected and it was shifted to the east. This meant that the portico had to be bricked up. A plaque in the portico commemorates one of the first-ever puppet shows in England, held near here in May 1662 and predictably enough witnessed by that ever-vigilant observer of the 1660s, Samuel Pepys. The portico also provided the back-drop to one of the most famous scenes in English theatre. George Bernard Shaw in *Pygmalion* (1914) has Professor Higgins first meet Eliza Doolittle, the Cockney flower-seller, in the portico of St Paul's. The phonetics expert roundly ticks Eliza off:

> A woman who utters such depressing and disgusting sounds has no right to be anywhere – no right to live. Remember that you are a human being with a soul and the divine gift of articulate speech: that your native language is the language of Shakespeare and Milton and The Bible; and don't sit there crooning like a bilious pigeon.

Inigo Jones completed St Paul's in 1633, and it soon became intimately linked with the acting profession because of the close proximity of the two theatres of Drury Lane and Covent Garden. Memorials to many actors and actresses line the inside walls, while the ashes of Ellen Terry, colleague of Sir Henry Irving and friend of George Bernard Shaw, are contained in a casket on the south wall. One figure associated with the church was the seven-teenth-century writer Samuel Butler, whose *Hudibras* was regarded in its day as a satirical masterpiece; Pepys 'tried by twice or three times reading to bring myself to think it witty' but finally gave up and sold his copy.

Throughout the seventeenth century the Strand remained an important highway. In May 1660 another diarist, John Evelyn, had stood here to watch the return from exile of Charles II, providing a graphic description of the streets hung with tapestries, the fountains running with wine and all the notables in their finery.[4] After the Restoration the district became increasingly populous. Also established in the neighbourhood were certain trades such as the coachmakers of Long Acre where in 1668 Samuel Pepys came to buy a status symbol, namely a secondhand coach which cost him £52. Pepys was later to be one of the area's new residents. He lived at 12 Buckingham Street from 1679, moved to number 14 in 1688 and finally in 1701 retired to Clapham in South London, where he died in 1703.

In 1670 the Duke of Bedford received a charter from Charles II to establish a market here, a privilege which might have brought him short-term financial gain but resulted in the deterioration of Covent Garden as a residential area and the exodus of the wealthy towards the west. Bedford House, which had stood roughly where today's Southampton Street now runs, was pulled down in 1704, and the market stalls and booths turned the piazza into an eyesore. This open space was also something of a playground; John Gay in his poem *Trivia; or, The Art of Walking the Streets of London* (1716) is strolling quietly around Covent Garden when suddenly:

> . . . lo! from far
> *I spy the furies of the foot-ball war:*
> *The 'prentice quits his shop to join the crew,*
> *Increasing crowds the flying game pursue.*
> *O whither shall I run? the throng draws nigh;*
> *The ball now skims the street, now soars on high;*
> *The dextrous glazier strong returns the bound,*
> *And jingling sashes on the pent-house sound.*

Covent Garden's easy morals had already been dealt with by the seventeenth-century poet John Dryden:

> *This town two bargains has not worth one farthing,*
> *A Smithfield horse – and wife of Covent Garden.*[5]

Dryden lived in Long Acre. One night on his way home in 1679 he was beaten up in Rose Street, a little side-street which is still rather gloomy and sinister. Despite a reward of £50 his assailants were never identified, although it was suspected that they were in the pay of the Earl of Rochester, who had felt himself slighted by one of Dryden's poems.

That Covent Garden was the 'red light' district of Georgian London is amply testified to by various writers and publications. Perhaps the century's bestseller was the annual Harris's *Lists of Covent Garden Ladies* which detailed the availability, price and much else besides of the neighbourhood's prostitutes.[6] Henry Fielding in his *Jonathan Wild* of 1743 refers to 'one of those eating-houses in Covent Garden, where female flesh is deliciously drest and served up to the greedy appetites of young gentlemen'. James Boswell was one gentleman who made full use of Covent Garden's resources, once picking up 'two very pretty little girls' and taking them to the Shakespeare's Head tavern in the north-east corner of the piazza where 'I solaced my existence with them one after the other, according to their seniority'.[7]

Henry Fielding, one of the most attractive of all English writers for the way in which he managed to combine his literary labours with a full public life, was instrumental in trying to clear up some of the district's worst abuses. Originally a playwright and then, after his marriage to Charlotte Cradock and the acquisition of a dowry of £1500, the manager of the Haymarket Theatre, Fielding had to find another career after the government of the day passed the Stage Licensing Act of 1737 instituting rigorous stage censorship. He became a barrister but was not very successful, using his excess time to write the novels *Joseph Andrews* and *Jonathan Wild*. Sadly his beloved wife Charlotte, later to be portrayed as Sophia in *Tom Jones* and as Amelia in the novel of that name, died in Fielding's arms in 1744. A few years later he made a servant pregnant; and, in an action typical of the man but far from typical of the age, he married Mary Daniel at Wren's church of St Benet Paul's Wharf, much to the derision of 'Polite Society'. For instance, his fellow-novelist Tobias Smollett remarked that Fielding had married 'his own cook-wench'.[8] In July 1748, Fielding was appointed a magistrate for Westminster and moved into 4 Bow Street, a house on the western side just up from Russell Street (the present magistrates' court on the other side of Bow Street was opened in 1880). Fielding quickly found that the old system of policing which relied on elderly watchmen was quite inadequate in enforcing law and order in a growing city. These 'Charleys' as they were called, because they had been introduced in the reign of Charles II, were often locked into their own stand-boxes and then thrown over by young men-about-town. In 1749, Fielding established the Bow Street Runners, a small force of about a dozen thieftakers who were paid from a secret service fund. Almost immediately the capital's crime rate began to decline.[9] Apart from organising the Runners and dispensing justice in a firm but fair manner at his Bow Street court – unlike the corrupt Justice Thrasher in *Amelia* – Fielding also worked on his lengthy novel *Tom Jones*, published in 1749. This rumbustious story of the young, ardent but often foolish Tom and his romantic pursuit of Sophia Western was an instant bestseller by eighteenth-century standards – 10,000 copies were sold in the first year of publication. *Tom Jones* prompted Sir Walter Scott to call Fielding 'the father of the English novel'.

Over the next few years Fielding battled effectively against the criminal gangs which then ran much of London, but with less success against his own failing health. In 1754 he resigned his magistrate's post in order to recuperate in Portugal. By this time he was so ill that he had to be carried on and off the ship – 'The total loss of limbs was apparent to all who saw me, and my face contained marks of a most diseased state, if not of death itself' – but his last book, *Journal of a Voyage to Lisbon*, recounts his adventures with his usual humour and courage. He died in Lisbon in October 1754 and was buried there. Notwithstanding his several distinguished careers as playwright, novelist, magistrate and founder of what proved to be the forerunner of the modern police force, and despite the fact that he lived for most of his life in the capital, London contains not a single statue or proper memorial to Henry Fielding.

Georgian Covent Garden boasted several coffee-houses such as Will's, which for many years was dominated by John Dryden who was a conversationalist on a par with Samuel Johnson; Button's and Tom's as well as taverns and alehouses, always a lure to young men out on a spree. In Smollett's novel *Roderick Random* (1748), Roderick embarks on a monumental binge here, ending up at the notorious Moll King's, a stall near to St Paul's portico which was shown by William Hogarth in his painting 'Morning'. At 8 Russell Street was Covent Garden's bookshop, run by Tom Davies. Here, on 16 May 1763, took place the famous first meeting of the young, nervous James Boswell with his idol Samuel Johnson:

> I drank tea at Davies's in Russell Street, and about seven came in the great Samuel Johnson, whom I have so long wished to see. Mr Davies introduced me to him. As I knew his mortal antipathy at the Scotch, I cried to Davies, 'Don't tell where I come from.' However he said, 'From Scotland.' 'Mr Johnson,' said I, 'indeed I come from Scotland, but I cannot help it.' 'Sir,' replied he, 'that, I find, is what a very great many of your countrymen cannot help.'[10]

Twenty years later Boswell lived in the area, in Great Queen Street, where he wrote most of his famous life of Johnson. The site of the house is now covered by the vast Freemasons' Hall.

The coffee-houses, brothels and taverns by no means exhausted all that Covent Garden had to offer the eighteenth-century seeker of noise and excitement. For instance, the Westminster elections and their hustings took place in the portico of St Paul's. They were almost like carnivals, lasting over two weeks and resulting in broken heads and spilled blood. One contemporary observer wrote that 'The vulgar abuse of the candidates from the vilest rabble is not rendered endurable by either wit or good temper'.[11]

The area was also famous for its two theatres, Drury Lane and Covent Garden, which were boisterous and often violent – Fielding's Sophia Western was frightened away from Covent Garden Theatre by its noise. The leading figure in the eighteenth-century theatre was the actor David Garrick, who as a young man in 1737 had travelled up to London from Lichfield to make his fortune, his companion on this journey from the provinces being Samuel Johnson. Garrick's natural style of playing marked a sharp break from the stilted declamatory manner which had formerly held the boards. Manager of Drury Lane from 1747, he lived nearby at 27 Southampton Street from 1750 to 1772. A plaque with a picture of him still survives on the building, appropriately called Garrick House. He then moved to the Adelphi, a new development built on the south side of the Strand by the Adam brothers (*adelphi* is the Greek word for 'brothers'). This was a fashionable address which was to be much patronised by literary names in subsequent years. When Garrick died in 1779 he left a fortune valued at all of £100,000.[12] Next year Tom Davies, manager of the Russell Street bookshop, published a biography of Garrick with the encouragement of Johnson.

At the end of the eighteenth century and the beginning of the nineteenth, several famous poets and writers either lived in Covent Garden or knew it well. Thomas Gray, author of 'Elegy Written in a Country Churchyard', always came to the market in order to buy the flowers with which he decorated his room. Charles Lamb lived with his sister Mary at 20 Russell Street from 1817 until 1823, calling Covent Garden 'dearer to me than any Garden of Alcinous, where we are morally sure of the earliest peas and 'sparagus'.[13] Coleridge lived at 10 King Street from 1798 to 1801 while he was working as a journalist on the *Morning Post*. Jane Austen occasionally stayed at 10 Henrietta Street where her brother was employed in the family bank. Charles Westmacott has described seeing Lord Byron at the Finish, a club in King Street, 'the light of genius beaming in his noble countenance, and an eye brilliant and expressive as the morning star; the rich juice of the Tuscan grape had diffused an unusual glow over his features, and inspired him with a playful animation'.[14] As for Thomas de Quincey, he wrote his *Confessions of an Opium Eater* when living at 36 Tavistock Street.

In contrast to the above writers, who figure in any pantheon of English literature, the Covent Garden area was also the home of the 'Seven Dials School' of street literature, comprising largely street ballads, 'Murder Sheets' and 'Last Dying Speeches and Confessions'. The foremost publisher in this field was Jemmy Catnach, who set up his business in 1813 and effectively cornered the market for street literature. He did well out of his trade but nevertheless experienced some unusual problems, as Leslie Shepard has revealed:

Most of Jemmy Catnach's fortune was accumulated in coppers, so he used to take them to the Bank of England in large bags in a hackney coach. His neighbours would not change them for silver, dreading infection from the filthy coins collected by his broadside sellers. Eventually Catnach used to boil up the coppers in strong vinegar and potash to make them look like new coins. But all his workers were obliged to take their wages in copper, and at weekends would bring their wives and mothers to help them carry home anything from ten to forty shillings all in pennies and halfpennies.[15]

Perhaps no writer has ever known Covent Garden so well as Charles Dickens. His biographer John Forster says that 'To be taken for a walk . . . especially if it were anywhere about Covent Garden or the Strand, perfectly entranced him [Dickens] with pleasure'. The family links with the area had started early – his father, John, had worked as a clerk at Somerset House and was married at St Mary-le-Strand. As a boy Charles slaved away at a blacking warehouse – sticking labels on cans – at 80 Hungerford Stairs for two years from 1822, moving with the business to Chandos Place, Covent Garden (now marked by a plaque). It was a profound experience for Dickens – 'No words can express the agony of soul as I sank into this companionship, and felt my hopes of growing up to be a learned and distinguished man crushed in my breast' – about which he only ever talked to John Forster, although *David Copperfield* does provide a fictional representation. Later, he once arranged a trial at Covent Garden Theatre as an actor.[16] Covent Garden and the Strand appear in almost all of his novels. The Micawbers, for example, set off for Australia from Hungerford Stairs (these stairs were wiped out by the building of Charing Cross station). In *Oliver Twist* the Artful Dodger ends up at Bow Street magistrates' court, while Pip in *Great Expectations* stays at the Hummums hotel at the corner of Russell Street when warned not to return home. Dickens was a member of the Garrick Club in Garrick Street, the club which P. G. Wodehouse, not the 'clubbable' sort, called 'The Pesthole' but which is nevertheless full of theatrical portraits.[17] Both *Household Words* and *All the Year Round* were edited from Wellington Street by Charles Dickens. Wilkie Collins was on the staff of *All the Year Round* in 1868 when the magazine serialised *The Moonstone*, regarded by many as the first detective novel written in English. So popular was it that eager crowds gathered outside 26 Wellington Street in order to snap up the latest issue as soon as it appeared.[18]

During the nineteenth century both Drury Lane and Covent Garden Theatre suffered disaster in that both were often burnt down. When Covent Garden was razed to the ground in 1804 its manager, the playwright Sheridan, sat quietly nearby taking a drink. When bystanders suggested he might do more to prevent the blaze spreading, he is reputed to have quipped: 'Surely a gentleman may warm his hands at his own fireside.'[19] Five years later the new theatre was torn apart by the 'Old Price' riots which lasted for sixty-seven consecutive nights when organised crowds campaigned violently against increased prices by blowing trumpets and whistles and letting pigs and pigeons loose in the auditorium. The rioters were eventually successful, and the proprietor John Philip Kemble – he can be seen on the signboard of the pub at the corner of Bow Street and Long Acre – had to back down.[20] Such turmoil, which was commonplace in theatres at this time, prompted the middle-class audience to desert the playhouse for the opera house. Covent Garden later opened as the Royal Opera House in 1858, and Drury Lane relied on its lavish Christmas pantomimes introduced by Augustus Harris, whose bust stands outside the theatre. However, towards the end of the nineteenth century several managers and proprietors of what was to be termed 'the West End theatre' began to woo back the wealthy and respectable. The key figure in this process was Sir Henry Irving, who for nearly thirty years ran the Lyceum Theatre in Wellington Street and whose statue stands outside the National Portrait Gallery. Irving's stage manager and biographer was an Irishman called Bram Stoker, better known as the creator of *Dracula*. Several new theatres were built along the Strand, including Richard D'Oyly Carte's Savoy which opened in 1881 and became famous for its Gilbert and Sullivan operas. A window in the Savoy Chapel commemorates the D'Oyly Carte family.

The Savoy was in fact only a hundred yards from 17 Southampton Street where W. S. Gilbert was born on 18 November 1836; he was baptised at St Paul's, Covent Garden. The leading actor in many of the Savoy operas was George Grossmith, later to collaborate with his brother Weedon on the marvellous *Diary of a Nobody* which recounts the life and mishaps of Mr Charles Pooter of 'The Laurels', Brickfield Terrace, Holloway. Mr Pooter comes to a shop in the Strand to buy his Christmas cards, with characteristically chaotic results. The Savoy Hotel above the theatre was where Oscar Wilde lived from April 1893, as did Noël Coward after he had been bombed out of his flat during the Blitz.

Apart from the Strand's theatres there were also the numerous music-halls, much appreciated by the young Rudyard Kipling when he lived at 43 Villiers Street between 1889 and 1901. Today a plaque is attached to Kipling House. Then, 'My rooms were above an establishment of Harris, the Sausage King, who for tuppence gave as much sausage and mash as would carry one from breakfast to dinner'.[21] Kipling slaved over his writing, even putting outside his door a sign which read 'TO PUBLISHERS: A CLASSIC WHILE YOU WAIT'.[22] For recreation he frequented the halls and also Gordon's Wine Bar which was, and still is, just around the corner near the Watergate. Gordon's was also a favourite resort of G. K. Chesterton. In view of Kipling's love of the music-hall it is appropriate that the Players' Theatre now stands opposite his old rooms, although its site is threatened by redevelopment.

At the turn of the nineteenth century the Strand was the Bohemian centre of London, its Gaiety Theatre with its famous girls and Romano's nightclub a must for any self-respecting man about town. The Strand appears in many of P. G. Wodehouse's novels, and he had written for the Aldwych and Gaiety Theatres in 1906 and 1907. Popular at the Gaiety in the years before the First World War was George Grossmith Junior, who played in what were called 'Dude' comedies featuring young innocents abroad in High Society. Grossmith was a tall, languid individual who became in large part the model for Wodehouse's Bertie Wooster. Many of Wodehouse's sketches were first published in the *Strand Magazine* as were all of Conan Doyle's Sherlock Holmes stories. The *Strand Magazine* had been founded in January 1891 by George Newnes out of the profits of his *Tit-Bits*, and as a successful monthly costing sixpence it was soon selling over 500,000 copies. Its editor asked Sidney Paget to illustrate the Sherlock Holmes stories, and Paget it was who introduced the now indispensable deerstalker.[23] From 1897 the *Strand Magazine* was published from the Newnes empire based on the east side of Southampton Street, an enterprise which also issued *Woman's Life*, the first weekly of its kind. Almost until its death in March 1950 the *Strand Magazine* was the country's leading fiction magazine.

On the other side of the Strand, the Adelphi was a popular residence for writers. J. M. Barrie lived in Adelphi Terrace between 1911 and 1937. In October 1917 during an air-raid several of his friends sheltered there with him. A direct hit that night would have killed Thomas Hardy, H. G. Wells, Arnold Bennett, George Bernard Shaw and Barrie himself. Hardy was in fact returning to an old stamping-ground; as a young man training to be an architect between 1862 and 1867 he had worked at 8

Adelphi, looking out of his window and watching the construction of the Embankment.[24] In the late 1930s most of the Adelphi was demolished.

In 1928, Victor Gollancz founded what turned out to be one of London's most influential publishing houses, based at 14 Henrietta Street. In 1936 he set up the Left Book Club, members being entitled to receive a selection of progressive and anti-fascist titles. The club chimed in perfectly with the mood of the 1930s and at its peak in 1938 claimed nearly 60,000 members. Political splits and disagreements in the Left Book Club at the beginning of the war weakened its influence and it was finally wound up in 1946. The publishing house is still in Henrietta Street and is now run by Gollancz's daughter.

In 1974 the Covent Garden market, after several hundred years on its site behind the Strand, moved to Nine Elms in South London. At one stage it looked as if Inigo Jones's piazza and the Market Buildings of 1830 would be destroyed; fortunately, however, they have survived. With its shops and restaurants, its theatres and its new Theatre Museum, its Royal Opera House and London Transport Museum, Covent Garden offers the same kind of opportunity to stroll and stare which has attracted literary figures throughout the ages.

7

The East End

In George Gissing's novel *The Nether World* (1889), Jane Snowden, Sidney Kirkwood and Jane's grandfather leave Liverpool Street station by train for a holiday in Chelmsford:

> Over the pest-stricken regions of East London, sweltering in sunshine which served only to reveal the intimacies of abomination; across miles of a city of the damned, such as thought never conceived before this age of ours; above streets swarming with a nameless populace, cruelly exposed by the unwonted light of heaven; stopping at stations which it crushes the heart to think should be the destination of any mortal; the train made its way at length beyond the outmost limits of dread, and entered upon a land of level meadows, of hedges and trees, crops and cattle.

The hostility in the tone of Gissing's description of the East End sums up the attitude taken by novelists towards the district in the last 200 years. Some writers have literally wished the East End out of existence. In William Morris's socialist Utopia, *News from Nowhere*, published the year after Gissing's novel, the narrator has woken up in the year 2003 and is told that 'Once a year, on May-day, we hold a solemn feast in those easterly communes of London to commemorate The Clearing of Misery, as it is called. On that day we have music and dancing, and merry games and happy feasting on the site of some of the worst of the old slums.'

71

Morris himself had little firsthand knowledge of the East End, though he did sometimes leave his splendid home at Kelmscott House in Hammersmith and his country mansion in Gloucestershire, Kelmscott Manor, to go there for political meetings. The fleeting nature of such encounters has never been an obstacle to writing about the East End. Thomas Burke, for instance, in 1916 wrote a very popular series of stories published as *Limehouse Nights* in which he populated Limehouse with hordes of opium-filled Chinese forever menacing innocent white girls. Yet in his autobiography, *Son of London*, and elsewhere Burke boasts of his ignorance about Limehouse: 'At the time of writing those stories I had only once spoken to a Chinese – for two minutes, outside the Chinese legation, when I was six years old.'[1] Sax Rohmer was another writer who did not let the facts get in the way of a melodramatic story. In his Fu Manchu novels Limehouse was the centre of 'the Yellow Peril', 'the greatest peril facing the White Man'. At the time Rohmer was churning out his 'shockers' one informed observer estimated the Chinese community at less than 300 people – hardly a world-threatening army.[2] Limehouse and the rest of the East End were so stereotyped that even Bertie Wooster can be found, in *Much Obliged, Jeeves*, authoritatively referring to 'one of those sinister underground dens lit by stumps of candles stuck in the mouths of empty beer bottles such as abound, I believe, in places like Whitechapel and Limehouse'.

In contrast with all this, Arnold Bennett was actually shown around 'Chinatown' in April 1925 by a police inspector: 'Then out with the Inspector to Pennyfields. No gambling after 8 o'clock, he said, usually not later than 7. We entered two Chinese restaurants (11 p.m.) where lots of people were drinking tea. Humble people. All very clean and tidy indeed, and the people looked decent.' After seeing a few more places Bennett concluded: 'On the whole a rather flat night. Still we saw the facts. We saw no vice whatever. Inspector gave the Chinese an exceedingly good character.'[3]

The rather lurid portrayal of the East End as a sort of Hell on Earth, however inaccurate such a picture may be, is a comparatively recent phenomenon. Until the late eighteenth century East London was one of Londoners' favourite resorts, its open fields and healthy air offering an excellent place in which to stroll far away from the crowded and dirty streets of the City. There were pleasant landmarks to visit: the chapel covered with whitewash which gave its name to Whitechapel; the pretty St Dunstan's church tucked away on Stepney Green; the stone bridge on bowed arches over the River Lea which gave the name 'Bow' to the neighbouring village. East London in the Middle Ages was also dotted with religious establishments such as the priory of St Mary Spital and the Royal Foundation of St Katharine. Another such institution was the Benedictine nunnery of St Leonard near Bromley by Bow. Here Chaucer's charming prioress, Madam Eglantyne, had learnt her French with an accent which was not quite Parisian:

> *And Frenssh she spak ful faire and fetisly,*
> *After the scole of Stratford atte Bowe. . . .*

Geoffrey Chaucer himself certainly knew East London because he lived for several years in rooms above the Aldgate, the most eastern of the City gates.[4] This was demolished along with the other six gates in the 1760s, but its site is now commemorated by a plaque on the south side of Aldgate High Street. In 1374 the Mayor and Aldermen had granted 'the whole dwelling-house above Aldgate Gate, with the chambers there on built and a certain cellar beneath the said gate, on the eastern side thereof, together with all its appurtenances, for the lifetime of the said Geoffrey'. Chaucer lived here until 1386. During these years he was working at the Customs House on the River Thames, but it seems he lived for the end of his official working day after which he could rush home and bury himself in what was then an enormous private library of sixty volumes.[5] An autobiographical passage in his poem 'The House of Fame' reveals his passion for literature:

> *For when thy labour doon al ys,*
> *And hast mad alle thy rekenynges,*
> *In stede of reste and newe thynges,*
> *Thou goost hom to thy hous anoon;*
> *And, al so domb as any stoon,*
> *Thou sittest at another book*
> *Tyl fully daswed ys thy look,*
> *And lyvest thus as an heremyte,*
> *Although thyn abstynence ys lyte.*

Chaucer's early career had in fact been as adventurous as anyone could wish. As a boy he had been a page in a noble household; as a soldier in France he had been captured in 1360 and ransomed for the grand total of £16. He had then been sent on several diplomatic missions to Italy as well as serving briefly in 1386 as a Member of Parliament representing Kent as its Knight of the Shire. Since June 1374, Chaucer had been Comptroller of the Customs and Subsidy of Wools, Skins and Hides in the Port of London. When these wide experiences were combined with his studies and learning the ingredients were present from which sprang *The Canterbury Tales*, begun some time in the late 1380s, after Chaucer had left the Aldgate.

Chaucer's twelve-year stay meant that he would have been living at the Aldgate when Wat Tyler and his peasants passed underneath during the revolt of 1381. The rebels confronted the young Richard II on Friday, 14 June 1381 at Mile End, where the fields easily held the 60,000–100,000 people gathered there. The peasants' demands have been summed up by the London historian John Stow in his *Chronicles* where he reported the words supposedly used by the hedge-priest John Ball, one of the uprising's leaders: 'If it had pleased God to have made bondsmen He would have appointed them from the beginning of the world, who should be slave and who lord. They ought to consider, therefore, that now was a time given them by God, in the which, laying aside their continual bondage, they might, if they would, enjoy their longwished liberty.'[6] Or, as the popular rhyme put it with powerful simplicity:

> When Adam delved and Eve span
> Who was then the gentleman?

At this Mile End meeting Richard agreed to the drawing-up of charters which in effect signified the end of feudalism in England. After a further meeting at Smithfield when Wat Tyler was murdered, the grant of the charters was withdrawn and retribution exacted by the king and his men.

Nearly 150 years later another rebel of a kind visited the district. Sir Thomas More seems to have loved its rural setting, remarking that 'Here you find nothing but bounteous gifts of nature and the saint-like tokens of innocence'.[7] A little later Stow in his *Survey of London* (1598) described the fields around Aldgate as 'fayre hedgerowes and Elme trees, with Bridges and easie stiles to passe over into the pleasant fieldes, very commodious for

Citizens therein to walke, shoote, and otherwise to recreate and refresh their dulled spirites in the sweete and wholesome ayre'.[8]

In the course of the sixteenth century there was in fact the beginning of some development based on the riverside hamlets, particularly at Wapping and Ratcliff, and houses were starting to line the Whitechapel Road. Yet for Pepys in the 1660s the area was still the place to enjoy an evening stroll and breathe the country air. He once visited a Captain Marsh who lived in the then isolated village of Limehouse, 'close by the Limehouse which gives the name to the place', but he did not enjoy the meal as he felt out of sorts because of 'not being neat in clothes'. Pepys was friendly, too, with Sir William Rider who lived in Kirby House beside Bethnal Green, a distant village several miles outside London. On one occasion Pepys came here to pick strawberries. He was to return early on 3 September 1666 as the Great Fire crept nearer his home on Tower Hill:

> About 4 a-clock in the morning, my Lady Batten sent me a cart to carry away all my money and plate and best things to Sir W. Riders at Bednall greene; which I did, riding myself in my nightgown in the Cart; and Lord, to see how the streets and the highways are crowded with people, running and riding and getting of carts at any rate to fetch away things. . . . I am eased at my heart to have my treasure so well served.

Pepys's treasure included his diary.

The year in which Pepys had begun his diary, 1660, was also the year in which Daniel Defoe was born. East London often appears in his writings. The narrator of *A Journal of the Plague Year* lives in Aldgate, and many of the book's most graphic details concern the area. Defoe tells of the grass which grew up in Whitechapel High Street during the plague because of the lack of traffic using the road, of the huge plague-pit near Aldgate church – 'A terrible pit it was, and I could not resist my curiosity to go and see it' – and of the delirious people who threw themselves into it. He describes a service at St Botolph's during which someone notices 'an evil smell':

> Immediately she fancies the plague was in the pew, whispers her notion or suspicion to the next, then rises and goes out of the pew. It immediately took with the next, and so to them all; and every one of them, and of the two or three adjoining

pews, got up and went out of the church, nobody knowing what it was offended them, or from whom.

The remedy adopted was to turn the church into 'a smelling bottle; in one corner it was all perfumes; in another, aromatics, balsamics, and variety of drugs and herbs; in another, salts and spirits, as everyone was furnished for their own preservation'.

St Botolph's, Aldgate, was the church in which Defoe himself had been married in 1683. By 1740, a few years after Defoe's death, the building was in ruins and it was pulled down. Its replacement was the church we see today and in which the nineteenth-century philosopher Jeremy Bentham was baptised. Its exterior is grimy and unattractive; its interior is wonderful, complete with some fine wood carving, a splendid organ case and a figured ceiling which is worth going a long way to see.

In Defoe's novels of the 1720s such as *Roxana* and *Moll Flanders* he still refers to the 'villages' of Stepney and Hackney, and maps of the time confirm East London's continuing rural character.[9] There had been some development around Spitalfields with the arrival of the Huguenot refugees from 1685 onwards, and Nicholas Hawksmoor's three East London churches – Christ Church, Spitalfields, St Anne's, Limehouse and St George's in the East – were all built between 1712 and 1730. Nevertheless, as late as 1757 when the London Hospital was opened along the Whitechapel Road, contemporary illustrations show it to be still surrounded by fields. The district's riverside villages were no more than pleasant curiosities for literary men; in 1783, Johnson advised Boswell to explore Wapping.

In the early nineteenth century increasing industrialisation and the construction of the docks led to the rapid expansion of London eastwards and the swallowing-up of the neighbouring villages. The 'stink' industries were located in this 'East End'; there had always been slaughterhouses in Aldgate and breweries along Mile End Road but they were now joined by sugar refineries, gluemaking, gasworks and any other trade which was smelly and dirty. Standards of health, housing and education were low or nonexistent, overcrowding was endemic, and labour cheap. Sam Weller in *Pickwick Papers* considers Whitechapel to be 'Not a wery nice neighbourhood this. . . . It's a wery remarkable circumstance, sir, that poverty and oysters always seems to go together. . . . Look here, sir; here's an oyster stall to every half dozen houses. The streets lined with 'em. Blessed if I don't think that ven a man's very poor, he rushes out of his lodgings, and eats oysters in reg'lar desperation.'

Dickens himself knew the East End fairly well, often going to Limehouse to see his godfather Christopher Huffam who lived in Church (now Newell) Street. Perhaps as a result of these trips the East End often appears in the novels but in a less negative fashion than with most of his contemporaries. Captain Cuttle in *Dombey and Son* is very 'punctual in his attendance' at St Anne's, Limehouse; David Copperfield disembarks at the Blue Boar coaching inn, Whitechapel, on his way to school; and Rogue Riderhood and his daughter Pleasant live at Limehouse Hole, while also in *Our Mutual Friend* is the Six Jolly Fellowship-Porters tavern which is thought to be based on the Grapes in Narrow Street.

Generally, however, the East End is written about in gloomy terms. Wilkie Collins, for instance, in *The Woman in White* (1860) uses the East End as a conveniently impersonal spot in which Laura, Walter and Marian can hide from the attentions of Count Fosco and Sir Percival Glyde, 'where there were fewest idle people to lounge about and look about them in the streets'. Sometimes the descriptions are couched in a patronising tone. In Oscar Wilde's *The Picture of Dorian Gray* Aunt Agatha makes periodic trips east to play piano duets – 'they are so unhappy in Whitechapel'. When engaged on his career of dissipation Dorian visits 'dreadful places near Blue Gate Fields' (Shadwell) and 'a little ill-famed tavern near the Docks'; there are even rumours that he brawls 'with foreign sailors in a low den in the distant parts of Whitechapel'. To be fair to Wilde, he did once apply for a job at the People's Palace along the Mile End Road, but his application was unsuccessful.[10] On the whole the tone of writing about the East End is exemplified by E. M. Forster's vacuous phrase in *Howard's End* when he says that the very poor should only be approached by the statistician or the poet. One writer who did go and see for himself was the American Jack London, who spent the winter of 1902–3 living in Flower and Dean Street, Spitalfields. He wrote to his wife Anna that 'I am made sick by this human hell-hole called the East End' and he recorded his experiences in *The People of the Abyss*, a searing book with an immediacy and a compassion which make Forster's quasi-socialism appear rather anaemic.[11] It has been suggested that it was London's example which encouraged George Orwell to go 'tramping' in the 1930s.[12]

Several mass murders happened here in the East End in the nineteenth century. In the Ratcliff Highway Murders of 1811 two families were found butchered.[13] Thomas De Quincey wrote about this slaughter in his satirical essay 'Murder Considered as One of the Fine Arts' – the murders were 'the sublimest and most entire in their excellence that ever were committed' – and more recently the crime writer P. D. James has co-written a detailed history of this gruesome event. In 1888 it was the 'Jack the Ripper' murders which grabbed the headlines after several women were found murdered and mutilated in Whitechapel alleys. This grisly episode has spawned many books, often fictional (whether deliberately so or not), of which the most popular has probably been Mrs Belloc Lowndes's novel *The Lodger*, first published in 1911, where Jack the Ripper is portrayed as 'The Avenger'. Within twelve years the sixpenny edition had sold more than half a million copies.[14] Even today some of the district's backstreets, notably the dark and gloomy Woods Buildings near Whitechapel Underground station, suggest how simple it must have been for the murderer to dispose of the women in these unlit alleys.

So far not a single writer other than Chaucer mentioned in this section has lived in the East End proper. However, one nineteenth-century writer who was brought up in the East End – although the biographical details he later supplied to dictionaries and directories tended to play down or omit this fact altogether – was Arthur Morrison. Born in Poplar in 1863, Morrison became the clerk to the educational Beaumont Trust in 1886, a few years after the historian and novelist Sir Walter Besant published the fictional *All Sorts and Conditions of Men*. The events in this book happened in Stepney and centred around the setting-up of a 'Palace of Delights', a cultural centre which would brighten up the lives of East Enders. Subtitled 'An Impossible Story', the ideas in Besant's novel were so influential that they led to the founding of the 'People's Palace', which was opened in 1887 under the aegis of the Drapers' Company and the Beaumont Trust. It is now Queen Mary College, a part of London University. From 1889, Arthur Morrison was the sub-editor of the *Palace Journal*, an appointment which seems to have prompted him into writing pieces himself. In 1890 he resigned from the People's Palace and set up as a full-time writer.[15]

Morrison's first short stories were published in 1894 in a volume called *Tales of Mean Streets*. In them he focuses not so much on the criminal nature of the East End but rather on 'its dismal lack of accent, its sordid uniformity, its utter remoteness of delight'. From this description it sounds as if these tales are just a gloomy catalogue, but that is very far from being the case. The stories include romance and humour as well as callous brutality – but the violence led to the book being banned by W. H. Smith. Morrison went on to write *A Child of the Jago* about Shoreditch and *The Hole in the Wall* about Wapping and a series of detective stories featuring Martin Hewitt, who was the only serious rival in terms of popularity to Sherlock Holmes.[16] In the last thirty years of his life Morrison established himself as an expert on oriental art and gave up writing. By the time of his death in 1945 his writings were largely forgotten. Although some of his novels have since been reprinted, Morrison's work deserves much greater attention, as does that of the two other East End novelists W. W. Jacobs and H. M. Tomlinson who feature in this book in the chapter on the Thames.

The very year in which Morrison was born in Poplar saw another family leave Walsall for the very same district, a neighbourhood in which the father obtained a job working on a Limehouse wharf. The son was Jerome K. Jerome, and in his autobiography *My Life and Times* Jerome's loathing of the East End is obvious, even at a distance of sixty years: '. . . about the East End of London there is a menace, a haunting terror that is to be found nowhere else. The awful silence of its weary streets. The ashen faces, with their lifeless eyes that rise out of the shadows and are lost.' There is no hint in this recollection of any of the humour or resilience of the East End character captured by Henry Mayhew in the interviews for *London Labour and the London Poor*. Jerome later wrote the autobiographical novel *Paul Kelver*, set in the East End.

By this time the East End was struggling to assimilate an influx of immigrants, namely the Jewish refugees who fled to London from pogroms in Poland and Tsarist Russia. Usually with no money or prospects and unfamiliar with the English language, the cheap East End was where many of the newcomers settled. Soon the traditional Jewish emphasis on study and learning began to produce writers, poets and painters, and for much of the last hundred years the East End in literature has been predominantly a Jewish affair. For example, Israel Zangwill, who had been brought up in Spitalfields, published *The Children of the Ghetto* in 1892, an evocative account of the new immigrants and their attempts to adapt to an alien environment. Later works by Zangwill continued to examine similar themes, as their titles make plain: *Dreamers of the Ghetto*, *Ghetto Tragedies* and *Ghetto Comedies*. Zangwill's residence at 288 Old Ford Road is now marked by a plaque.

Two institutions which figure largely in Jewish recollections of the East End are the Whitechapel Art Gallery and the Whitechapel Library, where many young Jews embarked on a strenuous programme of self-education. Both were warm and also offered a convenient place at which to meet friends. One person who made full use of the Gallery and the Library was the poet Isaac Rosenberg, whose family moved to Whitechapel in 1897 when he was seven. Whilst still a young man Rosenberg often read aloud his poems to his friends whilst standing under the gas-lamps of Whitechapel Road.[17] Perhaps his most poignant piece is 'A Ballad of Whitechapel', which deals with one of the neighbourhood's many streetwalkers:

> *I watched the gleams*
> *Of jagged warm lights on shrunk faces pale.*
> *I heard mad laughter as one hears in dreams,*
> *Or Hell's harsh lurid tale.*

The rest of the poem continues in this harshly realistic tone. Having studied at the Slade School of Art, Rosenberg made his name as a war poet after joining up in 1915 – he was placed in the Bantam Regiment because of his small size. Unlike almost all the other First World War poets, Rosenberg served in the ranks. He was killed near Arras in March 1918. Nearly twenty years later his *Collected Works* was published, and Rosenberg's reputation has been growing steadily ever since. More recent Jewish writers born and brought up in the East End have included Bernard Kops, author of such works as *The Hamlet of Stepney Green*, Arnold Wesker and Wolf Mankowitz.

In the last few years many of the books written in Hebrew and Yiddish have been removed from the shelves of the Whitechapel Library on the grounds of lack of use, a potent acknowledgement that in large part the Jewish community has dispersed since the Second World War, shifting further northwards. Now the library shelves offer volumes written in Bengali, catering for the latest wave of immigrants who have settled here in the East End. There are many striking similarities between the Jews and the Asians, particularly in their emphasis on hard work and self-help, and no doubt within a few years it will be Bengali writers who will be familiar to a much wider public. A first step has already been taken by Farruk Dhondy with his touching stories in *East End at Your Feet* and *Come to Mecca*.

One important theme for future writers about the East End will be the recent transformation of dockland into smart and very expensive dwellings and the impact on local communities of a rather different breed of immigrant – for the first time these newcomers are wealthy and arrive here in the East End from the west.

Fitzrovia

What and where is Fitzrovia? Surrounded by Underground stations and at the very heart of London, this district lies sandwiched between Euston Road to the north, Tottenham Court Road to the east, Oxford Street to the south and Great Portland Street to the west; and, although one of the least-known areas in the capital, it contains the headquarters of the BBC, ITN and Channel Four, the Middlesex Hospital, the Telecom (once the Post Office) Tower and any number of fine restaurants and pubs.[1] The roads which form its boundaries are dull in the extreme – V. S. Pritchett has called Tottenham Court Road 'the ugliest and most ludicrous street in London'[2] – but once inside them Fitzrovia's cosmopolitanism boasts an appealing vigour absent from many other places in London. The name itself comes from the Fitzroy family, who owned the land in the eighteenth century and who laid out Fitzroy Square, but it has also been known as 'London's Latin Quarter' and 'North Soho'.

In the 1930s and 1940s Fitzrovia's pubs and flats offered a home to an enormous and floating population of writers, artists, dramatists, poets, prostitutes and parasites. During the war years the BBC and the nearby Ministry of Information offered a host of minor jobs which attracted yet more would-be literary people who relished the exciting atmosphere heightened by the blackout.

This cultural 'fringe life', which spawned the term 'Fitzrovia', was very much in keeping with the district's past history – Fitzrovia has always been on the margin of things. In 1756 the New Road (now Marylebone and Euston Roads) was built so that drovers taking their cattle to Smithfield could bypass central London and particularly Oxford Street. The land was owned by Charles Fitzroy, a descendant of one of Charles II's many illegitimate children. Fitzroy could see that since the late seventeenth century the wealthy and prosperous had been moving away from the City towards the west, and he therefore decided to cash in on this migration by building an exclusive and aristocratic estate. Robert Adam was employed to create a square named after his employer, the east side of which was begun in 1792, the south side two years later. It was all too late. The westward migration had already swept past Fitzrovia by the end of the eighteenth century with the fashionable settling in Mayfair, Marylebone and, later, Belgravia. No one wanted to live in the stately houses of Fitzroy Square and Fitzroy Street, despite their fine views away to the north of the hills of Hampstead and Highgate. Fitzroy undertook no further development, and the neighbourhood reverted once more to being the pleasant semi-rural resort of which John Gay had written earlier in his 'Epistle to William Pulteney':

> *When the sweet-breathing spring unfolds the buds,*
> *Love flys the dusty town for shady woods.*
> *Then Totenham fields with roving beauty swarm. . . .*

The streets which led off Oxford Street to the north were in fact run-down and tatty, catering for the impoverished. Samuel Johnson lived at 6 Castle (now Eastcastle) Street with his wife Tetty in 1738. He had only recently arrived in the city, and it was here that he wrote his popular poem *London* which presented a rather jaundiced view of the capital:

> *. . . malice, rapine, accident, conspire,*
> *And now a rabble rages, now a fire;*
> *Their ambush here relentless ruffians lay,*
> *And here the full attorney prowls for prey;*
> *Here falling houses thunder on your head,*
> *And here a female atheist talks you dead. . . .*
> *Prepare for death, if here at night you roam,*
> *And sign your will before you sup from home.*

It is a vivid picture which might trouble those who think with wistful nostalgia about 'the good old days'. It was at Castle Street that Johnson met Edward Cave, owner of the *Gentleman's Magazine* in Clerkenwell, who first gave him regular employment.[3] Another of Fitzrovia's long-established thoroughfares was (Great) Portland Street, and it was here, at number 47, that Johnson's friend and biographer James Boswell died in 1795. Boswell's last few years in London were unhappy for he had been troubled by drink problems and avoided by friends and colleagues who worried about just how much of their conversation he might record for posterity. Number 47 Great Portland Street has since been demolished, but number 122 which stands on its site bears a plaque.

Another eighteenth-century street was Green Lanes, now called Cleveland Street. It appears in Dickens's *Barnaby Rudge* (1841) in one of the author's powerful descriptive passages as one of the spots at which the Gordon Rioters met in 1780, a piece of writing which underlines its still rural character:

> This was a retired spot, not of the choicest kind, leading into the fields. Great heaps of ashes; stagnant pools, overgrown with rank grass and duckweed; broken turnstiles; and the upright posts of palings long since carried off for firewood, which menaced all heedless walkers with their jagged and rusty nails, were the leading features of the landscape; while here and there a donkey, or a ragged horse, tethered to a stake and cropping off a wretched meal from the coarse stunted turf, were quite in keeping with the scene, and would have suggested (if the houses had not done so sufficiently of themselves) how very poor the people were who lived in the crazy huts adjacent, and how foolhardy it might prove for one who carried money, or wore decent clothes, to walk that way alone, unless by daylight.

As Dickens makes plain, the district was notorious in the eighteenth century for its thieves and highwaymen.

As a boy in the early 1820s Dickens himself knew the area well. On his daily walk from Camden towards the blacking factory at Charing Cross he 'could not resist the stale pastry put out at half price on trays at the confectioners' doors in Tottenham Court Road'. Between 1830 and 1833 he lodged at 15 (now 25) Fitzroy Street. In *Nicholas Nickleby*, published in 1839, he referred to 'the dowager barrenness and frigidity of Fitzroy Square', but in one respect at least this was quite wrong. At that time a family called the Mayhews were living at 16 Fitzroy Square of which two sons, Henry and Augustus, were famous Victorian literary figures – and they had fourteen other brothers and sisters. Henry Mayhew became a journalist and founded *Punch* in 1841, although he was eased out of the editor's chair within a year. He will always be best remembered for the four-volume *London Labour and the London Poor*, which first appeared from 1850. Unlike most other nineteenth-century observers, Mayhew was prepared to listen to, and report, his interviewees in full, and a bewildering galaxy of characters cross his pages, from costermongers and street-sellers to chimney-sweeps and rat-killers. Mayhew wanted to see everything at first hand, visiting Newgate prison and the prison hulks as well as doing a stint on the treadmill in order to experience what it was really like; rarely, unlike many of his contemporary journalists, did he engage in any ritualistic moral denunciation of 'the lower orders'. He influenced Charles Kingsley's novel *Alton Locke* (1850), and it has been suggested that his friend Charles Dickens took some information and even characters from Mayhew's writings.[4] He moved to 55 Albany Street, on the other side of Euston Road, and there is a plaque on the site recording his stay there.

During the nineteenth century the remaining open spaces of Fitzrovia were built over and the district became very overcrowded as the fine houses were split up and occupied by several families. The census of 1841, for instance, showed that the twenty-seven houses in Goodge Place were occupied by 485 people and, as a recent history of Fitzrovia has pointed out, 'When it is remembered that many occupants also carried on trades such as dressmaking in the same room, the extent of squalor and overcrowding can just about be imagined'.[5] Goodge Place still exists.

Apart from the furniture trade which flourished here, Fitzrovia was also popular with political refugees because of its cheapness. Although Karl Marx lived on the other side of Oxford Street in Soho, he once undertook a strenuous pub crawl along Tottenham Court Road.[6] At one pub Marx and his companions got into a row with some English workmen. On leaving the premises they began to break the street-lamps, as William Liebknecht, who was there, recalled:

Nonsense is contagious – Marx and I did not stay behind, and
we broke four or five street lamps – it was, perhaps, 2 o'clock
in the morning and the streets were deserted in consequence.
But the noise nevertheless attracted the attention of a policeman who with quick resolution gave the signal to his colleagues on the same beat. And immediately counter-signals
were given. The position became critical. Happily we took in
the situation at a glance; and happily we knew the locality. We
raced ahead, three or four policemen some distance behind us.
Marx showed an activity that I should not have attributed to
him. And after the wild chase had lasted some minutes, we
succeeded in turning into a side street and there running
through an alley – a back yard between two streets – whence
we came behind the policemen who lost the trail.

On a sadder note, three of Marx's children were buried at Whitfield's Tabernacle.[7] The churchyard was destroyed by a flying
bomb during the Second World War, but a little of it remains as a
public garden, close by what is now 'The American Church in
London'.

The Communist Club was at 49 Tottenham Street from 1878
until 1902, when it moved to 107 Charlotte Street. It was raided
by police on the outbreak of the First World War and closed
down. The club had functioned as a kind of social centre for
political refugees, providing a library, a billiards room and a cheap
restaurant – and always clouds of tobacco smoke accompanying
heated debate. Marx and Lenin were visitors – as, too, were
William Morris and George Bernard Shaw.[8]

Shaw was another writer who knew Fitzrovia well, having
lived at 29 Fitzroy Square from 1887 until his marriage in 1898 to
Charlotte Payne-Townsend. It was a busy eleven years in which
Shaw established his name both as the music critic 'Corno di
Bassetto' for the *Star* and as an outspoken drama critic; he wrote
his first plays and was also heavily involved in the Fabian Society.
Ever a great self-publicist, he would sometimes write scurrilous
attacks on himself which he then published under different
pseudonyms, thus keeping his name before the public. When
Shaw moved out of Fitzroy Square the literary tradition was
continued by a newcomer to the house a few years later. Virginia
Stephen (later Woolf) lived here from 1907 until 1911.

The cheapness of Fitzrovia was a great attraction to aspiring writers, and at the end of the nineteenth century several later-to-be-successful young men resided in the neighbourhood. Jerome K. Jerome was living in Whitfield Street when he began his first book *On the Stage – and Off*, which was published in 1885. Jerome had spent three years as a touring actor, and the subtitle 'The Brief Career of a Would-Be Actor' tells it all, and in a style just as witty as *Three Men in a Boat*. To save on lighting, Jerome wrote chapters of the book late at night standing underneath the street-lamps in Portland Place.[9]

George Gissing lived at 22 Colville Place in 1878. His *New Grub Street* of 1891 depicts a rather tatty Fitzrovia, whilst a passage in the semi-autobiographical *The Private Papers of Henry Ryecroft* (1903) reads: 'I see that alley [Colville Place] hidden on the west side of Tottenham Court Road where, after living in a back bedroom on the top floor, I had to exchange for a front cellar. There was a difference, if I remember rightly, of sixpence a week, and sixpence in those days was a great consideration – why it meant a couple of meals.' Colville Place is still there today, a rather select little row of houses facing a newly opened garden.

One of Gissing's few friends, H. G. Wells, once lived at 181 Euston Road. He, too, was watching the pennies, but his main complaint, like that of so many people throughout London's history, was about the boring Sundays: 'I found the Sundays terrible. They were vast, lonely days.'[10] Another famous literary figure who flitted briefly through the district was Rupert Brooke, who lived at 76 Charlotte Street towards the end of 1911 when he was working on his dissertation at the British Museum.

Between the wars Fitzrovia acquired a reputation as a literary and artistic Bohemia, very different from the rather more refined ambiance of Bloomsbury only a few hundred yards away. Rents here were much lower than in Chelsea, thus attracting the young, the impecunious and the not-yet- or never-to-be-famous who frequented the many cheap eating-places such as Bertorelli's and the Scala in Charlotte Street as well as Fitzrovia's many pubs.[11] One devotee has written that 'the pubs mysteriously combined the qualities of a railway station buffet at rush hour with those of a literary and artistic salon', whilst another categorised the patrons as 'Regulars', 'Wits' and 'Bums'.[12] The Fitzroy Tavern in Charlotte Street and the Wheatsheaf in Rathbone Place were the two pubs most favoured by writers.

One man who managed to be regular, wit *and* bum was Dylan

Thomas. He spent much of the 1930s and 1940s careering from one pub and bed to another, enduring what he called 'the capital punishment'[13] before retreating to his parents in Wales or, later, to his wife Caitlin in order to recuperate. Thomas himself wrote that life in London was 'promiscuity, booze, coloured shirts, too much talk, too little work'.[14] It was in April 1936 during a hectic stint in the capital that he was introduced to Caitlin by the painter Augustus John in the Wheatsheaf. He proposed to her almost immediately. During their exhausting, tumultuous marriage, Caitlin consistently tried to lure Thomas away from London, while he was drawn irresistibly to Fitzrovia and 'Comrade Bottle'. In her recent autobiography *Caitlin: A Warring Absence*, she has written that this was to be the pattern: '. . . he needed London for talk and pubbing – for stimulation – but he could only write away from it. He wrote well in Cornwall. As soon as I could get him away into my little dull country places he would settle down and start working.'

Of course other would-be artists and writers were drawn to the area by its slightly raffish atmosphere, but in the end Fitzrovia virtually destroyed some of them. For example, Julian Maclaren-Ross (who is depicted as X. Trapnell in Anthony Powell's series of novels *A Dance to the Music of Time*) was warned early in his career against succumbing to 'Sohoitis': 'If you get Sohoitis . . . you will stay there always day and night and get no work done. You have been warned.'[15] It was no good. Maclaren-Ross's literary promise was quickly dissipated, and his excellent *Memoirs of the Forties* was left unfinished at his death in 1964. Two other important pubs much frequented by the denizens of Fitzrovia and many other writers besides were the George and the Stag, both of which were near Broadcasting House. One recent historian of radio drama has written that 'For twenty years after the war The George became not merely the green room for writers, actors and technicians; it became the British equivalent of Les Deux Magots in Paris and there can be very few writers and composers who never stood at its bar.'[16]

Two other places in Fitzrovia should be mentioned because of their literary associations. The first is the Middlesex Hospital, founded in 1745 in what were then the fields to the north of Oxford Street, and where Rudyard Kipling died in 1936. The second is Holy Trinity Church, Marylebone Road, built in 1828 by Sir John Soane. In July 1935, aged only thirty-two, Allen Lane launched the first ten Penguin books. At first the response was muted, but the breakthrough came when Woolworths ordered 63,500 copies. The firm became so successful that it was necessary to lease the derelict crypt under Holy Trinity as an office and warehouse. Sir W. E. Williams, who worked closely with Lane, recalls the slightly bizarre surroundings in which they toiled away:

The rent was £200 a year, and there were no rates. Around the walls of this desolate cellar were bricked-in coffins, each with its nameplate attached. There was no water, no sanitation, so a utensil was provided which the office boy took upstairs every night and tipped in the shabby churchyard. The girls on the staff were given sixpence a week each to pay for visits to the public lavatory at Great Portland Street Station. As this Black Hole of the Crypt was below ground it was cool in summer but perishing cold in the winter.

Working in this cramped crypt was arduous and inconvenient. But it had lighter moments. Loud noises were carried upstairs by the ventilation grille to the church above, and caution had to be particularly observed when a service was in progress. There were inevitably 'incidents', as when a packer hit his thumb with a mallet and bellowed an oath just when the parson conducting a wedding upstairs had put the question, 'Wilt thou take this woman to be thy wife?'[17]

By November 1937 the crypt was too crowded. Lane was afraid that a move to another part of central London with all its attendant costs would endanger the sixpenny cover-price of Penguins. He therefore bought some land fifteen miles away at Harmondsworth, paying £2000 and an extra £200 for the cabbages then growing in the field. Penguin is still there.[18] As for Holy Trinity, it is now the headquarters of the Society for Promoting Christian Knowledge (SPCK). Appropriately enough, it contains a large bookshop.

Today, largely through the efforts of the Fitzrovia Neighbourhood Association, the district has been smartened up, while still retaining its beguilingly mixed atmosphere. Fitzrovia's long association with food and drink remains; as David Piper has written, 'Bacchus brooded over Charlotte Street; it is still rich in the altars of booze and food'.[19] In Eastcastle Street there is the Welsh Chapel and in Margaret Street the extraordinary mid-Victorian redbrick All Saints. The young Laurence Olivier attended the school attached to All Saints, and it was here that he first trod the boards.[20] Close to Fitzroy Square is the comprehensive French's Theatre Bookshop. My own favourite place is Pollock's Toy Museum at 1 Scala Street. In the 1870s Benjamin Pollock took over his father-in-law's toy theatre business, which was then situated at 73 Hoxton Street. Generations of children (and adults, too) have used the characters cut from printed cardboard sheets in order to re-enact scenes from popular plays or pantomimes in their toy theatres.

One lover of the toy theatre was Robert Louis Stevenson, and in an essay about Pollock's which he called 'A Penny Plain and Tuppence Coloured', he indicated just how important the toy theatre had been to him:

> Indeed, out of this cut-and-dry, dull, swaggering, obtrusive and infantile art, I seem to have learned the very spirit of my life's enjoyment; met there the shadows of the characters I was to read about and love in a late future; got the romance of *Der Freischutz* long ere I was to hear of Weber or the mighty Formes; acquired a gallery of scenes and characters with which, in the silent theatre of the brain, I might enact all novels and romances; and took from these rude cuts an enduring and transforming pleasure.[21]

In 1944, Pollock's was bombed out, but the venture continued. J. B. Priestley wrote a play especially for the toy theatre. In 1969, Pollock's moved away their main premises from Covent Garden to an eighteenth-century house here, premises which combine a shop with a museum. Stevenson ended his essay with the words 'If you love art, folly, or the bright eyes of children, speed to Pollock's!' If you love variety, food, drink and a unique atmosphere, then speed to Fitzrovia.

Hampstead

In Wilkie Collins's novel *The Woman in White*, serialised in Charles Dickens's magazine *All the Year Round* from late 1859, the young artist Walter Hartright has been to see his mother and sister who live in Hampstead:

> The idea of descending any sooner than I could help into the heat and gloom of London repelled me. . . . I was determined to stroll home in the purer air by the most roundabout way I could take; to follow the white winding paths across the lonely heath; and to approach London through its most open suburb by striking into the Finchley Road, and so getting back, in the cool of the new morning, by the western side of the Regent's Park.

It is on his journey home that Hartright meets 'the woman in white' and Collins's absorbing novel begins to unfold.

It is clear from this novel that by 1860 Hampstead was still not a part of London; that the inhabitants of the village would not then have considered themselves Londoners. Collins in fact had personal experience of this village life, having been brought up in Pond Street and then Hampstead Square in the 1830s. Hampstead's recorded history begins in AD 975, but it was not until 1888 that Hampstead was joined officially to the capital. For the first 900 years of its existence Hampstead was a village some miles away from the metropolis, possessing a sense of local pride

and community which is still evident today and visibly demonstrated by the special black plaques, sponsored by the Hampstead
Plaque Fund, which supplement the more familiar blue plaques.
Hampstead residents tend to remain Hampstead residents, and
even newcomers from very different parts of the country often
develop a fierce love of the place. John Braine is one example of
this; famous for *Room at the Top* set in his native Yorkshire, he
spent his latter years in Hampstead and at his death in late 1986
he was working on a eulogy of the village called 'Those Golden
Days'.[1] For some, 'Hampstead' is synonymous with the word
'intellectual', often uttered in a slightly dismissive tone of voice.
Certainly scores of writers, historians and 'thinkers' have lived
here.

The name comes from the Saxon word 'homestead', and it
appears first of all to have been a pig-farm in the forest of Middlesex. Lying high up in the hills over London, its Underground
station is the deepest in the capital. At the junction of Heath
Street and East Heath Road a plaque informs the passer-by that
he or she is now 440 feet above sea-level and several feet higher
even than the spire of St Paul's Cathedral. Hampstead's position
meant that it quickly earned a reputation for the wholesomeness
of its air, thus attracting writers and their relatives who have
hankered after its therapeutic qualities. Samuel Johnson brought
his wife Tetty to Hampstead in 1746 in order to cheer her up,[2]
whilst nearly 200 years later the short-story writer Katherine
Mansfield moved to the village in 1918 in the hope that its fresh
air would help her tuberculosis. Some observers found the rarefied air too much to take; Daniel Defoe in *A Tour Through the
Whole Island of Great Britain* noted ''tis so near heaven, that I dare
not say it can be a proper situation, for any but a race of moun-
taineers, whose lungs have been used to a rarefied air, nearer the
second region, than any ground for 30 miles around it'. William
Blake, who stayed with his friend the painter John Linnell at 'Old
Wyldes' farm in North End, also found the air sometimes too
much: 'When I was young, Hampstead, Highgate, Hornsey,
Muswell Hill, and even Islington, and all places north of London,
always laid me up the day after.'[3]

Hampstead has also had a spring since time immemorial, ever
since – so the story rather nicely has it – a monk carrying a bottle
of the Virgin Mary's tears tripped over the root of a tree, stumbled, dropped the bottle and the spilled tears turned into a spring.

In the late seventeenth century a spa was opened which was expanded to include a Long Room, wells, a coffee-house, an assembly room, a racecourse, gardens and even a chapel where couples could be married at any time of the day for a fee of five shillings.[4] From about 1703 until 1713, Hampstead Spa was a fashionable resort, but then it declined. It was too near to London and thus attracted too many 'common people', rivals had taken away some of the clientele, and the spa gained a bad reputation for the riotous behaviour of its patrons. Defoe in his *Tour*, undertaken in the 1720s, wrote that 'ladies who value their reputation, have of late more avoided the wells and walks at Hampstead, than they had formerly done'. Various attempts to woo back the now-departed gentry failed, and today only a few place-names remain of the spa's former existence – Flask Walk, Well Road, Well Walk and the Wells Tavern. A little fountain on the north side of Well Walk is marked with a warning that the water is 'Not Fit for Drinking'. The finest legacy of the Spa is Burgh House, a lovely Queen Anne creation built for the Spa's physician, Dr William Gibbons. From 1934 to 1937, Burgh House was occupied by Rudyard Kipling's daughter, who has written that 'the delightful old house and garden which we rented in Hampstead was a source of happiness to my father to the end of his life'.[5] Kipling's last outing before his death in 1936 was in fact to Burgh House to see his daughter and son-in-law. At one time threatened with demolition, Burgh House is now run by a trust and offers a venue for many concerts and meetings. It also contains the original staircase, a panelled music-room and the Hampstead Museum. Burgh House alone is worth a trip to Hampstead.

Even if Hampstead Spa had declined by the 1720s, several of the village's taverns continued to offer an attractive haven for London writers. One was the Upper Flask tavern, which stood at the top of Heath Street on the site now occupied by Queen Mary's Maternity Hospital. In the summer months members of the literary Kit Cat Club met here – gatherings which included Jonathan Swift and the critics Joseph Addison and Richard Steele. Steele later moved to Hampstead because it was far enough away from London to deter his creditors. In similar fashion Samuel Richardson's heroine in his novel *Clarissa Harlowe* (1748) hides in Hampstead in order to escape the advances of Lovelace. The Upper Flask tavern appears in that book, too, as does the Lower Flask in Flask Walk, still there but since rebuilt.

Richardson describes it as 'a place where second-rate persons are to be found occasionally in a swinish condition'.

Three other Hampstead pubs, amongst the most famous in London, still ring Hampstead Heath. There is Jack Straw's Castle, near Whitestone Pond, which has been a tavern since the early seventeenth century, although this modern building is barely twenty years old. It contains a Dickens Room, a reminder of the fact that Charles Dickens loved to ramble over Hampstead Heath, pausing here for refreshment. The Spaniards Inn supposedly gets its name either from the Spanish ambassador of the seventeenth century who lived nearby, or more romantically from two brothers of Spanish extraction who killed each other in a duel. Again it was known to Dickens – Mrs Bardell in *Pickwick Papers* plots Mr Pickwick's downfall here. Finally there is the Bull and Bush, which, like Jack Straw's Castle, brings an old pedigree to a new building.

Within Hampstead Heath is the exquisite Kenwood House. Originally built in the early seventeenth century, it was remodelled by Robert Adam in the 1760s. In 1780 it was the home of the Chief Justice of England, Lord Mansfield. Having already burnt down his house in Bloomsbury Square, the Gordon Rioters set off for Hampstead to raze Kenwood House to the ground. However, the proprietor of the Spaniards, a Giles Thomas, saved the day by offering plentiful supplies of free drink to the mob while at the same time sending for the militia, who arrived in time to guard Kenwood House.[6] Open to the public, the finest room is the library. In the grounds is Dr Johnson's summerhouse, which originally stood in the garden of the home of his friends the Thrales in Streatham.

As for Hampstead Heath itself, Dickens could often have been found striding over its acres, setting such an impossibly fast pace that few of his friends could keep up for long. A very different man from Dickens, Karl Marx, also praised the Heath, leading an expedition up here every Sunday from cramped Soho where he and his family lived.[7] Family and friends read the newspapers, went for donkey-rides, played chess and wrestled. On one occasion they bombarded a chestnut-tree; not used to this sudden exertion, Marx's arm was so stiff that he could not move it for a week. Today a stroll around the Heath is highly productive for those wanting to collect sightings of the famous: Michael Foot,

Melvyn Bragg and John le Carré all live nearby and frequently exercise here.

Another who has hymned the Heath's beauties did so in these lines:

> . . . *where sweet air stirs*
> *Blue hare-bells lightly, and where prickly furze*
> *Binds lavish gold.*

John Keats knew the Heath well from 1816 when he travelled to the Vale of Health to visit his friend, the critic and journalist Leigh Hunt. Hunt came to live in Hampstead in 1815 after his release from gaol, having been imprisoned for libelling the Prince Regent. Hunt and the young Keats got on well together and Keats moved to 1 Well Walk in April 1817, partly to be close to his friend. Keats lived with the local postman, a Mr Bentley, in a small house (now demolished) where the noise of Bentley's young family sometimes distracted the poet from his work. He had already had two books of poetry published, neither of which had been favourably reviewed. Some of the critics wrote sneeringly of 'the Cockney School of poetry' which they claimed had gathered around Hunt.

In 1818, John Keats's brother Tom died of consumption at Well Walk, and when Coleridge was introduced to John he whispered to Leigh Hunt after shaking hands: 'There is death in that hand.'[8] Keats moved to Wentworth Place (now Keats Grove) where a new house had just been built on the edge of the Heath. It was here that his gifts found their full expression, most famously in his 'Ode to a Nightingale' which was written under a plum tree in the front garden. The tree has now gone but a plaque marks where it stood. The house had been split into two dwellings, and a family called Brawne hired the other half. Mrs Brawne had a young daughter, Fanny, with whom Keats fell in love and to whom he became engaged. Under this stimulus Keats produced most of his finest poetry in the summer of 1819. However, early in 1820 Keats went on a walking tour in the north, and it was on his return in February that he was taken ill. Put to bed at Wentworth Place he coughed up blood into a handkerchief, and his medical training told him that he, like his brother, had consumption: 'I know the colour of that blood – it is arterial blood – I cannot be deceived in that colour – that drop of blood – it is my death-warrant – I must die.' Later that year, after his doctors had told him that his only hope was to live in a warm climate, Keats left for Italy with his friend Joseph Severn. There he died on 23 February 1821, at the age of twenty-five. Tragedy attended the Brawnes, too: Fanny married, but Mrs Brawne was accidentally burnt to death at Wentworth Place. The house had a series of occupants before it was opened in 1925 as Keats House. Quite apart from its connections with the poet, Keats House is well worth visiting because of its early-nineteenth-century decoration and furniture. The staff are also unfailingly helpful. Amongst the exhibits are a bust of Keats at his correct height – he was barely five feet tall – as well as Fanny's engagement ring and first editions of Keats's poems. Thomas Hardy came to Keats House in July 1920 and composed a poem called 'At a House in Hampstead' which begins by remarking on how much the neighbourhood must have changed since the poet's day:

> *O Poet, come you haunting here*
> *Where streets have stolen up all around,*
> *And never a nightingale pours one*
> *Full-throated sound?*

Nevertheless Hardy ends saying that there is more of Keats here than in Rome where he died:

> *Pleasanter now it is to hold*
> *That here, where sang he, more of him*
> *Remains than where he, tuneless, cold,*
> *Passed to the dim.*

Nearby is the Keats Memorial Library with a collection of over 6000 volumes about the poet and his poetry.

At the other end of Hampstead yet more literary associations may be discovered. Hampstead's oldest residence, Fenton House, built in 1693 and possibly designed by Wren, is in Hampstead Grove and now houses the Morley Fletcher Collection of Keyboard Instruments. Just down the Grove is the splendid Bolton House with its magnificent wrought-iron gates and a plaque to Joanna Baillie. Even if her works such as *Plays on the Passions* are little known today, Baillie's literary fame in her own day as a playwright meant that Wordsworth and Keats were visitors here – as, too, was Sir Walter Scott. At their first meeting here in 1806 she confessed herself disappointed: 'She had looked for a creature of elegant and romantic aspect; she saw a solid, prosaic-looking square-built man destitute of poetic externals.'[9] Miss Baillie was soon to learn that, despite the Romantics, a dashing appearance did not guarantee good poetry and that a more commonplace appearance was not an insuperable obstacle. She died at Bolton House in 1851 at the age of eighty-nine.

Further up Hampstead Grove on the left is New Grove House, where the *Punch* cartoonist and writer George du Maurier lived. His literary fame will always rest on his novel *Trilby*, published in 1894, in which an opera singer falls under the dominating influence of a musician called Svengali. Opposite New Grove House is the Admiral's House, built in 1700 although with later additions, where one of George IV's admirals is supposed, erroneously, to have paced the quarterdeck. The house appears as Admiral Boom's House, Cherry Tree Lane, in P. L. Travers's *Mary Poppins* (1934). Just to the side of the Admiral's House is the early-eighteenth-century Grove Lodge where John Galsworthy lived for the last fifteen years of his life. When he moved here in 1918, Galsworthy had already made his name in the Edwardian period as a playwright with such works as *The Silver Box*, *Strife* and *Justice*. He had also, in 1906, published *A Man of Property*, the first part of *The Forsyte Saga*, the last five volumes of which were written at Grove Lodge. In 1932, Galsworthy was awarded the Nobel Prize for Literature but he was so ill that despite repeated efforts he was unable to travel to Stockholm. The prize Gold Medal along with the illuminated scroll was therefore brought to Grove Lodge. Galsworthy died here in 1933.[10]

If one walks down from Hampstead Grove – on the left is the Holly Bush pub, an attractive early-eighteenth-century building – and into Mount Vernon, a plaque on Abernethy Lodge commemorates the relatively brief stay of Robert Louis Stevenson, who like so many others before him came to Hampstead to sample its fresh air. As one walks down the hill, passing a charming little Roman Catholic chapel on the left, Hampstead's parish church of St John lies before one. The church has two burial-grounds, the older one to the south containing the graves of John Constable and his family, the newer extension (although still of 1810) those of George du Maurier, the politician Hugh Gaitskell and also Sir Walter Besant, Victorian novelist and historian, who lived at 17 Frognal Gardens. Although his novels have not retained their popularity, his histories of London are still of value to the social historian. Besant also founded the Society of Authors in 1888. Inside St John's are memorials to John Keats and Joanna Baillie. Opposite St John's is another of Hampstead's glories, the early-eighteenth-century Church Row. H. G. Wells lived at number 17 from 1909. In 1914 he invited D. H. Lawrence to dinner here – an occasion which does not seem to have been a success because Wells expected his guests to wear dinner-jackets. Lawrence had to borrow one, and spent the whole evening complaining about it.

It was not an experience which prevented Lawrence and his wife Frieda moving into Hampstead themselves the next year when they rented 1 Byron Villas in the Vale of Health (this name belies the fact that the vale was once a swamp). Lawrence came here because it was hoped that the climate would help his always precarious health, not because the Vale of Health has probably contained more literary figures per house than any other part of London. Leigh Hunt has already been mentioned at Vale Lodge, but there have been Edgar Wallace at Vale Lodge; the Harmsworth brothers, later to be influential newspaper proprietors, at Hunt Cottage; Compton Mackenzie at Woodbine Cottage; the Indian poet Tagore at 3 The Villas; and the social historians Barbara and J. L. Hammond at Hollycot. Most of the above seem to have liked both Hampstead and the Vale of Health, but rather typically Lawrence did not. As his German wife Frieda wrote later: 'He didn't like the Vale of Health, and he didn't like the little flat and he didn't like me or anybody else.' It was a busy time for Lawrence: visitors to Byron Villas included E. M. Forster, Katherine Mansfield, who was living up the road at 17 East Heath Road, Aldous Huxley (himself 'a Hampstead man' having spent part of his youth at 16 Bracknell Gardens), Bertrand Russell, W. B. Yeats and Ezra Pound. Whilst at the Vale of Health, Lawrence's novel *The Rainbow* was published, which resulted in the successful prosecution of his publishers Methuen by the police. In 1915, Lawrence watched the first major Zeppelin raid on London from the comparative safety of Hampstead Heath. In his novel *Kangaroo* of 1923, Harriet – the character based on Frieda – looks up and says as the Zeppelins pass over: 'Think, some of the boys I played with when I was a child are probably on it.' After less than six, albeit eventful, months the Lawrences left Byron Villas.[11]

The First World War saw other Hampstead writers sometimes placed in unusual situations. The biographer Lytton Strachey, author of *Eminent Victorians*, claimed to be a conscientious objector. Strachey had a house for many years in Belsize Park and he was summoned to Hampstead Town Hall for examination by a committee in 1917. He was asked the by now standard question as to what he would do if he came across a German soldier attempting to violate his sister, and replied that he would endeavour to interpose his body between them.[12] In 1918, Marie Stopes, occupant of 14 Well Walk directly opposite Burgh House, published her *Married Love*, a book which resulted from her disastrous first marriage and whose great popularity prefaced a new frankness in sexual matters. Later that year she issued *Wise Parenthood*, another bestseller. For the last few years of her life Marie Stopes lived near Dorking and published several volumes of poetry. She died in 1958.

Between the wars the flow of literary figures into Hampstead continued unabated, although one young man came here not to write but to beg money by singing in the streets. Early in 1919, C. S. Forester, desperate to raise some money in order to take out a new girlfriend, 'stepped off the kerb, and began to blare ballads in my tuneless baritone': 'To try to sing a song when one does not know the words at the same time as one cannot sing the tune gives a certain formlessness to one's efforts not likely to produce many coppers. The three songs I could sing right through I had never liked . . . and after about the hundredth repetition I simply hated them.' He did, however, succeed in his aim, making nearly £1.[13]

Noël Coward staged his play *The Vortex* at the Everyman Theatre (now Cinema) in November 1924, only just managing to obtain a licence from the Lord Chamberlain on the morning of the first performance.[14] It was just as well that he did as it was *The Vortex* which made Coward's name.

The Waugh family were then living at 'Underhill', North End Road, in a house designed by the father, Arthur, who was a director of the publishers Chapman & Hall. The two sons Alec and Evelyn both became novelists. Apparently Evelyn thought it witty and amusing to drop pennies on his way home from Hampstead Tube station and see how many remained in the morning.[15]

One fine novel set in interwar Hampstead is Vita Sackville-West's *All Passion Spent* (1931), in which the recently widowed Lady Slane decides to live in what her relatives and family regard as a distinctly unfashionable part of London. Lady Slane travels to Hampstead, searching for the house which she recalls seeing many years before:

> The passers-by ignored her, standing there, so well accustomed were they to the sight of old ladies in Hampstead. Setting out to walk, she wondered if she remembered the way; but Hampstead seemed scarcely a part of London, so sleepy and village-like, with its warm red-brick houses and vistas of trees and distance that reminded her pleasantly of Constable's paintings.

She finds the house and moves in, renewing, too, her acquaintance with Mr FitzGeorge, strolling with him on the Heath and visiting Keats's house – 'that little white box of strain and tragedy marooned among the dark green laurels'. One commentator has suggested that Lady Slane's house was in Church Row, and it is here that she dies.[16]

In 1934, George Orwell began work in a bookshop called Booklovers' Corner on the edge of South End Green, living rent-free in a flat above the shop in return for working there in the afternoons. It was an experience which he used in his novel *Keep the Aspidistra Flying* (1936), although no one could have been less of a self-portrait than the forever whining Gordon Comstock, the novel's protagonist. Orwell's second novel, *A Clergyman's Daughter*, was issued in 1935, by which time he had moved to 77 Parliament Hill. In January 1936 the publisher Victor Gollancz commissioned him to write what became *The Road to Wigan Pier* and Orwell was able to establish himself as a full-time writer. Booklovers' Corner is now 'The Perfect Pizza' – one can imagine a stinging Orwell essay on the theme 'From bookshop to takeaway' – but on the outside there is a small bust of Orwell. Two years after Orwell moved away from Hampstead, Sigmund Freud moved to 20 Maresfield Gardens where he lived for the last two years of his life from 1938 to 1939. The plaque calls Freud the 'Founder of Psychoanalysis' and the house is now a museum. One of the objects on display is Freud's famous consultant's couch.

Since the war Hampstead has retained its reputation as one of London's most popular literary addresses.[17] There are several bookshops, fine architecture – it is revealing that Sir Nikolaus Pevsner chose to live at 2 Wildwood Terrace, North End, from

1936 until his death in 1983 – and the Heath. Though traffic hurtles through the village now, and Church Row in particular seems always to be in imminent danger from lorry and juggernaut, much of Hampstead's rural charm remains, and it is no surprise to find it as popular with literary figures today as it ever was.

Highgate

After Bill Sykes had murdered Nancy in Charles Dickens's *Oliver Twist* he escaped from London through Islington and 'strode up the hill at Highgate, on which stands the stone in honour of Whittington'. This stone is still to be seen on the west side of Highgate Hill, placed there in 1821, and it is the third memorial to Whittington on this spot. The only change since Sykes's day is the black cat, added in 1964, which now sits on the stone. The Whittington stone commemorates the place at which the young Dick, leaving the capital after an unhappy period as an undercook at the Priory of St Bartholomew the Great in Smithfield, was persuaded by the sound of the bells of St Mary-le-Bow in Cheapside to 'turn again'. Apparently the bells told him that he would be 'thrice Lord Mayor of London' – which just shows the unreliability of relying on portents such as these. He was in fact elected Lord Mayor of London four times. It is of course a legend which has launched a thousand pantomimes, but before these comparatively recent shows the tale of Dick and his cat was popular in broadsides and chapbooks, no doubt much favoured by employers trying to goad lazy apprentices into doing some work. The hospital nearby, which originally cared for lepers, is now named after Whittington – as, too, is the pub.

In order to reach Whittington's stone the pedestrian leaving Archway Underground station has to trek up a steep hill. Keep toiling up the gradient – now one understands only too well all those poetic references to the hills of Hampstead and Highgate – and stop at the Catholic church of St Joseph, familiarly known as 'Holy Joe's'. Here is a splendid view down towards London. One final push up the hill takes one past a terrace of fine seventeenth-century houses to the right and Lauderdale House to the left, and finally into Pond Square at the top of Highgate Hill. Now one is at the heart of what was once Highgate village. In the Middle Ages the village was hidden away in the Great Park of Haringey, which belonged to the Bishops of London. A 'high gate' at the top of the hill, roughly where the modern Gatehouse tavern now stands, restricted access to the park. This gate was supposedly looked after by a hermit who also found the time and the inclination to dig out a pond close to the gate – hence the name Pond Square, although the pond has since been filled in. The story then goes on to suggest that the hermit used the rubble and mud from this excavation to fill in the 'hollow way' or road at the bottom of Highgate Hill. Anyway, it makes for a good story.

After the Reformation in the 1530s the land in and around Highgate was acquired by several noblemen who built themselves fine country houses in what was an attractive and above all healthy setting. John Norden wrote in 1593: 'Upon this hills is most pleasant dwelling, yet not so pleasant as healthful; for the expert inhabitants there report that divers that have beene long visited with sickness, not curable by physicke, have in short time repayred their health by that sweet salutarie air.'[1] Elizabeth I was a frequent visitor to, and admirer of, Highgate, but another famous guest found the place less conducive to his health. The seventeenth-century biographer John Aubrey in his *Lives* recounts what happened to Francis Bacon, eminent lawyer, scholar and, according to some, the author of Shakespeare's plays:

Towards Highgate snow lay on the ground, and it came into my lord's thoughts why flesh might not be preserved in snow as salt. They were resolved they would try the experiment. Presently they alighted out of the coach, and went into a poore woman's house at the bottom of Highgate Hill, and bought a hen, and made her exenterate [i.e. disembowelled it], and then stuffed the bodie with snow, and my lord did help to doe it himself. The snow so chilled him that he immediately fell so ill that he could not return to his lodgings [I suppose then at

Gray's Inn], but went to the Earl of Arundel's house at Highgate, where they put him into a good bed, warmed with a panne; but it was a dampe bed that had not been layn in for about a year before, which gave him such a colde that in two or three days he died of suffocation.[2]

As the 1st Viscount of St Albans, Bacon was buried in that town.

The place at which Bacon died, Arundel House, has not survived. Much of it was demolished in 1694 and replaced by the lovely Old Hall, still at 17 South Grove. The rest of the buildings were pulled down in 1828. However, one house of that vintage which would have been known to Bacon and that still stands is Lauderdale House, beautifully positioned with views down to London to the south and over Waterlow Park to the west. Built in the sixteenth century, although with later additions, its first owner was Sir Richard Martin, three times Lord Mayor of London (perhaps the Bow Bells were calling to Dick Martin and not Dick Whittington?). In the 1660s the house was owned by a Lord Lauderdale, who in July 1666 invited Samuel Pepys to dinner. In his diary Pepys recorded that 'at supper there played one of their servants upon the viallin, some Scotch tunes only – several – and the best of their country, as they seemed to esteem them by their praising and admiring them; but Lord, the strangest ayre that ever I heard in my life, and all of one cast'.

Besides Pepys, Lauderdale House is linked with two other famous seventeenth-century characters. In 1670, Nell Gwyn was living here when she gave birth to Charles Beauclerk, later the Duke of St Albans. The boy's father, Charles II, was a frequent visitor to Lauderdale House to see Nell Gwyn, and only the dullest of imaginations can fail to visualise Charles and Nell strolling hand-in-hand through the gardens. There is a certain irony in Charles coming here to Lauderdale House since both it and the houses on the other side of Highgate Hill, notably Cromwell House, had formed part of a Parliamentary community during the Civil War. One of those employed by Cromwell, the poet Andrew Marvell, lived in a little house by the side of the hill, and a plaque informs the pedestrian that 'Four feet below this spot is the stone step, formerly the entrance to the cottage in which he lived'. Originally from Yorkshire, Marvell came to London and was a friend of John Milton, helping to save the latter's life after the Restoration in 1660. Marvell became MP for Hull and spent several years abroad as a diplomat before dying of 'an ague' in 1678.

In the nineteenth century Lauderdale House was occupied by yet another Lord Mayor of London, Sir Sydney Waterlow, who made his fortune printing a new genre of literature introduced in the Victorian age: railway tickets and timetables. He gave the extensive grounds of the house, comprising some twenty-six acres, to the public and in 1891 they were formally opened as Waterlow Park. With its lake, aviary and open-air theatre it is one of London's nicest parks. A statue of Sir Sydney, complete with umbrella, stands at the top end. Lauderdale House was briefly used by Bart's Hospital at the end of the nineteenth century for its tubercular patients but it is now a leisure and arts centre offering a restaurant, concerts, auctions and craft bazaars.

Throughout the seventeenth century the village of Highgate was still separated from London by acres of fields and countryside. On 7 September 1666 the diarist John Evelyn came here a few days after the Great Fire, afterwards extolling the behaviour of the refugees:

> I then went towards Islington and Highgate, where one might have seen some 200,000 people, of all ranks and degrees, dispersed and lying along by their heaps of what they could save from the fire, deploring their loss; and yet ready to perish for hunger and destitution, yet not asking one penny for relief, which to me seemed a stranger sight than any I had yet beheld.

A few years after Evelyn visited Highgate, work started on a strip of housing called The Grove, still perhaps the village's most fashionable address. To the rear the residents enjoy a wonderful view over Hampstead Heath, and sometimes they are obliging enough to leave the shutters open so that everyone can have a look. Out in the front The Grove faces some fine elm trees and also the Flask tavern, which dates from the eighteenth century. Highgate seems to attract London legends: Dick Turpin, no doubt on Black Bess, is supposed to have jumped the high gate when pursued by the authorities and hidden himself in the Flask's cellars. What we do know for certain is that the poet Samuel Taylor Coleridge occupied 3 The Grove from 1816 until his death in 1834, living with the local doctor James Gillman and his wife Ann. After leaving Christ's Hospital, Coleridge had enjoyed a varied career. Once intended for the Church, he had even joined the Light Dragoons under the name Silas Tomken Comber-bache.[3] At his interview he had been asked whether he could run a Frenchman through the body with a sword. Coleridge replied: 'I don't know, as I never tried; but I'll let a Frenchman run me through before I'll run away.' 'That'll do', replied the officer.

After leaving the Army, Coleridge became friendly with William and Dorothy Wordsworth, writing poetry but having also become addicted to the opium which he first began taking in order to ward off rheumatic pains. It was an addiction which produced the fragment 'Kubla Khan'. His play *Remorse* was staged at Drury Lane in 1813, but by 1816, after the break-up of his marriage and on the verge of suicide, Coleridge was taken in by the Gillmans. Gradually Coleridge regained some of his health, helped by the rural seclusion of the village and also by the visits of friends such as the painter William Collins – ironically Collins's own son, the novelist Wilkie, later had his own drug problems – and by Thomas Carlyle, who has left us in his *The Life of John Sterling* (1851) a·charming picture of 3 The Grove and also of semi-rural Highgate in the early years of the nineteenth century:

> He [Coleridge] would stroll about the pleasant garden with you, sit in the pleasant rooms of the place, – perhaps take you to his own peculiar room high up, with a rearward view, which was the chief view of all. A really charming outlook, in fine weather. Close at hand, wide sweep of flowery leafy gardens, their few houses mostly hidden, the very chimney-pots veiled under blossomy umbrage, flowed gloriously down hill; gloriously issuing in wide-tufted undulating plain-country, rich in charms of field and town. Waving blooming country of the brightest green; dotted all over with handsome villas, handsome groves; crossed by roads and human traffic, here inaudible or heard only as a musical hum: and behind all swam, under olive-tinted haze, the illimitable limitary ocean of London, with its domes and steeples definite in the sun, big Paul's and the many memories attached to it hanging high over all.

All Coleridge's visitors remarked upon his extraordinary powers of conversation. William Hazlitt came to The Grove and noted that Coleridge 'talked on forever; and you wished him to talk on for ever'. Carlyle was not so appreciative; he was fond of the sound of his own voice, but Coleridge talked for two and three-quarter hours of their three-hour interview. At his death in 1834, Coleridge was buried in the chapel attached to Highgate School, but in 1961 was reburied at St Michael's, the church which stands in The Grove and is the highest point of the village, loftily surveying the rest of London to the south.

For many people, however, mention of Highgate is inseparable from its cemetery, opened in 1839 and containing the remains of several notable literary figures. Sir John Betjeman has called Highgate Cemetery 'a Victorian Valhalla',[4] and it was indeed one of the most fashionable of the seventy cemeteries built in Victorian London in a desperate attempt to deal satisfactorily with the needs of a rapidly expanding population. Most of London's churchyards were already full by the early nineteenth century, and huge new cemeteries such as those at Kensal Green, Abney Park, Brompton and Highgate were laid out on what were then the outskirts of London. Highgate Cemetery's architect was Stephen Geary, himself buried here, and he was clearly much influenced by the Egyptian style, creating an Egyptian Avenue and Cedar of Lebanon Catacombs as well as Gothic Catacombs under St Michael's, together with the obligatory high walls necessary to deter grave-robbers. Highgate Cemetery proved so popular that within fifteen years the older or western section had to be supplemented by an extension to the east.

In all there are some 51,000 graves at Highgate, containing over 160,000 bodies. The most famous of course is that of Karl Marx, whose tomb lies in the eastern section, surmounted by the large bust of his head which bears the injunction 'Workers of All Lands Unite'. Originally buried a hundred yards away, his remains were moved to this more prominent position in 1954 and the bust erected two years later. Here also lie his wife Jenny, his daughter Eleanor, his grandson Henry and the Marxes' maid-servant Helene Demuth, by whom Marx had an illegitimate son. Every day a constant stream of visitors comes to pay respects, one of the first being William Morris who trudged up here in 1884, the year after Marx's death '(with a red-ribbon in my button-hole) at the tail of various banners and a very bad band'.[5]

Marx's grave is easy to find. Much more hidden, although only fifty yards away, is the grave of the novelist George Eliot, which lies close to that of George Henry Lewes, the journalist and philosopher with whom she lived for many years. Eliot died in 1880, and her coffin bore the inscription 'Quel la fonte che spande di

parlar si largo fiumi' ('This is the fountain which sheds light') –
ironic in view of the orienteering needed to find her grave. Also
buried in this east side are John Cross, George Eliot's husband for
the last seven months of her life, who later edited her journals
and letters; Sir Leslie Stephen, first editor of the *Dictionary of
National Biography* and father of Virginia Woolf; and also William
Foyle, succinctly described in the guide to Highgate Cemetery:
'Founder of the Charing Cross Road bookshop. He and his
brother entered the bookselling business as a result of their
experience selling their used textbooks after failing their civil
service exams.'[6] In the older west section are Charles Dickens's
parents and his wife Catherine; Radclyffe Hall, author of the
lesbian novel *The Well of Loneliness*, banned in Britain in 1928;
and Mrs Henry Wood, responsible for one of the most popular
Victorian novels, *East Lynne*. John Galsworthy's parents, and also
most of his fictional Forsytes, are buried in Highgate; although
Galsworthy's ashes were scattered on the Sussex Downs, there is
a memorial on his parents' grave.

Yet another famous writer's parents lie in this cemetery, those
of John Betjeman. His father wanted him to enter the family
furniture business near the Angel in Islington:

> *And now when I behold, fresh-published, new,*
> *A further volume of my verse, I see*
> *His kind grey eyes look woundedly at mine,*
> *I see his workmen seeking other jobs,*
> *And that red granite obelisk that marks*
> *The family grave in Highgate Cemetery*
> *Points an accusing finger to the sky.*

Betjeman was born in Highgate in August 1906, and much of
his early childhood was spent at 31 West Hill, 'Safe, in a world of
trams and buttered toast'. The house is still there – as, too, are
most of the places mentioned in his verse autobiography, *Summoned by Bells*. There Betjeman tells of his preparatory school,
Byron House, in North Grove at which he falls in love with Peggy
Purey-Cust:

> *Your ice-blue eyes, your lashes long and light,*
> *Your sweetly freckled face and turned-up nose*
> *So haunted me that all my loves since then*

Have had a look of Peggy Purey-Cust.
Along the Grove, what happy, happy steps
Under the limes I took to Byron House,
And blob-work, weaving, carpentry and art,
Walking with you; and with what joy returned.

At Byron House the young Betjeman was already writing poetry, and when he went to Highgate Junior School in 1914 one of his masters was a certain T. S. Eliot, known to the boys as 'the American master'.[7] The nine-year-old Betjeman bound his early verses into a book which he called 'The Best Poems of Betjeman', presenting a copy to Eliot. Eliot failed to respond to what Betjeman later called his 'terrible' poems and appeared to have forgotten about them. Twenty years on, however, he reminded Betjeman of the incident.[8] The Betjeman family later moved away to Chelsea, taking with them young John, who was homesick for Highgate. Eliot himself was only at Highgate School for a couple of terms. Another poet who had attended Highgate School was Gerard Manley Hopkins, fifty years before.

Today, like its neighbour Hampstead, Highgate is firmly a part of London, but it, too, retains in part the air of elegance and style which has characterised its history. The Highgate Literary and Scientific Institution of 1839 stands in Pond Square as testimony to the community's long links with learning. The village has continued to attract literary 'names': J. B. Priestley, for instance, lived at 3 The Grove, Coleridge's old residence, from 1935 to 1939. The one drawback to living in Highgate is that the continuous thunder of the traffic threatens to tear the village apart.

Perhaps worst affected are the houses sandwiched between North Road and Southwood Lane, one of which carries a plaque. One hundred years ago A. E. Housman lived at 'Byron Cottage', 17 North Road, then a pleasant Georgian house overlooking the grounds of Highgate School.[9] Housman had moved here in 1886, working during the day at the Patent Office in Chancery Lane and in the evenings studying at the British Museum. In 1892 he was appointed Professor of Latin at London University. It was at Byron Cottage that Housman produced his most famous work, *A Shropshire Lad*, published in March 1896. The sixty-three separate poems contained within the overall work are imbued with a quiet nostalgia for a 'lost' rural England. Housman left Highgate in

1905, just before the motorcar began its concerted assault on the London landscape. Its effects would no doubt only have confirmed in his mind these lines from *A Shropshire Lad*:

> *By bridges that Thames runs under,*
> *In London, the town built ill,*
> *'Tis sure small matter for wonder*
> *If sorrow is with one still.*

Holborn
and Lincoln's Inn

It is difficult to identify quite what or where Holborn is. Lying between Covent Garden to the west, Bloomsbury to the north, Clerkenwell and Smithfield to the east and the Strand and Fleet Street to the south, Holborn seems rather squeezed by its more distinct neighbours. The area known as Lincoln's Inn on the other hand is easier to define since it centres on the Inn of Court, while Gray's Inn sits on the north side of High Holborn. One reason for Holborn's relative anonymity – and in 1965 the borough of Holborn was subsumed into that of Camden – is that, although it has an Underground station and also an excellent public library in Theobalds Road, Holborn contains few residential areas. There were rather more in Victorian times, though they were mostly slums. Today traffic hurtles through Holborn causing a tremendous din, just as it did a hundred years ago; J. M. Barrie in his first novel, *When a Man's Single* (1888), describes Rob entering the capital via Gray's Inn Road: 'He walked into the roar of London in Holborn, and never forgot the alley into which he retreated to discover if he had suddenly become deaf.

Holborn has often been an area through which people have passed on their way to somewhere else. In the Middle Ages it might have been merchants travelling to the City, or drovers taking their herds to Smithfield. The cattle used to stray into

Lincoln's Inn Fields, leading to the erection of turnstiles designed to keep them out: hence Great and Little Turnstile Streets. Until 1783 the condemned were brought along High Holborn on their final journey to Tyburn. In John Gay's *The Beggar's Opera* Polly imagines her lover, Captain Macheath, passing along here:

> Now I am a wretch indeed; methinks I see him already in the cart, sweeter and more lovely than the nosegay in his hand! I hear the crowd extolling his resolution and intrepidity! What volleys of sighs are sent from the windows of Holborn that so comely a youth should be brought to disgrace! I see him at the tree! the whole circle are in tears! even butchers weep! Jack Ketch [the hangman] himself hesitates to perform his duty, and would be glad to lose his fee by a reprieve! What then will become of Polly?

Yet despite its use as a convenient thoroughfare Holborn is full of unexpected pleasures and well repays a visit. There is Ely Place, still a private road guarded by top-hatted and frock-coated beadles and with an iron bar at the entrance to stop horses turning around in this cul-de-sac. Halfway down it is the Catholic church of St Etheldreda, parts of which date back to the Middle Ages. The atmospheric undercroft, for example, was built in 1251 and boasts walls which are eight feet thick. From the thirteenth century much of the land here had been occupied by the Bishops of Ely as their town residence, a property which then stood on the edge of the Fleet river – Holborn derives its name from 'the stream in the hollow' – and was surrounded by farmland. Ely Palace possessed an orchard and a seven-acre vineyard, and in Shakespeare's *Richard III* the Duke of Gloucester says to the Bishop of Ely that 'when I was last in Holborn, I saw good strawberries in your garden there: I do beseech you, send for some of them'. In *Richard II*, John of Gaunt is at Ely House when he speaks of England as 'this scepter'd isle . . . this precious stone set in a silver sea . . . this blessed plot, this earth, this realm, this England'. John of Gaunt actually died here in 1399. Most of the medieval buildings were demolished in the late eighteenth century and what was left was very badly treated. In 1874 when the church was bought back by the Roman Catholics it was found to be full of 'inconceivable filth, living and dead'. St Etheldreda's is the oldest Catholic church building in Britain.[1]

At the back of St Etheldreda's is the Mitre tavern of 1546,

another reminder of the former importance in this neighbour-
hood of the Bishops of Ely and originally built for the Palace
servants. Although rebuilt, the Mitre is one of the oldest pubs in
London. In the bar is the trunk of a cherry tree around which
Elizabeth I is supposed to have danced with a favourite courtier,
Sir Christopher Hatton. Elizabeth certainly knew Holborn, forcing the then Bishop of Ely to disgorge part of his property to
Hatton. His name lives on in Hatton Garden, the home of
London's jewel and gem trade. When Hatton lived in Holborn he
would have been familiar with the beautiful timber-framed
Staple Inn, complete with overhanging gables, which lies further
to the west and was built in 1586. Its picturesque quality con-
trasts with the blatant *Mirror* offices which dominate Holborn
Circus. Formerly an Inn of Chancery, Staple Inn was severely
damaged by a flying bomb in 1944 but it has been well restored
and has a charming garden to the rear. It features heavily in
Charles Dickens's last and unfinished novel, *The Mystery of Edwin
Drood*, and his description of the little enclave could not be
bettered:

> It is one of those nooks, the turning into which out of the
> clashing street, imparts to the relieved pedestrian the sensation
> of having put cotton in his ears, and velvet soles on his boots. It
> is one of those nooks where a few smoky sparrows twitter in
> smoky trees, as though they called to one another, 'Let us play
> at country', and where a few feet of garden-mould and a few
> yards of gravel enable them to do that refreshing violence to
> their tiny understandings. . . . Moreover, it is one of those
> little nooks which are legal nooks; and it contains a little Hall,
> with a little lantern in its roof.

In its essentials Dickens's evocation remains true today.

Apart from St Etheldreda's, the oldest building in the vicinity is
the Old Hall of Lincoln's Inn, one of the four Inns of Court, with
records which date back to 1422. Seven years after the Old Hall
was completed in 1489, the Inn accepted the eighteen-year-old
Thomas More as a student. The next-oldest building in Lincoln's
Inn is the chapel, built between 1619 and 1623. The man who
inaugurated this chapel was the poet John Donne, who had himself studied at the Inn from 1592. A contemporary described him
in these youthful years as 'a great visiter of Ladies, a great
frequenter of Playes, a great writer of conceited Verses'.[2] When

Donne returned, however, it was as the Divinity Reader, paid £60 per annum and responsible for preaching fifty sermons each year. At Lincoln's Inn to this day a bell is tolled between 12.30 and 1.00 when a bencher (or member) of the Inn dies, in a custom which goes back to Donne's day.[3] Perhaps the bell was an inspiration to him in his *Devotions*:

> No man is an island, entire of itself; every man is a piece of the continent, a part of the main; if a clod be washed away by the sea, Europe is the less, as well as if a promontory were, as well as if a manor of thy friend's or of thine own were; any man's death diminishes me, because I am involved in mankind; and therefore never send to know for whom the bell tolls; it tolls for thee.

From 1737 the Old Hall of Lincoln's Inn was sometimes used as the High Court of Chancery, and no book about literary London would be complete without a quotation from Dickens's *Bleak House*, which opens with the Lord Chancellor in the Old Hall: 'Never can there come fog too thick, never can there come mud and mire too deep, to assort with the groping and floundering condition which this High Court of Chancery, most pestilent of hoary sinners, holds, this day, in the sight of heaven and earth.' And always the case of Jarndyce and Jarndyce proceeds down the years, 'perennially hopeless' – except of course to the lawyers themselves, who are amply remunerated.

Several writers have been students at Lincoln's Inn, apart from More and Donne. Benjamin Disraeli was here in 1824, as was his rival William Gladstone later on and also the historian Macaulay, the novelist Wilkie Collins and the adventure-writer Rider Haggard. The last was responsible not just for fifty-eight novels full of action and heroics but also for an excellent survey of rural England at the close of the nineteenth century.[4]

The students at Lincoln's Inn have always been very keen, quite rightly, to protect the rural seclusion of their Inn. In the past several attempts were made to build over the land to the west, and in the seventeenth century the builders found themselves confronted by stone-throwing lawyers – a bit of hooliganism which did in fact pay off. Houses were built around Lincoln's Inn Fields from the 1630s, but the open space in the middle was left untouched. Not that this has always been the attractive garden it is now; John Gay in his long poem *Trivia; or, The Art of Walking the Streets of London* (1716) refers to:

> *Where Lincoln's Inn, wide space, is rail'd around,*
> *Cross not with venturous step; there oft is found*
> *The lurking thief, who, while the daylight shone,*
> *Made the walls echo with his begging tone,*
> *That crutch, which late compassion moved, shall wound*
> *Thy bleeding head, and fell thee to the ground.*
> *Though thou art tempted by the linkman's call,*
> *Yet trust him not along the lonely wall,*
> *In the mid way he'll quench the flaming brand*
> *And share the booty with the pilfering band.*

Red Lion Square to the north also survives as open land because of a violent campaign similar to that conducted over Lincoln's Inn Fields. Both squares were often used for executions and duels. In 1660, Oliver Cromwell's body was dug up from its Westminster resting-place, brought here to Red Lion Square overnight and then removed the next day to Tyburn where it was gibbeted and buried once more. In the eighteenth century Jonas Hanway lived in Red Lion Square at number 23 in the north-east corner. Hanway had been an intrepid explorer in his youth. Among other experiences he spent a year in Russia and wrote several books about his adventures. When Hanway settled here in Holborn he founded the Marine Society, an organisation which trained boys for the Royal Navy and lessened the need for press-ganging, and helped with the administration of the Coram Hospital. Most famously of all, Hanway introduced the umbrella into this country. At first passers-by in the street mocked both him and his accessory, but by the time of his death in 1786 the umbrella had become accepted. Hanway House now stands on the site of his residence in Red Lion Square.[5]

Whilst Hanway was living at 23 Red Lion Square a literary tragedy occurred elsewhere in Holborn. In the spring of 1770 a seventeen-year-old boy called Thomas Chatterton left Bristol in order to find fame and fortune in London. He knew no one there and began to forge manuscripts, pretending that they were original poems written by a fifteenth-century poet. His fraud was quickly discovered and, in August 1770, Chatterton killed himself by swallowing arsenic in his rooms at Brooke Street, Holborn. A plaque attached to 29 Brooke Street marks the former site of his lodgings.[6] Several of the Romantic poets later wrote about the poignant life and death of Chatterton – 'The marvellous boy . . . perished in his pride' (Wordsworth). Another tragedy which took place in Holborn came in 1796 when Charles Lamb's sister Mary killed their mother with a knife in a fit of insanity. For the rest of his life Charles devoted much time and energy to caring for Mary. The site of the house in which the killing took place is now occupied by Holy Trinity, Kingsway, the church which faces Holborn Underground station.

In the nineteenth century the Holborn area was familiar to Charles Dickens. At fifteen he was an office boy with the legal firm of Ellis & Blackman at 1 South Square in Gray's Inn; the desk at which he worked is in Dickens House. Mr Pickwick's attorney, Mr Perker, has his offices at Gray's Inn, and in *David Copperfield* Tommy Traddles also has his chambers here. Dickens lived at Furnival's Inn between 1834 and 1837, writing much of his first novel, *Pickwick Papers*, here. He moved away to 48 Doughty Street after his marriage. Furnival's Inn has gone, replaced by the garish red brick of the Prudential Assurance Company on the north side of High Holborn, but there is a bust of Dickens just inside the gateway on the left. Dickens was also acquainted with 58 Lincoln's Inn Fields where his friend John Forster lived and which he fictionalised as the home of Mr Tulkinghorn in *Bleak House* where the lawyer is in fact murdered. John Forster wrote the first and still one of the most informative biographies of Dickens. He does not exactly take a back seat in the book, prompting one critic to remark that it should more properly have been entitled 'The Life of John Forster, with occasional anecdotes of Charles Dickens'.[7] At the south-west corner of Lincoln's Inn Fields is the Old Curiosity Shop, bearing foot-high letters which proclaim that this building was immortalised by Charles Dickens. It wasn't: Dickens did not base his story on this shop, and there is in fact no need to inflate the shop's historic worth. It is quite enough that it dates back to 1567 and is the oldest shop in London. Ignore the synthetic roof!

Another nineteenth-century resident of Holborn was William Morris, who lived at 17 Red Lion Square from 1856 to 1859, after he had come down from Oxford. Morris's companion here was the painter Edward Burne-Jones. Their predecessor at this address five years before had been the painter and poet Dante Gabriel Rossetti, whose landlord had stipulated that 'the models are to be kept under some gentlemanly restraint, as some artists sacrifice the dignity of art to the baseness of passion'.[8] Morris was already distinguished by his violent outbursts of bad temper, so virulent that one critic has suggested that he may well have been epileptic.[9] Nearby at 8 Red Lion Square he began the firm which later became Morris & Co. In 1859, Morris married Jane Burden and the couple moved away to a house specially built for them, the Red House at Bexleyheath in Kent. The name of 'the Red House' did not derive from Morris's politics; only later was he active in the labour movement. Someone who would have approved of Morris's political work was Bertrand Russell, whose statue stands in the east section of Red Lion Square. In his philosophical, mathematical and political books, Russell wrote with sufficient style and imagination to be awarded the Nobel Prize for Literature in 1950.

By the end of the nineteenth century several parts of Holborn had become slum districts. The Victorian solution was to build either institutions on, or roads over, such spots. In this area a start was made with the construction of the Law Courts in the Strand which replaced a nest of 'rookeries' or foul alleys. One of the sites wiped out had once held a fruit and vegetable market called Clare Market – it stood where the Clare Market building of the London School of Economics is now. It was this market which led to the lines in the nursery rhyme:

> *Oranges and lemons,*
> *Say the bells of St Clement's.*

St Clement Danes is the church in the middle of the road opposite the Law Courts (or, more properly, the Royal Courts of Justice). The slum clearance here was then followed by the construction of Kingsway, opened in 1905 and named after King Edward VII, and by the Aldwych. One of the side-streets demolished to make way for the Aldwych was called Holywell Street, or, as it was more commonly known, Booksellers' Row.[10] For many years this had been the centre of London's secondhand book trade, and several devotees lamented its passing. One of them, E. Beresford Chancellor, has left behind a portrait of Booksellers' Row:

> . . . overhanging first floors, the mysterious (and lord! how dirty as Pepys would have remarked) upper windows forming such an antithesis to the multi-coloured volumes that crowded the shop fronts beneath and bulged in their trays or boxes over

the pavements – those exiguous pavements where you were jostled by crowds, and sometimes were forced into the kennel (no one could have used so modern a word as gutter in such a connection). But there was so little vehicular traffic in Holywell Street that it did not matter.

The secondhand book trade moved off to Charing Cross Road.

Another famous institution which has also disappeared is the Holborn Empire, a grand music-hall which stood near Little Turnstile Street. Between the wars one of its regular star performers was Nellie Wallace. On one occasion Edith Sitwell was innocently passing the Holborn Empire when she was suddenly besieged by fans who had mistaken her for Nellie Wallace.[11] The Empire was demolished in 1960, but still very much present is St Andrew's, one of Wren's largest parish churches. Many of the items from the Coram Hospital's chapel are now here, including Captain Coram's tomb (see the chapter on Bloomsbury). It was also where the critic William Hazlitt was married – his best man, Charles Lamb, got a fit of the giggles during the service[12] – and where the young Benjamin Disraeli was received into the Christian faith in 1817.

Another survival is the amazing treasure-trove of Sir John Soane's Museum on the north side of Lincoln's Inn Fields. Soane was a leading architect at the turn of the eighteenth century – he designed the Bank of England amongst other buildings – and also an avid collector of virtually anything and everything, from the sarcophagus of King Seti I to paintings by Hogarth and Turner. Of literary interest are the busts of Homer and Ben Jonson, a Shakespeare Recess, several medieval manuscripts and a watercolour of 'Milton composing *Paradise Lost*'. On his death in 1837 Soane left his collection to the nation. For many years its curator was Sir John Summerson, author of several excellent books on the architects and architecture of London. To live in London, or to visit it for more than a day, and yet not to have been to Sir John Soane's Museum is an omission which should be rectified immediately.

The slum clearance schemes in Holborn reduced its residential population, and much of the neighbourhood today comprises such institutions as the Law Society and the Land Registry Office. To escape from the legal character of Holborn and Lincoln's Inn, stroll around the charming Garden or 'Walks' of Gray's Inn which were laid out by Sir Francis Bacon in 1606 and which are open to the public during the summer at certain times. Samuel Pepys came to see 'the fine ladies walk there', and 150 years later in the autumn of 1814 Shelley, heavily in debt, used to meet his lover Mary here in secret.[13] Nowadays the buses travelling along Theobalds Road would discourage such brief and furtive encounters, but the 'Walks' confirm that even Holborn, plagued as it is by heavy traffic, offers moments of peace and quiet.

Islington

In 1700, Islington's population was around 2000. By 1800, when it had increased to 10,000, Islington was still little more than a town some distance from London. By 1900, however, Islington's population numbered more than 300,000 and it was very firmly a part of the metropolis. In the course of 200 years the 'Merrie Islington' once familiar to Londoners as pleasant countryside in which they could relax had ceased to exist.

In literary terms one way of bringing home this transformation is by comparing the experiences of two writers who both knew the area well: Oliver Goldsmith and George Orwell. Goldsmith enjoyed strolling around the Islington fields in the mid-eighteenth century, organising walking expeditions from London to the Highbury Barn, a noted pleasure resort.[1] One of Goldsmith's friends called Cooke wrote of these trips from the Temple where Goldsmith lived:

There was then a very good ordinary, 'of two dishes, and a pastry, kept at Highbury Barn, at tenpence per head, including a penny for the waiter; and the company consisted of literary characters, a few Templars, and some citizens who had left off trade; the whole expenses of the day's fete never exceeded a crown, and oftener were from three-and-sixpence to four shillings, for which the party obtained good air and exercise, the example of good manners, and good conversation.

Nearly 200 years later, in 1945, George Orwell moved into 27 Canonbury Square and an Islington which had been badly bombed during the Second World War. Here Orwell began work on what proved to be his final novel, *1984*, and he based his description of the district inhabited by the 'proles' in that book on the Islington through which he often walked:

> He [Winston Smith] was somewhere in the vague, brown-coloured slums to the north and east of what had once been Saint Pancras Station. He was walking up a cobbled street of little two-storey houses with battered doorways which gave straight on the pavement and which were somehow curiously suggestive of ratholes. There were puddles of filthy water here and there among the cobbles. In and out of the dark doorways, and down narrow alley-ways that branched off on either side, people swarmed in astonishing numbers – girls in full bloom, with crudely lipsticked mouths, and youths who chased the girls, and swollen waddling women who showed you what the girls would be like in ten years' time, and old bent creatures shuffling along on splayed feet, and ragged barefooted children who played in the puddles and then scattered at angry yells from their mothers. Perhaps a quarter of the windows in the street were broken and boarded up.

Today Islington is perhaps a mix of Goldsmith and Orwell. Parts of it are elegant and fashionable, particularly the many squares of Barnsbury, the district around Duncan Terrace and Colebrooke Row and the landscaped New River. Other neighbourhoods in Islington are less attractive.

Islington was originally owned in the Middle Ages by several religious bodies. For example, there was the Order of St John, whose fourteenth-century prior, Sir Robert Hales, built himself the fine Highbury House. A contemporary chronicler recorded of Hales that 'He constructed afresh the manor house of Highbury and made it as elegant as the alternative Paradise, as good as the Garden of Eden'.[2] However, Hales was not to enjoy his mansion for long: it was his imposition of the poll tax which sparked off the Peasants' Revolt in 1381 and he was beheaded on Tower Hill. The canons of St Paul's owned what is now Barnsbury, and the canons of St Bartholomew the Great in Clerkenwell controlled the land further north. The latter built themselves a residence here which they called Canonbury (from the canons' 'burgh' or manor). Although often rebuilt, a part of this building – namely the Canonbury Tower which dates from 1562 – still exists.

This tower would have been familiar to Islington's first famous literary figure, Sir Walter Ralegh, who lived here in the countryside in the late sixteenth century. It was at his Islington home in 1583 that Ralegh first began to smoke tobacco, with at first unfortunate results:

> . . . sitting one day, in a deep meditation, with a pipe in his mouth, he inadvertently called to his man to bring him a tankard of small ale; the fellow, coming into the room, threw all the liquor into his master's face, and running downstairs bawled out: 'Fire! Help! Sir Walter has studied till his head is on fire, and the smoke bursts out of his head and nose!'[3]

Ralegh's studies did, however, result in several poems, travel books and an erudite *History of the World*. His Islington home stood near Upper Street until 1830 when it was pulled down and the site covered over by other houses. Ralegh is also thought to have owned several taverns in the district, two of which are still in their original positions: the Old Queen's Head in Essex Road and the Pied Bull in Upper Street. Although the Old Queen's Head was rebuilt in the early nineteenth century, it contains the original parlour chimney.

Samuel Pepys was another writer who admired the rural charms of what Londoners called 'Merrie Islington', often coming here to eat at 'the great Chescake house'. He sampled the milk of the Islington dairy farms which supplied London and he would have known, too, of the nearby spa. In 1683 a Mr Dick Sadler, surveyor of the King's Highway, discovered a well which he astutely developed into a spa, calling it Sadler's Wells in order to profit from the popularity of Tunbridge Wells. Much was made of the allegedly medicinal properties of the waters. Gardens and a 'Musick House' were soon added to Sadler's Wells' amenities, and for much of the eighteenth century it prospered. In Fanny Burney's novel *Evelina* of 1770, Mr Braughton tells the heroine that she has seen nothing until she has been to Sadler's Wells, and in Smollett's *Humphry Clinker* (1771) Elizabeth Jenkins struggles to convey the wonders of what she has witnessed:

> I was afterwards of a party at Sadler's-wells, where I saw such tumbling and dancing upon ropes and wires, that I was frightened, and ready to go into a fit. I tho't it was all inchant-

ment; and believing myself bewitched, began for to cry. You know as how the witches in Wales fly upon broom-sticks; but here was flying without any broom-stick, or thing in the varsal world, and firing of pistols in the air, and blowing of trumpets, and swinging, and rolling of wheel-barrows upon a wire (God bless us!), no thicker than a sewing-thread; that, to be sure, they must deal with the devil.

It was the theatrical side of Sadler's Wells which proved most successful, and the Musick House was converted into a stone theatre in 1765.[4] Forty years on William Wordsworth wrote in *The Prelude* of the variety of acts staged at Sadler's Wells, himself witnessing singers, rope-dancers, giants, dwarfs, clowns, conjurors, posture-masters and Harlequins. Its heyday came at the end of the eighteenth century and the beginning of the nineteenth with the immense popularity of the clown Joe Grimaldi, who had first appeared here at the age of two, dressed as a monkey and being swung around on the end of a chain by his father Giuseppe Grimaldi. For nearly thirty years Joe Grimaldi's inspired clowning brought in the crowds and brought himself fame and the managership of the Wells. The audience which journeyed here to see him had to brave the highwaymen who skulked in the fields between London and Islington; playbills often specified if it was to be a 'Moonlight Night'.

Grimaldi lived close to Sadler's Wells in Exmouth Street, also owning a cottage away in the fields of Finchley at Fallow Court. One of his greatest admirers was Lord Byron, and poet gave clown a silver snuff-box before his fatal departure to Greece.[5] Just before his death in May 1837, Grimaldi finished his *Memoirs* which were published the next year under the editorship of Charles Dickens and with twelve illustrations by George Cruikshank.[6] Grimaldi was buried at St James, Pentonville Road; the churchyard has recently been turned into Grimaldi Park and the clown's tombstone is clearly visible.

After Grimaldi's departure Sadler's Wells experienced mixed fortunes until 1844, when Samuel Phelps took over the management. Phelps, who lived at 8 Canonbury Square, established a reputation for his Shakespearean productions, staging all but three of Shakespeare's plays during the eighteen years he was at the Wells. On his leaving the playhouse in 1862 it again passed through a patchy period, being used as one of London's first cinemas and also a roller-skating rink. At one point it was nearly turned into a pickle factory. In the 1920s the formidable Lilian Baylis of the Old Vic took over the theatre and rebuilt it in 1931. The first night saw a performance of *Twelfth Night* with a youthful John Gielgud and Ralph Richardson. Both the Royal Ballet and the English National Opera have since grown out of Sadler's Wells.

If the Wells has survived since the seventeenth century, Oliver Goldsmith's Highbury Barn has not. A concert-hall had been added to its facilities during the Victorian period, but in 1865 the Highbury Barn was acquired by a former clown called Giovanelli, who presented what were widely regarded as scandalous dancing acts.[7] In 1870 the exhibition given by the Colonna troupe was considered so obscene that the place was closed down for good. The five-acre grounds were soon built over, but at least the public house now partly on their site is called 'The Highbury Barn'.

A third Islington pleasure resort has also not survived. The White Conduit Fields were just to the north of Pentonville Road and had been opened in the 1730s. Like Sadler's Wells and the Highbury Barn, it offered various indoor entertainments as well as the opportunity to walk in its gardens. In the 1780s some of the first cricket matches in London were played here in White Conduit Fields, but by 1786 the players and their patrons thought the ground too public and delegated Thomas Lord to find another, more suitable site. The first 'Lord's' was opened in Marylebone in May 1787. The fields themselves were built over in the first half of the nineteenth century, their only legacy being today's White Conduit Street.[8]

One feature of rural Islington which can still be seen is the New River, opened in 1613 by Sir Hugh Myddelton, whose statue stands on Islington Green. Disturbed by London's lack of a fresh water supply, Myddelton built a river which brought water to the capital from Ware in Hertfordshire, a distance of nearly forty miles, at a cost of £18,500.[9] The New River ended at a reservoir near Sadler's Wells which is now the headquarters of the Thames Water Authority. The young Samuel Taylor Coleridge and his friend Charles Lamb often walked to Islington from their school, Christ's Hospital near Newgate, in order to enjoy a swim in the New River.[10] Charles Lamb later described these excursions: 'How merrily we would sally forth into the fields and strip under the first warmth of the sun, and wanton like young dace in the streams getting appetites for noon. How faint and languid finally we would return towards nightfall to our desired morsel.' These dips did have one unfortunate consequence for Coleridge: it has been suggested that he failed to dry himself properly afterwards, an omission which led to the severe rheumatic pain and consequent opium addiction which played such a significant part in his later life.

Lamb lived briefly in Islington in 1799 at 45 Chapel Market, returning in the 1820s to live for several years at what was then Colebrook Cottage but is now 64 Duncan Terrace. Although by then Camden Passage and Charlton Place had been built and Barnsbury was in the process of development, Islington was still not much more than a village. He described his new home in a letter of September 1823:

> I have a cottage in Colebrooke Row, Islington; a cottage, for it is detached; a white house with six good rooms; the New River (rather elderly by this time) runs (if a moderate walking pace may be so termed) close to the foot of the house; and behind is a spacious garden with vines (I assure you), pears, strawberries, parsnips, leeks, carrots, cabbages, to delight the heart of old Alcinous. . . . I feel like a great lad, never having had a house before.[11]

On one occasion Lamb's friend George Dyer took a wrong turning after leaving Lamb's cottage and fell into the New River; Lamb wrote some ironic lines in which he called it 'Mockery of a river – liquid artifice, wretched conduit! henceforth rank with canals and sluggish aqueducts.'

Lamb's return to Islington did in fact have a sad purpose. Thirty years earlier his sister Mary had killed their mother in a fit of insanity. Charles looked after Mary for the rest of his life, and Colebrook Cottage was conveniently near to the Islington Lunatic Asylum in which she was periodically incarcerated. Lamb's high spirits were not downcast, and William Hazlitt often came here to accompany him on long walks through the Islington fields. They particularly liked going to see the Canonbury Tower: 'He [Lamb] was never weary of toiling up and down the winding and narrow stairs of this suburban pile, peeping into its quaint corners and cupboards.' In 1827, Charles and Mary Lamb moved away to Enfield.

Another 'Islingtonian' of the time was the writer and artist

Edward Lear, born in 1812 at Bowman's Lodge which then stood out in the country. If it still existed, then Bowman's Lodge would be on the busy junction of Seven Sisters Road and Holloway Road – there is in fact a Bowman's Place nearby. Lear was one of twenty-one children, although not all of them survived. His City stockbroker father went bankrupt, and the sickly child was brought up by an older sister. Lear's epilepsy was not helped by the dirty London climate – he often called the capital 'Foggopolis'[12] – and for most of his adult life he lived abroad, although he always retained affectionate memories of his boyhood in rural Islington. In 1846, Lear published *A Book of Nonsense* and in 1871 *Nonsense Songs*, a collection which includes 'The Owl and the Pussy-Cat'. Lear was educated at home, but Islington was noted for its good schools. The novelist Wilkie Collins came here in the 1830s as a young boy. Picked on by the school bully, Collins found that he could appease him by telling story after story like some nineteenth-century Scheherazade until the older boy eventually fell asleep.[13]

Lying some miles out of London, Islington High Street and Essex Road contained several taverns and coaching inns in which travellers stayed before the last stage of their journey into the city. The most famous of these establishments, giving its name to the neighbourhood, was the Angel, situated on the corner of Pentonville Road. Here, in November 1790, Thomas Paine is thought to have written the first part of his influential *Rights of Man*. Published in 1791, it is believed to have sold one and a half million copies in Paine's lifetime alone. The most famous coaching inn was the Peacock in Islington High Street. In Thomas Hughes's *Tom Brown's Schooldays* (1857) Tom and his father halt at the Peacock on their way to Rugby:

> . . . having heard with unfeigned joy the paternal order, at the bar, of steaks and oyster-sauce for supper in half an hour, and seen his father seated cozily by the bright fire in the coffee-room with the paper in his hand, Tom had run out to see about him, had wondered at all the vehicles passing and repassing, and had fraternized with the boots and ostler, from whom he ascertained that the Tally-ho was a tip-top goer – ten miles an hour including stoppages – and so punctual that all the roads set their clocks by her.

By Tom Brown's day Islington was expanding rapidly, covering the fields in which Ralegh, Pepys and Goldsmith had once savoured the country air. Parts of Islington became very run-down and squalid – ideal for the pen of Dickens, one would have thought, except that Islington hardly appears in his pages. The Peacock is mentioned in the short story 'Boots at the Cherry Tree Inn', but that is about it, even though the illustrator of *Oliver Twist*, George Cruikshank, lived at 22 Myddelton Terrace for several years. The best description of shabby nineteenth-century Islington is the few pages in Michael Sadleir's *Fanny by Gaslight* when Fanny tries to find Chunks, now the proprietor of the Jolly Bargee near the canal in River Row:

> Low houses, so lifeless and shuttered that they might have been abandoned, edged the street. One lamp, set in a project-ing bracket, shone feebly in the distance. Beyond it there seemed to be a faint glow, but why or whence there was no knowing. River Row had no pavements; uneven setts sloped slightly toward the centre, so as to make a central drain, in which rubbish, liquid and otherwise, lay stagnant. I hardly knew whether to keep under the lee of the black house-fronts or brave the horrid jetsam of the street's middle.

Much of Islington became similarly seedy. The New River, full of rubbish and a potential cholera hazard, had to be covered over, and the fine terraced houses were split up into multiple dwell-ings. Someone, however, who did occupy a terraced house and was inordinately proud of this fact, was George and Weedon Grossmith's Mr Pooter, who resides with his wife Carrie at 'The Laurels', Brickfield Terrace, Holloway Road. Published in 1892, Mr Pooter's *Diary of a Nobody* records the day-to-day events in the life of a City clerk plagued by a wayward son called Lupin, self-important tradesmen and all the problems of keeping up the right sort of appearance. 'Why should I not publish my diary? I have often seen reminiscences of people I have never even heard of, and I fail to see – because I do not happen to be a "Somebody" – why my diary should not be interesting.' Apart from Mr Pooter, however, Islington seems to have slid out of sight of literary London, whether it be writers living there or using it for their fiction. When Arnold Bennett decided to explore Barnsbury in 1925, his taxi was as much a curiosity to the residents as the area was to him.[14] Canonbury Square retained a certain social cachet, although even here housing was cheap. This asset explained why

Evelyn Waugh and his first wife, also called Evelyn, moved into 17a Canonbury Square in September 1928 after their marriage. That same year Waugh's first novel, *Decline and Fall*, was published. It was while he was working on his second novel, *Vile Bodies*, that his wife ran off with another man and Waugh left Islington.

One great admirer of Mr Pooter, and who himself lived in Islington between the wars, was John Betjeman. He lived with his parents in Highbury New Park. Nearby is Aberdeen Park, one of London's first housing estates, and in the middle rises St Saviour's, built in 1859 almost entirely in brick. One of Betjeman's finest poems, 'St Saviour's, Aberdeen Park, Highbury, London, N.', evokes interwar Islington:

> *Stop the trolley-bus, stop! And here, where the roads unite*
> *Of weariest worn-out London – no cigarettes, no beer,*
> *No repairs undertaken, nothing in stock – alight;*
> *For over the waste of willow-herb, look at her, sailing clear,*
> *A great Victorian church, tall, unbroken and bright*
> *In a sun that's setting in Willesden and saturating us here.*

The poem goes on to call St Saviour's 'Great red church of my parents' and ends 'Christ, at this Highbury altar, I offer myself To Thee'. After several years when the church was closed and in imminent danger of demolition, St Saviour's is now being restored.[15] Betjeman was also a devotee of the secondhand bookstalls which then lined Essex Road.

George Orwell moved to Islington in 1945 in order to escape what he regarded as the time-wasting obligations of literary London, particularly the draining pub life. He moved into the first-floor flat at 27 Canonbury Square with his wife Eileen and their adopted son Richard. Orwell's literary career was flourishing: *Animal Farm* was finally published in 1945 and as literary editor of the weekly newspaper *Tribune* he wrote some sparkling essays. His private life on the other hand was blighted by the tragic death of Eileen during a hospital operation. T. R. Fyvel often visited Orwell's flat and has recalled its utter cheerlessness, describing it as 'emphatically bleak'.[16] Orwell seems to have needed only his typewriter, strong rolled cigarettes, 'tea as dark and almost as thick as treacle' and a carpenter's bench on which he relaxed by doing a bit of joinery.[17] A nanny looked after Richard. Renewed tuberculosis was eating away at Orwell's health, and he often left London – which he disliked anyway – to live for long spells on an isolated farmhouse on Jura off the Scottish coast. There he kept hammering away at *1984* (or 'The Last Man in Europe' as it was first called) between periods in sanatoriums. In September 1949 he was taken into University College Hospital where he died in January 1950.

Nine years after Orwell's death Joe Orton and his lover Kenneth Halliwell moved into flat 4, 25 Noel Road. Out of work and with few prospects in front of them, Orton and Halliwell began to deface the library books which they had borrowed from the public library in Holloway Road. They typed false 'blurbs' inside the covers, especially Dorothy L. Sayers's Lord Peter Wimsey novels to which the pair had apparently taken particular exception, and then stood discreetly amongst the stacks trying to watch the reaction of unsuspecting browsers.[18] In 1962, Orton and Halliwell were caught and given sentences of six months' imprisonment. After their release and return to the small one-bedroom flat, Orton went on to make his name as a playwright with such works as *Loot* and *Entertaining Mr Sloane*. The increasingly jealous Halliwell found both Orton's sudden fame and his continued infidelities, often committed in Islington lavatories, too much to bear and on 9 August 1967 Halliwell killed Orton and then himself. One irony is that, as a journalist in *Time Out* observed, 'The same library which prosecuted them and pushed for their six-month prison sentence, now cherishes these jackets in the Orton archives'.[19]

Over the last fifteen years much of Islington has shot rapidly up the social scale. There has been a rediscovery of its fine squares – Barnsbury alone has Arundel, Barnsbury, Thornhill, Cloudesley, Gibson and Milner Squares – its excellent terraces and the landscaped New River. Camden Passage Market is fashionable and expensive, the Camden Head offers an authentic Victorian gin-palace atmosphere with appropriate fittings and décor, and the Royal Agricultural Hall (the 'Aggie') has been opened as a design and exhibition centre. The coaching inns along Islington High Street and Collins's music-hall which once overlooked the Green may have gone, but Canonbury Tower now houses the Tavistock Repertory Company and in Dagmar Passage there is the remarkable Little Angel Puppet Theatre, the only one of its kind in London. Today's Islington is crammed full of journalists, publishers and authors, and any *Literary London* written in a hundred years' time will probably have to devote two chapters to Islington.

Kensington

For centuries Kensington was a village several miles away from London, and the fields which lay between it and the capital were plagued by highwaymen. In June 1664, for example, Samuel Pepys had to escort Lady Paulina Mountagu back to Kensington – 'I was even afeard myself, though I appeared otherwise'. As late as the mid-nineteenth century, when the critic Leigh Hunt wrote a history of Kensington, it was still a semi-rural retreat. In *The Old Court Suburb* (1855) Hunt paints an idyllic picture of a journey from London to Kensington: 'The way to it is the pleasantest out of the town; you may walk in high-road, or on grass, as you please; the fresh air salutes you from a healthy soil; and there is not a step out of the way, from its commencement at Kensington Gore, to its termination beyond Holland House, in which you are not greeted with the face of some pleasant memory.'

It was not until the last decades of the nineteenth century that Kensington was swallowed up by London: by 1901 its population had risen to over 175,000, nearly twenty times as large as it had been a hundred years before. And yet, despite the rapid development of the district, parts of Old Kensington have survived as a reminder of 'the old court suburb', particularly Kensington Palace and Gardens, Holland House, Kensington Square and Kensington Church Walk.

Kensington's reputation for fine healthy air attracted William of Orange in 1689 when he bought what was then Nottingham

House for 18,000 guineas. William suffered from asthma and he refused to live at Whitehall where the Thames mists pervaded the Palace.[1] Sir Christopher Wren was employed to turn Nottingham House into Kensington Palace, which he certainly did to the satisfaction of the diarist John Evelyn, who visited in 1696, noting that 'The House is very noble, tho not greate', that there was a fine art gallery and 'a pretty private Library', and finally that 'the Gardens about it [are] very delicious'.[2] Four years later Evelyn was back again, this time accompanied by Wren himself in order to show William the plans for the new Greenwich Hospital. Both Mary and William died at Kensington Palace – as, too, did Queen Anne. Unlike her predecessors, Anne was interested in the arts, and Swift, Addison and Steele came here on several occasions, although Swift in particular complained about the Queen's limited conversation. During the winter of 1712–13, Swift lived at Kensington Gravel Pits, a spot to the north of the village and close to today's Notting Hill Gate, which was a fashionable resort for invalids.[3]

When William of Orange moved into Kensington Palace it was not the only mansion in the neighbourhood. Holland House was originally erected in 1607 for Sir Walter Cope. Parts of the seventeenth-century building have survived even though it was badly bombed in the Second World War. The two wings which remain are now occupied by a Youth Hostel, but at the back of the garden is an orangery and an eighteenth-century ice-house which suggest the splendours of aristocratic life in the past. Cope House, as it was first called, was far enough away from London to stage plays during the puritan Commonwealth when such activities were illegal. After the Copes the house was acquired by the Holland family, celebrated as staunch Whigs and patrons of the arts and literature. The then Lady Holland married the founder of the *Spectator*, Joseph Addison, in 1716. Addison was the first to popularise the still barely known poetry of John Milton. Addison wrote a long essay in 1711 on the 'London cries' which were bellowed freely in the streets:

> . . . they may be divided into vocal and instrumental; milk is generally sold in a note above E-la, and it sounds so exceedingly shrill that it often sets our teeth on edge. The chimney-sweep is confined to no certain pitch, he utters himself in the deepest bass and sometimes in the sharpest treble. . . . The

same observation might be made of the retailers of small coal, not to mention broken glasses or brick dust.

Addison died at Holland House in 1719. The road to the west of the house is named after him.

In the 1760s the Lord Holland in residence was one of the earliest admirers of Goldsmith's *The Vicar of Wakefield*, which had been largely ignored by the reviewers. His championing of the work to his friends ensured its success.[4] The poet Samuel Rogers was a frequent visitor to Holland House, being allowed his own seat in a garden alcove. In 1812 the 3rd Lord Holland wrote some lines about Rogers, and the inscription is still there:

> *Here Rogers sat, and here for ever dwell*
> *With me those pleasures that he sings so well.*

In the Victorian period Holland House was the focus for many salons, its garden-parties attracting Byron, Dickens and even Victoria and Albert. In this century the Holland line came to an end and the Ilchester family took up residence. Lady Ilchester is thought to have been the model for P. G. Wodehouse's Aunt Dahlia, the only aunt with whom Bertie Wooster gets on;[5] as Bertie remarks in *The Mating Season*: 'In this life it is not aunts that matter, but the courage that one brings to them.' In 1952 the damaged Holland House was bought by the London County Council. It now looks down to the Commonwealth Institute with its distinctive green-coloured copper roof and the perpetually busy Kensington High Street. Until the nineteenth century this was little more than a country lane.

On the south side of Kensington High Street is Kensington Square, tucked away behind several department stores. Laid out in the late seventeenth century, it has always been a fashionable address, as the number of plaques which adorn the houses testify. Especially attractive are numbers 11–12, built in the late seventeenth century. From 1837 to 1851 the busy John Stuart Mill lived at 18 Kensington Square, writing his *Political Economy*, working for several magazines and yet also still employed at the East India House in Leadenhall Street in the City. What is more, as he wrote to a friend, 'I am quite well and strong, and now walk the whole way to and from Kensington without the self-indulgence of omnibi' – a fair step.[6] In 1851 he married Harriet Taylor and moved out of the square. On the west side of Kensington Square lived the actress Mrs Patrick Campbell, with whom

George Bernard Shaw corresponded over a number of years. In 1912, Shaw met her for the first time when he read aloud his new play *Pygmalion*, selecting her for the role of Eliza Doolittle. Shaw fell in love with 'Mrs Pat';

> I could think of nothing but a thousand scenes of which she was the heroine and I the hero. And I am on the verge of 56. There never has been anything so ridiculous, or so delightful, in the history of the world. On Friday we were together for an hour; we visited a lord; we drove in a taxi; we sat on a sofa in Kensington Square; and my years fell from me like a garment. I was in love for nearly 35 hours; and for that be all her sins forgiven her![7]

The road leading into Kensington Square from the north-east is Young Street. William Makepeace Thackeray lived at number 16 from 1846 to 1853, a period during which he was just starting to make his name. In these seven years he wrote his first novel, *Vanity Fair*, as well as *Pendennis* and *The History of Henry Esmond*. In later years Thackeray once passed 16 Young Street with a friend to whom he remarked: 'Down on your knees you rogue, for here *Vanity Fair* was penned, and I will go down with you, for I have a high opinion of that little production myself.'[8] It was also at Young Street that Thackeray hosted a reception for Charlotte Brontë after the success of *Jane Eyre*. Thackeray found the formidable Miss Brontë rather too much and he fled to the security of his club.[9] From Young Street Thackeray moved to 36 Onslow Square, another attractive part of Kensington, where he was living when he contested the parliamentary election in Oxford, losing by just sixty-seven votes. In 1862, Thackeray moved to 2 Kensington Palace Gardens and a house which he designed himself: 'My dear relations are furious at my arrogance, extravagance and presumption in building a handsome new house. . . .' He died here in December 1863, aged only fifty-two, and was buried in Kensal Green Cemetery. Most of the residences in Kensington Palace Gardens now house embassies.

Almost opposite Kensington High Street Underground station can be found a path called Kensington Church Walk which meanders through what was once a burial-ground. Further on is a small parade of shops with some houses and flats off to the left. It is a charming enclave, relatively remote from the traffic. The American poet Ezra Pound lived at number 10 from 1908 to

1911. The church of the Church Walk is clearly visible from all over Kensington because of its spire of 278 feet, the tallest in London. To begin with, St Mary Abbots was a small building catering for a village congregation, but as Kensington grew so, too, did the church have to be rebuilt. Thackeray often worshipped in the late-seventeenth-century building, as did the historian Macaulay when he lived at Holly Lodge, Campden Hill, from 1856 until his death in 1859. His four-volume *History of England* had been completed in 1855 but its success brought him a peerage whilst he was living in Kensington. W. S. Gilbert was married at St Mary Abbots in August 1867. The present building by Sir Gilbert Scott dates from 1872 but retains the fine old seventeenth-century pulpit. Thomas Hardy remarked on the opulence of the congregation in 1888: 'When the congregation rises there is a rustling of silks like that of the Devil's wings in *Paradise Lost*.'[10] G. K. Chesterton was married at St Mary Abbots in 1901, as was Ezra Pound in 1914.

As well as novelists and historians, Kensington also attracted artists in the nineteenth century, many of whom had houses built for them in Melbury Road. Open to the public is Leighton House, designed in the 1860s by Frederic Leighton, later to be President of the Royal Academy and the first artist to be raised to the peerage. Leighton was an immensely cultured man with friends in every sphere of the arts, and his paintings often dealt with literary themes. He had a taste for oriental art, and his Leighton House contains a splendid Arab Hall complete with a little fountain. Upstairs is his huge studio, whilst statues are dotted around the garden. He was not keen, however, for his friends and visitors to stay; Leighton House has only one bedroom!

Although Kensington was devoured by the expanding metropolis in the later nineteenth century, it established itself as a fashionable area for the wealthy to live – a process reinforced by the continuing royal connections of Kensington Palace. The future Queen Victoria was born here in 1819 and brought up at the Palace. It was also where she first met Prince Albert. These fond memories ensured that despite her move to Buckingham Palace she steadfastly resisted the periodic attempts during the nineteenth century to pull down Kensington Palace. This association explains, too, why in 1901 it was named the 'Royal Borough of Kensington'. Many of the elegant terraces and squares built in the nineteenth century for Kensington's prosperous newcomers have remained: Edwardes Square, Pembroke Square, Hyde Park Gate, Queen's Gate, Ennismore Gardens, Prince's Gardens. The dwellings in Prince's Gardens were aptly described by Leigh Hunt as resembling 'a set of tall thin gentlemen, squeezing together to look at something over the way'.[11]

But more people meant more churches, and away to the north of Kensington was built St George's, Campden Hill, in 1864. The cover of early editions of *Peter Pan* shows Peter and Wendy flying around its spire (demolished in 1950). Why? Because J. M. Barrie lived in Campden Hill Square in the early years of this century, as did the Llewelyn Davies children who inspired *Peter Pan*, first performed in 1904. Two years later Barrie wrote the short story *Peter Pan in Kensington Gardens* and he also commissioned the statue which stands there. The rabbits' ears on the statue are being slowly worn away by the thousands of children (and adults) who stroke them. There does seem to be something about Kensington and children. Kenneth Grahame lived at 16 Phillimore Place between 1900 and 1906, years in which he was employed at the Bank of England. The stories which he told to his son Alastair at bedtime and on walks in Kensington Gardens became *The Wind in the Willows*, published in 1908. Initially the book received only a lukewarm reception; *The Times* considered that 'Grown-up readers will find it monstrous and elusive, children will hope, in vain, for more fun'.[12] Fortunately the general public proved to be better judges than the critics.

A few years after Barrie moved to Lancaster Gate and then to the Adelphi, Siegfried Sassoon moved into 23 Campden Hill Square. He had made his name as a soldier in the trenches – his bravery earning him the nickname 'Mad Jack' as well as the Military Cross which he later threw into the Mersey – and as a war poet whose conversational style of writing had contrasted the carnage of the front line with the stupidity of the men in command and the illusions surrounding the war at home. At Campden Hill Square he embarked on another genre of writing, that of the semi-fictional autobiography, beginning with *Memoirs of a Foxhunting Man* and then *Memoirs of an Infantry Officer*. In 1933, Sassoon moved down to Heytesbury House in Wiltshire, where he lived for the rest of his life. However, his connection with Kensington was not finished. In 1956 a volume of his poems called *Sequences* was published. Mother Margaret Mary, Superior of the Convent of the Assumption at 23 Kensington Square, wrote to him and eventually Sassoon was received into the Catholic Church in 1957.[13] Both the convent and the pleasant sloping Campden Hill Square remain.

Next to St George's was the Water Tower, which figures in G. K. Chesterton's novel *The Napoleon of Notting Hill*, published in 1904. Chesterton had been born nearby, at 32 Sheffield Terrace, and he was baptised at St George's. Later he lived at 11 Warwick Gardens. *Napoleon* is a fantasy about districts of London setting themselves up as autonomous republics and the resulting chaos and warfare which result. Chesterton was an extremely versatile writer, turning his pen to anything if he could be inveigled away from pubs and friends. He became rather corpulent. During the First World War an irate lady asked him why he was not out at the front. 'Madam,' was the reply, 'if you look at me sideways you will see that I am!'[14]

In 1851 the Great Exhibition, or 'Crystal Palace' as it was called by *Punch*, was held in Hyde Park close to Kensington Gardens. From May to October over 6 million visitors came here, an enormous figure which comprised some 17 per cent of the total population. It marked the heyday of Britain as the 'Workshop of the World', but it signified, too, the beginning of the end for Kensington as a village. The Great Exhibition made a profit of £186,000, and it was decided to use this money to create a network of cultural and educational institutions here in South Kensington in what were then fields. One such institution was the South Kensington Museum, now the Victoria and Albert, much frequented by Oscar Wilde – several pages in his *The Picture of Dorian Gray* read like an extract from the museum catalogue – and by William Morris: 'Perhaps I have used it as much as any man living.'[15] The irony here is that when Morris had visited the Great Exhibition he fled in disgust at what he saw as its blatant commercialism. The 'Crystal Palace' itself was dismantled once the exhibition was over and re-erected in South London.

Other institutions here in Kensington include the Oratory on Brompton Road, completed in 1884. Its interior, designed in the style of the Italian Renaissance, is among the sights of London. Outside is a statue of one of the Oratory's founders, Cardinal Newman, who had become a Catholic convert in 1845. Famous for his *Tracts for the Times*, Newman was also the author of two novels and the poem *The Dream of Gerontius*. Unfortunately the unceasing traffic passing up and down Brompton Road results in

his statue being always covered in grime. Roughly on the site of
Gore House, a mansion which was once the venue for Lady
Blessington's Whig salons attended by Charles Dickens and
others, is the Albert Hall – once described by P. G. Wodehouse as
'round in the middle and not much above'.[16] Opposite is the
Albert Memorial which shows not just Prince Albert holding the
catalogue of the 1851 exhibition but also a mass of statuary
ranging from the reliefs on the pedestal depicting famous men of
letters, musicians and painters, to allegorical figures representing
Agriculture, Manufacture, Commerce and Engineering. Unfortunately the Memorial was built in a slapdash manner and
today is near to collapse.

On the south side of the Albert Hall are various educational
establishments, one of which was named the Normal School of
Science at the end of the nineteenth century but is now called the
Imperial College of Science and Technology. The young H. G.
Wells came here in 1884, feeling shy and overawed: 'When I first
took my fragile, unkempt self and my small black bag through its
portals, I had a feeling of having come at last under definite
guidance and protection.' The feeling was not to last: he later
wrote of his years in South Kensington as wasted. His novel *Love
and Mr Lewisham* (1900) is partly autobiographical – like Wells,
the socialist Mr Lewisham wears a red tie to the Normal School.[17]
The book is also a fine study of a marriage between two poor
young people and the stress this lack of money causes, as Wells
experienced himself: 'The stress of perpetual worry was upon
them, of dwindling funds and the anxious search for work that
would not come.'

Of the other writers resident in Kensington at the end of the
nineteenth century, Robert Browning lived at 29 De Vere
Gardens for the last two years of his time in England, leaving for
Venice in 1889 where he died. His near neighbour had been
Henry James, who lived at 34 De Vere Gardens from 1886,
believing that 'I shall do far better work than I have ever done
before'. His fourth-floor apartment, which is still there and
marked by a plaque, was 'excellent in every respect, improves on
acquaintance every hour and is, in particular, flooded with light
like a photographer's studio. I commune with the unobserved
sky and have an immense bird's eye view of house tops and
streets.' In 1902, James moved out of London to Rye.

Opposite Kensington Gardens is Hyde Park Gate, where in

1882 the legal writer Sir Leslie Stephen, the first editor of the *Dictionary of National Biography*, was living at number 22. That year saw the birth of his daughter Virginia, later to be Virginia Woolf. Sir Winston Churchill, certainly this century's most widely read historian, died at number 28 in 1965. His neighbour at number 30 for many years was Enid Bagnold, author of *National Velvet*. Several other, rather contrasting, literary figures lived in Kensington between the wars. James Joyce resided at 28b Campden Grove with his wife Nora in the summer of 1931. The Joyces had planned to stay indefinitely, but they soon got fed up with Kensington and left – Joyce wrote that their street was full of mummies and should be renamed 'Campden Grave'.[18] E. F. Benson lived at 25 Brompton Square between 1920 and 1940, turning out a flood of books of which the Lucia series has recently been rediscovered, whilst Ivy Compton-Burnett lived at 5 Braemar Mansions in Cornwall Gardens from 1934 to 1969.

None of the last three writers dealt much with Kensington or their experiences here, but one world-famous author who did was T. S. Eliot. *Four Quartets* was originally called 'The Kensington Quartets'. After the break-up of his first marriage in the early 1930s, Eliot lived for a time in a boarding-house at 33 Courtfield Road, South Kensington. His neighbour Miss Bevan had a tabby cat called Bubbles which proved to be the inspiration for *Old Possum's Book of Practical Cats*, first published in 1939.[19] Two of the cats, the naughty Mungojerrie and Rumpelteazer, live in Victoria Grove, which is just off Gloucester Road. Eliot was attracted to the Anglo-Catholic St Stephen's in Gloucester Road, moving into the church's clergy house in 1934 and living there for six years. Eliot was a churchwarden at St Stephen's from 1934 until 1959, even though he lived in Chelsea after the Second World War. In January 1957, Eliot remarried at St Barnabas, Addison Road, and moved to 3 Kensington Gardens, where he died in 1965. There is a commemorative tablet inside St Stephen's.

Sometimes the seemingly endless Kensington terraces, always neat, elegant and overlooking pleasant gardens, can appear a bit pompous and smug. The best antidote to this mood is a stroll in what is certainly Kensington's most priceless asset, namely its Gardens complete with Palace, Orangery, Dutch Garden, Round Pond and 'Elfin Tree' by the children's playground. Matthew Arnold came here in the 1850s and in his 'Lines Written in Kensington Gardens' he welcomes the respite which this royal park offers from the hustle and bustle of London life, sentiments no less true today than in Arnold's time:

> *Calm soul of all things! make it mine*
> *To feel, amid the city's jar,*
> *That there abides a peace of thine,*
> *Man did not make, and cannot mar.*

Lambeth

Today Lambeth is dominated by the South Bank complex of Festival Hall, National Theatre, National Film Theatre and Hayward Gallery. Despite the concrete severity of these buildings it is appropriate that such a cluster of places of entertainment should be here on this side of the river, because for centuries Lambeth was full of pleasure gardens and resorts. In fact Lambeth's most prominent position in popular memory results from its links with entertainment, namely the song 'The Lambeth Walk' from the 1930s musical *Me and My Girl* which has recently been revived. Sadly, Lambeth is now but a shadow of its former self. Nondescript roads, uninteresting modern buildings – at first sight there appears to be little here to interest any London enthusiast, let alone someone trying to ferret out literary associations.

And yet if one devotes a little time to exploration, then, like almost everywhere in the capital, attractive nooks and crannies reveal themselves. The first place to aim for is the church of St Mary-at-Lambeth which stands beside Lambeth Palace and near to Lambeth Bridge. Just another church? Not quite – the building now houses the Museum of Garden History, run by the Tradescant Trust and its devoted band of voluntary helpers.

The seventeenth-century poet Andrew Marvell wrote a poem called 'The Garden' which contains the lines:

> *What a wondrous life is this I lead!*
> *Ripe apples drop about my head;*
> *The luscious clusters of the vine*
> *Upon my mouth do crush their wine;*
> *The nectarine and curious peach*
> *Into my hands themselves do reach;*
> *Stumbling on melons, as I pass,*
> *Ensnared with flowers, I fall on grass.*

Marvell's account of the exotic new fruits which were being introduced into this country in the seventeenth century is a tribute to the travels of the two John Tradescants, father and son, both of whom were royal gardeners to Charles I. Apart from laying out the grounds of Hatfield House, the Tradescants owned a sixty-acre garden here in Lambeth which they stocked with the results of their ceaseless foreign travel in search of new fruits and vegetables – a series of intrepid journeys which took them to America, Africa and Russia. Calling their garden 'The Ark', they opened it to the public in the middle of the seventeenth century – it was arguably this country's first-ever museum – and in 1656 issued *Musaeum Tradescantianum*, the first printed catalogue.[1] The writer and businessman Izaak Walton visited the Ark:

> You may there see the Hog-fish, the Dog-fish, the Dolphin, the Cony-fish, the Parrot-fish, the Shark, the Poyson-fish, sword-fish, and not only other incredible fish! but you may see there the Salamander, several sorts of Barnacles, of Solan Geese, the bird of Paradise, such sorts of Snakes, and such birds-nests, and of so various forms, and so wonderfully made, as may beget wonder and amusement in any beholder: and so many hundred of other rarities in that collection, as will make the other wonders I spake of, the less incredible; for, you may note, that the waters are natures store-house, in which she locks up her wonders.[2]

And Walton does not even mention the range of flowers and fruits on display! The first edition of the catalogue now owned by the Tradescant Trust was once John Evelyn's copy. After the death of John Tradescant the younger the collection of curiosities was acquired by Elias Ashmole, who in turn opened the Ashmolean in Oxford in 1683.

The Tradescants were buried at St Mary-at-Lambeth beneath a fine sculptured tomb in the garden to the rear of the church, close by the tomb of Captain Bligh of *Mutiny on the Bounty* fame. Five Archbishops of Canterbury were also buried here, but such exalted connections did not prevent the church from becoming very run down and tatty before it was deconsecrated and closed completely in 1972. Fortunately John and Rosemary Nicholson set up the Tradescant Trust in 1977 which has now saved the church from demolition and also laid out the church garden in seventeenth-century style. The tower is fourteenth century, the rest of the church a Victorian reconstruction of 1851.

When the Tradescants were designing their garden the only building in the immediate vicinity was Lambeth Palace. The explanation for this tardy development of Lambeth lay in the damp and marshy nature of the land – the name Lambeth is derived from 'mud-haven' – and until the building of the Embankment in the 1860s it was frequently flooded by the Thames. For centuries, therefore, Lambeth was a little-inhabited district notorious as a place for the furtive burial of mysterious corpses.[3] The Archbishops of Canterbury initially moved here in order to escape the prying eyes of the monks down at Canterbury who were always eager to criticise their superior. The Palace was built in the thirteenth century, and although Lambeth was not a salubrious site it did mean that the successive archbishops had easy access to the kings based at Westminster Palace over the Thames, crossing via the horse-ferry which they owned and which until the opening of Westminster Bridge in 1750 was the easiest method of transport between Lambeth and Westminster.

One martyr associated with Lambeth Palace was Thomas More, who once worked in the household of Cardinal Morton. This cleric built the red brick gateway in 1495 by which the visitor approaches the Palace and which is still known as 'Morton's Tower'. In 1534, More was back at the Palace and being examined in the guard room on his refusal to take the Oath of Supremacy, the first step in the process which led to his death on Tower Hill the following year. Inside the Palace is a unique library of ecclesiastical works, numbering over 150,000 books and 3000 manuscripts, amongst them the 'Lambeth Bible' of about 1150, a first edition of Francis Bacon's *Essays* of 1597 and, ironically, a first edition of More's *Utopia*, published in 1516. The Library was opened to the public in 1610 and is sometimes claimed to have been this country's first public library.[4] In the late nineteenth century the historian J. R. Green, author of *A History of the English*

People, became the Librarian after a spell working as a vicar in the East End: '. . . the quiet of Lambeth Library is like still waters after the noise of the East.'[5]

Of Lambeth's pleasure gardens there were Cuper's Garden and the Paris Gardens, but the most famous were the Vauxhall Gardens, second only to Ranelagh in Chelsea for their fashionableness and popularity. Samuel Pepys was an early visitor, noting in his diary for May 1667 that he went 'by water to Foxhall . . . and it is very pleasant and cheap going thither, for a man may go to spend what he will, or nothing, all is one. But to hear the nightingale and other birds, and hear fiddles, and there a harp and here a Jew's trump, and here laughing and there fine people walking, is mighty diverting.' During the eighteenth century the gardens were expanded under the proprietorship of Jonathan Tyers, who ran them from 1728 until 1764.[6] For an admission fee of a shilling one could walk in shady groves hung with thousands of lamps and adorned by statues; or watch the frequent firework displays; or listen to the music in the concert-hall.

All the literary figures of the day sampled the delights of Vauxhall. For instance, Oliver Goldsmith in his *Citizen of the World* describes how the supposed Chinese author of these sketches found 'every sense overpaid with more than expected pleasure'; 'the lights everywhere glimmering through the scarcely moving trees; the full-bodied concert bursting on the stillness of the night, the natural concert of the birds in the more retired part of the grove vying with that which was formed by art; the company gaily dressed, looking satisfaction, and the tables spread with various delicacies . . .'. Tobias Smollett in his novel *Humphry Clinker* (1771) records the differing reactions of a niece and her uncle, the niece dwelling on the 'gayest company', the uncle on the noise. Samuel Johnson was often a visitor, as was James Boswell, and also the diarist, letter-writer and gossip Horace Walpole, even if the last did find himself stuck in a traffic jam because of the numerous carriages cluttering up the road. Fanny Burney in her novel *Evelina* (1778) refers to the Vauxhall Gardens as being 'the first pleasure in life', although she mentions, too, the 'dark walks' which sometimes prompted activities that led to the temporary closure of the gardens.

In the nineteenth century Vauxhall Gardens still retained some of its former fashionableness. In *Vanity Fair* Thackeray sends a party of young people to the gardens. Becky Sharp and Joseph Sedley head off for one of the supposedly quiet walks – 'in which there were not above five score more of couples similarly straying' – and where the shy Mr Sedley is desperately trying to pluck up the courage to propose to Becky. The moment has come, 'for he puffed and panted a great deal, and Rebecca's hand, which was placed near his heart, could count the feverish pulsations' when suddenly 'oh, provoking! the bell rang for the fireworks, and, a great scuffling and running taking place, these interesting lovers were obliged to follow in the stream of people'. Joined by George Osborne and Amelia in their private box, Joseph Sedley proceeds to get drunk on the notorious rack punch dispensed at Vauxhall. Not only has the opportunity to propose to Becky gone, but he has to pay the penalty of his over-indulgence the next morning – an experience which clearly Thackeray had also undergone:

> Oh, ignorant young creatures! How little do you know the effect of rack punch! What is the rack in the punch, at night, to the rack in the head of a morning? To this truth I can vouch as a man; there is no headache in the world like that caused by Vauxhall punch. Through the lapse of twenty years, I can remember the consequence of two glasses! – two wine glasses! – but two, upon the honour of a gentleman; and Joseph Sedley, who had a liver complaint, had swallowed at least a quart of the abominable mixture.

Only a few years after Mr Sedley's unfortunate escapade at the Vauxhall Gardens they had closed down for good in 1859. The gardens were quickly buried under a wave of bricks and mortar. Nothing remains today, though the eighteenth-century proprietor Jonathan Tyers is remembered in the names of Jonathan Street and Tyers Street, and the pretty Vauxhall Park does its best to recall bygone glories.

Much of Lambeth was occupied by St George's Fields, a huge open space which often hosted important meetings and celebrations. Here it was that the Lord Mayor and the Aldermen of the City of London gave a banquet in 1660 to the returning Charles II, and in 1780 Lord George Gordon rallied his followers to protest against a measure of relief for Roman Catholics – a demonstration which later developed into the Gordon Riots described so vividly by Charles Dickens in *Barnaby Rudge*. Ironically it is thought that the altar of St George's Roman Catholic Cathedral may well stand roughly on the spot from which Gordon spoke to the 60,000 ardently Protestant crowd. By Gordon's time the construction of Westminster and Blackfriars Bridges had led to the start of building on the fields of Lambeth – a process which accelerated in the early nineteenth century. A plaintive little poem of 1812 by two poetical brothers and residents of Lambeth called Smith lamented:

> *Saint George's Fields are fields no more,*
> *The trowel supersedes the plough;*
> *Huge inundated swamps of yore*
> *Are changed to civic villas now.*[7]

The Smiths were exaggerating with their remark about 'villas'; in fact most of the housing erected in Lambeth was distinctly cheap and shoddy. Nevertheless Lambeth, though deprived of its pleasure garden, still retained a reputation as a quarter for entertainment because of its circus and music-hall. In the early 1770s Philip Astley opened Astley's Amphitheatre, the first proper circus in this country, on the Westminster Bridge Road. As an ex-dragoon Astley had originally intended to run a riding-school, but he soon found that the occasional entertainments which he presented in the afternoons were far more profitable. He built a series of 'amphitheatres' here which were often burnt down but were always replaced. Inside the always splendid exterior Astley and his successors offered an extraordinarily mixed bill of fare which ranged from 'equestrianised' Shakespeare to medieval plays, often an adaption of Sir Walter Scott's novels, to military melodrama. Most popular of all proved to be the highwaymen plays which usually featured Dick Turpin and his famous ride to York on Black Bess, a story culled from Harrison Ainsworth's immensely popular novel *Rookwood* (1834).[8]

Horace Walpole was an early visitor to Astley's, his trip in 1783 providing delights 'much beyond my expectation'. Queen Victoria came with Prince Albert in 1846, but the most assiduous attender of them all was Charles Dickens, with the inevitable result that Astley's often appears in his writings – for instance, in *Sketches by Boz* and in *Bleak House*. In *The Old Curiosity Shop* the excitement of a trip to Astley's is conveyed through the eyes of Kit, Barbara and little Jacob who marvel at the crowds, 'the vague smell of horses, suggestive of coming wonders', the orchestra and the glow of the lights. And then

> . . . the play itself! . . . the firing which made Barbara wink –
> the forlorn lady, who made her cry – the tyrant, who made her
> tremble – the man who sang the song with the lady's maid and
> danced the chorus, who made her laugh – the pony who
> reared up on his hind-legs when he saw the murderer, and
> wouldn't hear of walking on all fours again until he was taken
> into custody – the clown who ventured on such familiarities
> with the military man in boots – the lady who jumped over
> the nine-and-twenty ribbons and came down safe upon the
> horse's back, – everything was delightful, splendid, and sur-
> prising! Little Jacob applauded till his hands were sore; Kit
> cried 'an-kor' at the end of everything, the three-act piece
> included; and Barbara's mother beat her umbrella on the floor,
> in her ecstasies, until it was nearly worn down to the gingham.

By the second half of the nineteenth century Astley's
popularity began to wane, and in any case the building was
something of a fire trap, with few fire exits. For its last twenty
years it was run by 'Lord' George Sanger, who was later to write
an autobiography called *Seventy Years a Showman*, one edition of
which has a sparkling introduction by Kenneth Grahame, author
of *The Wind in the Willows*. Not even Sanger's efforts could save
Astley's from closure in March 1893, and now everything,
including the plaque on 225 Westminster Bridge Road which
once marked its site, has gone.

Apart from Astley's, Lambeth was also the home of the first
proper music-hall in London, which was opened by Charles
Morton in May 1852, just off the Westminster Bridge Road.
Before Morton, music-halls had been attached to the backs of
pubs as the afterthoughts which in fact they were. Morton put
the emphasis on the hall rather than on the pub, and his Canterbury Hall held over 2000 spectators, offering an aquarium and an
art gallery, too.[9] By the turn of the nineteenth century it was to
become a cinema. During the Blitz it was bombed out of existence
and, again like Astley's, nothing remains. Its site is now used as a
carpark for St Thomas's Hospital.

Happily the third of Victorian Lambeth's places of entertainment is still in existence, namely the Old Vic theatre. When it
was built in 1818 as the Royal Coburg Theatre the semi-rural

character – which as late as 1800 had been enjoyed by William Blake and his wife when they lived at 13 Hercules Buildings – had vanished, which meant that the Coburg's audience was often rough and eager to make its feelings very plain. In 1820 the critic William Hazlitt snobbishly wrote of its clientele as comprising 'Jew-boys, pickpockets, prostitutes and mountebanks',[10] while at the end of one performance Edmund Kean rebuked the spectators with the statement that 'in my life I have never acted to such a set of ignorant, unmitigated brutes as I now see before me'.[11] Dickens with his wider range of sympathy painted a more complimentary picture in a sketch by 'Boz', but Charles Kingsley described in his novel *Alton Locke* how 'Half the evil, low-browed, lowering faces in London are wedged in, twelve-hundred deep, perspiring, watchful, silent'. The theatre's management specialised in presenting gory melodramas, and its Shakespearian adaptations had to have a happy ending: in its *Hamlet* King Hamlet ends up marrying Queen Ophelia![12]

In 1880, Emma Cons and later her formidable niece Lilian Baylis began to transform the Old Vic, as it was by now called, and make it notable less for the behaviour of the audience than for the quality of the acting in its Shakespearian productions. One rather unlikely spectator was Lenin, who came here in May 1905 to see *Hamlet*.[13] Lilian Baylis discouraged frivolity – on one occasion she clambered up the 'flies' in evening dress in order to eject a drunken fireman.[14] When Bertie Wooster is bang in the middle of another crisis at Totleigh Towers in *Stiff Upper Lip, Jeeves* he remarks that 'The atmosphere was sombre. The whole binge might have been a scene from one of those Russian plays my Aunt Agatha sometimes makes me take her son Thos to at the Old Vic in order to improve his mind, which, as is widely known, can do with all the improvement that's coming to it'. On another occasion Bertie takes Thos to see Chekhov's *The Seagull* at the Old Vic, 'and what with the strain of trying to follow the cockeyed goings-on of characters called Zarietchnaya and Medvienko and having to be constantly on the alert to prevent Thos making a sneak for the great open spaces, my sufferings had been intense'.[15] Even if it is not Bertie Wooster's favourite place, everyone else must be glad that the Old Vic is still with us.

The squalor and poverty of much of Victorian Lambeth are powerfully depicted by the journalist John Hollingshead in his book *Ragged London in 1861*. Hollingshead was later to run the

Gaiety Theatre in the Strand for eighteen years and he is often claimed to have been responsible for introducing matinée performances. Conditions in Lambeth were so bad that, during the cholera epidemic of 1849, 544 people died in two streets alone. Prostitution was widespread. Michael Sadleir in his novel *Fanny by Gaslight* refers to the terrible scenes along and just off the Waterloo Road in the second half of the nineteenth century: '. . . side streets in which girls, even in broad daylight, sat at open doors in nothing but a chemise, called to men, and often, before going indoors, danced with them to the music of barrel-organs.'

One writer who knew the area well, and who wrote his first novel about it, was Somerset Maugham. After the death of his father Maugham enrolled as a student at St Thomas's teaching hospital, which had moved from Southwark to the Embankment in 1872. During his course he spent three weeks in 1895 as an obstetric clerk: 'I had to attend a certain number of confinements to get a certificate and this meant going into the slums of Lambeth, often into foul courts that the police hesitated to enter, but in which my black bag amply protected me: I found the work absorbing.'[16] Maugham used the experience to good effect in his first novel, *Liza of Lambeth*, published in 1897 when he was twenty-three years old. The reviewer in *The Times* considered that 'It is difficult to imagine how any writer with pretensions to refinement can have grovelled to acquire the necessary knowledge [of such conditions], or, having acquired it, should have forgotten self-respect so far as to embody it in fiction. . . . He consistently aims at shocking sensibilities or scandalizing average delicacy' – a review which reveals more about the limited experience of many Victorian critics than the novel itself, which is in fact a fine study of a doomed love-affair between Liza and a married man.[17]

It is an intriguing thought that when Maugham was working in the Lambeth slums he might have come across a six-year-old boy called Charles Chaplin, who was brought up in Lambeth in the 1880s and 1890s, spending some time in the Lambeth workhouse. The first hundred pages of Chaplin's *My Autobiography* are a wonderful picture of South London at the end of the nineteenth century; the rest of the book deals with Chaplin in Hollywood and is much less interesting.

Literary accounts of Lambeth in the first decades of this century suggest that little had changed; dreary Gordon Comstock in

George Orwell's *Keep the Aspidistra Flying* (1936) lives in an attic near Lambeth Cut in 'a room shaped like a wedge of cheese', and where 'in the cracks in the pink wallpaper dwelt multitudes of bugs'. Orwell must have based this description on personal experience; in *Down and Out in Paris and London*, published three years earlier, Orwell stayed at a cheap lodging-house in the Waterloo Road. For a shilling he shared a cramped room with several others: 'The walls were leprous, and the sheets, three weeks from the wash, were almost raw umber colour . . . every basin was streaked with grime – solid, sticky filth as black as bootblacking. I went out unwashed.'

But it would be wrong to complete this account of twentieth-century Lambeth on such a note. George Orwell and Gordon Comstock could have visited two pleasant green oases which had opened in the neighbourhood early this century. The first was Archbishop's Park at the back of Lambeth Palace, which had been thrown open to the public in 1901. The second was a gift from Lord Rothermere, the newspaper proprietor, in honour of his mother Geraldine Mary Harmsworth, after whom the park is named. The grounds had once belonged to the Bethlehem or Bedlam Hospital, whose buildings now contain the Imperial War Museum.

Nowadays Lambeth seems a rather sad, empty place. Vauxhall, for example, means nothing to most people except as a stop on the Victoria Line. But at least one part of Lambeth is once again synonymous with entertainment. After a period of decline in the nineteenth century the South Bank is once again throbbing with activity, and thousands cross the river every day to experience what is on offer there.

Marylebone

Marylebone derives its name from the old church of St Mary which once stood beside the River Tyburn. St Mary's-on-the-Burn gradually evolved into 'Marylebone'. The Tyburn now flows underground, but its course is marked roughly by the twisting path of Marylebone High Street and Marylebone Lane.

The church of St Mary is still with us, though the present building dates only from the early nineteenth century and sits not on the bank of a river but at the edge of Marylebone Road. Until the last decades of the eighteenth century the church was some distance from London, surrounded by fields and with one of Henry VIII's hunting parks, now Regent's Park, to the north. Because of its isolation St Mary's was much favoured by couples marrying in a hurry or in secret, away from the supervision of parents or guardians. In Hogarth's 'The Rake's Progress', for example, Tom Rakewell marries the elderly spinster here. Forty years later it was the turn of the playwright Richard Brinsley Sheridan to walk down the aisle of St Mary's. In 1772 he had fallen in love with the beautiful Miss Linley, but he was not alone and had to fight a duel with a Captain Mathews who was also a suitor. Their combat started at the Ring in Hyde Park, but crowds of onlookers interrupted the fight, forcing Sheridan and Mathews to try again at Hyde Park Corner. The same thing happened once more, and they eventually finished up at the Castle tavern in Henrietta Street, Covent Garden. Both men were badly injured.[1]

From this time onwards pistols replaced swords as duelling weapons. Five years later the same church witnessed the baptism of the infant Byron, born nearby at 24 Holles Street, and in 1803 the baptism of the son of Horatio Nelson and Emma Hamilton.

By the early nineteenth century St Mary's was proving too small for the district's expanding population – the parish's 577 houses of 1739 had become 6200 houses by 1795 – and it was rebuilt between 1813 and 1817, complete with the fine portico we see today.[2] Yet the old tradition of speedy marriages lived on in the new church. Between 1838 and 1846 the Barrett family lived at 50 Wimpole Street, a household dominated by the irascible father. One of the daughters, Elizabeth, corresponded with, met and then fell in love with a young poet and playwright, Robert Browning. They eloped together, Elizabeth taking with her a maid and a dog, and were married at St Mary's in September 1846 before leaving for Italy. The Brownings' dog Flush was the subject of a biography published by Virginia Woolf in 1933; Woolf modelled Flush's character on that of her own cocker spaniel, Pinka, which had been a present from Vita Sackville-West. Until 1861, when Elizabeth died, the Brownings lived mainly in Florence. After his wife's death Robert returned to London, and took up residence in what was then still rural Paddington. He lived at 19 Warwick Crescent, near 'Little Venice', where the island is commonly known as 'Browning's Island'. Browning is thought to have returned often to Marylebone church and to have kissed the altar steps at which he and Elizabeth had been married. Today the church has a Browning Memorial Chapel dedicated to the couple which contains memorabilia and mementoes. At the rear of the church is a small garden that was once the churchyard of the previous church and where there is an obelisk to Charles Wesley, younger brother of John and composer of many hymns. Also buried here is Edmund Hoyle, the eighteenth-century author of several books on card games. Before Hoyle's works, earlier books had often provided advice on cheating, but Hoyle's *Short Treatise* of 1742, originally written for his pupils, set whist on a fair footing based on skill rather than on pot luck. He then produced books which drew up the rules for other card games.[3]

Old maps of Marylebone, such as that published by John Rocque in 1746, show that apart from the church the only other prominent landmark here in the eighteenth century was the

Marylebone Gardens, one of several pleasure gardens then on the outskirts of London.[4] Samuel Pepys came here in May 1668 with the actress Elizabeth Knipp: 'Then we abroad to Marrowbone, and there walked in the garden; the first time I ever there, and a pretty place it is; and here we eat and drank and stayed until 9 at night; and so home by moonshine', Pepys attempting certain familiarities with Mrs Knipp but for once being repulsed. In about 1737 the Gardens were redesigned and extended, and for nearly forty more years they attracted an influential clientele, even though the journey home at night was often hazardous because of the highwaymen infesting Marylebone Fields. It was little consolation that English highwaymen were remarkably gentle when compared with their European counterparts. Sir John Fielding, half-brother of novelist Henry, wrote that

> Robberies on the highway in the neighbourhood of London are not very uncommon; these are usually committed early in the morning, or in the dusk of the evening, and as the times are known, the danger may be for the most part avoided. But the highwaymen here are civil, as compared with other countries; do not often use you with ill-manners; have been frequently known to return papers and curiosities with much politeness; and never commit murder, unless they are hotly pursued and find it difficult to escape.[5]

By 1776 the Gardens were threatened by the tide of building sweeping towards them, and that year a spell of bad weather and a subsequent decline in attendance led to their closure. Within a few years their green walks and arbours had been built over, but a small reminder of their existence is still visible today. A pub called the Rose of Normandy was once attached to them, and its frontage can still be seen at 32–3 Marylebone High Street, now the home of BBC Publications and more particularly the weekly *Listener* magazine.

One other former establishment in Marylebone which has generated an extensive literature was Lord's Cricket Ground. Founded in 1787 by a wine merchant and demon underarm bowler called Thomas Lord, the ground lay in what is now Dorset Square, as testified by a small plaque on the back of the garden shed. Within a few years the spread of Marylebone meant that what had once been an isolated spot was now on the verge of a huge metropolis, and Lord moved the ground first to Regent's

Park and finally, in 1814, to St John's Wood. Of all British sports, cricket has been responsible for the largest volume of words, and the library at Lord's possesses the finest collection of such material in the world.

The few residential streets belonging to the eighteenth-century village of Marylebone were situated close to Tyburn Road (today's Oxford Street), and their inhabitants even had their own church, that of St Peter in Vere Street, built between 1722 and 1724 to the designs of Sir Robert Harley, 1st Earl of Oxford, who owned much of the land here. St Peter's is now the home of the London Institute for Contemporary Christianity. It is well worth a visit if only to see the beautiful stained-glass windows designed by Edward Burne-Jones and installed by William Morris.

Sir Robert Harley, who gave his name to Harley Street and Oxford Street, was a patron of both Daniel Defoe and Jonathan Swift. The latter, a member of the Scriblerus Club which also included Alexander Pope and John Gay, often complained of the late hours kept by his patron. In his *Journal to Stella*, for instance, Swift writes: '"Tis now eleven, and a messenger is come from Lord Treasurer [Harley] to sup with them, but I have excused myself, and am glad I am in bed, for else I should sit up till two.' Swift also composed a few words of self-advice which seem to be of wider application:

> *Drink little at a time,*
> *Put water with your wine,*
> *Miss your glass where you can,*
> *And go off the first man.*[6]

Harley's personal library of pamphlets and manuscripts was acquired by the British Museum after his death.

Close to St Peter's is Bentinck Street, where the historian Edward Gibbon lived at number 7 from 1773 to 1783 in a household made up of six servants, a parrot and a Pomeranian lapdog. Gibbon thought it 'the best house in the world', and it was while he was here that he wrote and published the first two volumes of *The History of the Decline and Fall of the Roman Empire*. The house has since been demolished but its successor carries a plaque.[7] The years in which Gibbon was in Bentinck Street saw the building of one of London's finest houses, Home House, on the north-west corner of Portman Square. Designed by Robert Adam between 1773 and 1776, it contains a wonderful staircase which curves up four flights, and a music room overlooking the square. It is now the home of the Courtauld Institute of Art.

By the early nineteenth century Marylebone had become very firmly a part of London, bringing much and continuing profit to the Portman family who owned the land. It was laid out as a fashionable district with several squares such as Cavendish, Bryanston and Montagu, usually deriving their name from the Portman family associations. Baker Street, for example, is named after the John Baker who was once an associate of the Portmans.

Like Chelsea, Hampstead and Highgate, Marylebone had a reputation for its healthy air, and it was the sort of district in which already successful writers lived. In December 1839, Charles Dickens, at the age of twenty-seven a leading author, moved here to 1 Devonshire Terrace from Doughty Street. For the next twelve years Dickens and his family lived in Marylebone, years in which he wrote amongst other works the much-loved *The Old Curiosity Shop* and his own favourite, *David Copperfield*. The house has now gone, but a bas-relief on its site depicts several of the characters which he created here. A number of the more wealthy Dickensian protagonists live in Marylebone, amongst them Mr Dombey near Bryanston Square, and Mr Podsnap from *Our Mutual Friend* near Portman Square. Dickens was also a devotee of the waxworks run by Madame Tussaud which had settled in London close to Portman Square in 1835 at the Portman Rooms. Madame Tussaud had begun her career producing death-masks of the victims of the French Revolution. After she fled to England she spent thirty years on the road with her touring exhibition, surviving a shipwreck in the Irish Sea and riots in Bristol. She died in 1850 at the age of eighty-nine.[8] In 1884 the establishment moved to its present site in Marylebone Road.

Between 1860 and 1863, George Eliot and George Henry Lewes lived together 'in sin' at 16 Blandford Square, on the north side of Marylebone Road. These were productive years for the novelist, in which she issued *The Mill on the Floss*, *Silas Marner* and *Romola*, but her personal life was blighted by the refusal of Lewes's wife to give him a divorce.

Wilkie Collins lived almost his entire adult life in the neighbourhood. At various times Collins resided at 38 Blandford Square, 2 Harley Place, 12 Harley Street, 8 Melcombe Place and 90 (now 65) Gloucester Place, of which the last is marked by a plaque. As a young man Collins was apprenticed to a firm of tea importers in the Strand, but he gave up this occupation in favour of reading for the Bar. Although he passed his examinations, Collins never practised as a barrister and instead worked as a novelist and playwright, producing much of the melodrama so popular in the Victorian age. The bulk of his work has been forgotten, but he was responsible for two acknowledged masterpieces, *The Moonstone* and *The Woman in White*, both of which are as powerful today as they were a hundred years ago. The Victorian popularity of *The Woman in White*, published in 1860, led to a spin-off industry marketing 'Woman in White' perfumes, cloaks and dances, whilst Collins was pestered by men eager for the address of the female character Marian Halcombe.[9] Unlike so many of his friend Charles Dickens's weedy heroines, Marian Halcombe is a strong, self-sufficient but still feminine character.

Collins's private life was thoroughly complicated: he lived at times with two women and had children by both of them. He seems to have met one of them, Caroline Graves, whilst walking near Regent's Park late one night with the painter Millais and another friend. This strange encounter seems to have given Collins the idea for *The Woman in White*: in the words of Millais' son, they suddenly heard a scream from a nearby garden:

> The iron gate leading to the garden was dashed open, and from it came the figure of a young and very beautiful woman dressed in flowing white robes that shone in the moonlight. She seemed to float rather than to run in their direction, and, on coming up to the three young men, she paused for a moment in an attitude of supplication and terror.[10]

Collins pursued her – it seems that Caroline had been held captive in a villa. The whole incident is shrouded in mystery. The couple lived together for several years.

Collins suffered from rheumatic gout of the eyes, and a friend has described one occasion when 'his eyes were literally enormous bags of blood!' Lying on his bed dictating *The Moonstone* in 1868 – the book justly described by T. S. Eliot as 'the first, the longest, and the best of modern English detective novels' – Collins's cries of pain were such that all his male secretaries left. He finally engaged a young woman, 'stipulating that she must utterly disregard my sufferings and attend solely to my words'.[11]

This she did, and the novel was successfully completed. Understandably Collins took huge doses of laudanum in order to alleviate the pain, and clearly the strange figure of Ezra Jennings in *The Moonstone* is in part semi-autobiographical. His novels declined in quality, probably due to the effects of the drug. Collins died in September 1889 and he was buried at Kensal Green cemetery after a service which was sparsely attended because of the disapproval felt at his private life.

In Dickens, George Eliot and Collins, Marylebone can claim as residents three of the nineteenth century's most successful writers; but there was a fourth, Anthony Trollope, who lived from 1871 to 1880 at 39 Montagu Square. Trollope's output was prodigious. Place his six Barsetshire novels and the six Palliser books alongside *The Way We Live Now* and anyone's shelves begin to buckle and groan; yet this represents less than one-third of his total output as a novelist. When it is remembered that for most of his life Trollope worked full-time for the Post Office (he is credited with the introduction of the postbox to this country) and that his first love was hunting, one wonders how on earth he managed it all. The answer is in *An Autobiography*:

> It was my practice to be at my table every morning at 5.30 A.M.; and it was also my practice to allow myself no mercy. An old groom, whose business it was to call me, and to whom I paid £5 a year extra for the duty, allowed himself no mercy. . . . By beginning at that hour I could complete my literary work before I dressed for breakfast.

Of the three hours, half an hour was spent by Trollope rereading yesterday's work, after which he wrote steadily at the rate of 250 words every quarter of an hour. His autobiography was written at Montagu Square. Sadly, it contributed to the decline in his reputation because it challenged the Romantic idea of the writer and artist as tormented genius. Trollope likened his work to that of a shoemaker, and he listed the sums of money he had made from his books, totalling nearly £70,000. He died in a nursing home at 34 Welbeck Street in November 1882.

If the above writers appreciated Marylebone's qualities, several did not. Thackeray, for instance, hated Baker Street because of its noise and bustle, and Benjamin Disraeli referred scathingly to the district in his novel *Tancred*:

> Mary-le-bone alone ought to have produced a revolution in

our domestic architecture. It did nothing. It was built by Act of Parliament. Parliament prescribed even a façade. It is Parliament to whom we are indebted for our Gloucester Places, and Baker Streets, and Harley Streets, and Wimpole Streets, and all those flat, dull, spiritless streets, resembling each other like a large family of plain children, with Portland Place and Portman Square for their respectable parents.

In *North and South*, published in 1855, Mrs Gaskell's Margaret Hale grows dissatisfied with life in Harley Street and what she considered to be its smug complacency:

> She was getting surfeited of the eventless ease in which no struggle or endeavour was required. She was afraid lest she should even become sleepily deadened into forgetfulness of anything beyond the life which was lapping her round with luxury. There might be toilers and moilers there in London, but she never saw them; the very servants lived in an underground world of their own, of which she knew neither the hopes nor the fears; they only seemed to start into existence when some want or whim of their master or mistress needed them.

Nine years later Wilkie Collins moved out of Harley Street, not because he felt isolated but because it was too noisy. In a short period he had lost 'five working days through nothing but pianos at the back of the house and organs, bagpipes, bands and Punches in front'. The surfeit of music in the streets of London was a distraction which annoyed many Victorian men of letters. In 1864, the year that Collins left Harley Street, the Metropolitan Police Act which regulated street-performers came into force.[12] It had been legislation supported by Carlyle, Tennyson, Dickens and other writers who suspected that musicians played outside their windows on purpose as a form of blackmail!

Mention of Harley Street of course summons up images of doctors and medical practice – from the mid-nineteenth century the medical profession had colonised the street and its immediate neighbourhood. Most Harley Street doctors have been too busy to write, but with one doctor it was the other way around; he wrote because he had nothing else to do. Arthur Conan Doyle spent several years after his medical training at Edinburgh University as a general practitioner near Portsmouth, writing stories in his spare time and playing football for Portsmouth

Football Club. In 1887 the first Sherlock Holmes novel, *A Study in Scarlet*, was issued in *Beeton's Christmas Annual*, to be greeted by a resounding lack of interest. Doyle also published various historical novels such as *Micah Clarke*, which deals with the Monmouth Rebellion of 1685. The year of this book's publication saw an extraordinary literary meeting here in Marylebone. In 1889 an agent for the American publishers Lippincott was over in England looking for new novels. He arranged dinner at the Langham Hotel with Thomas Gill, MP, editor of the *Catholic World*, Oscar Wilde and Arthur Conan Doyle. Wilde was clearly in sparkling form, and over thirty years later in his autobiography *Memories and Adventures* Doyle recalled Wilde's conversation with great clarity: 'He towered above us all, and yet had the art of seeming to be interested in all that we could say.' As a result of that meeting, Wilde wrote his only novel, *The Picture of Dorian Gray*, whilst Doyle produced a second Holmes story, *The Sign of Four*, but again to little response. The Langham Hotel had been built in 1864 as one of the capital's first modern hotels. What remains of the building, which was badly damaged during the Second World War, was used by the BBC but is to be turned back into a hotel.

After eight years in Southsea, Doyle sold his general practice and spent six months in Vienna specialising in ophthalmics. In 1890 he returned to London and for the annual sum of £120 took a front room and part use of a waiting-room at 2 Devonshire Place, just off the top of Wimpole Street and still there. Dr Doyle sat back waiting for the patients to come streaming through the door, but he waited in vain for even a single one! Being a man of great energy and initiative, he decided not to waste his time. Instead he hit upon the idea of writing a series of short stories featuring the same characters in self-contained episodes, rather than the serial format favoured by authors such as Dickens, where if one issue was missed the reader faced the difficulty of catching up with the story. Doyle resurrected Sherlock Holmes and in the late spring of 1891 sent his two stories 'The Adventure of the Red-Headed League' and 'The Adventure of a Scandal in Bohemia' to the *Strand Magazine*. The editor immediately realised the potential of what he was being offered, and sales of the *Strand Magazine* quickly shot past the half-million mark.[13] Doyle wrote in his surgery from ten o'clock in the morning until three or four in the afternoon. There were no patients to interrupt him but, even if there had been, it would have made little difference.

Jerome K. Jerome recalled how Doyle would sit in his drawing-room at home surrounded by a dozen noisy friends but still writing away: 'Sometimes, without looking up from his work, he would make a remark, showing he must have been listening to our conversation; but his pen had never stopped moving.'[14]

After a few months Doyle gave up the struggle to be an eye specialist and decided instead to set up as a full-time writer. He left Marylebone for 12 Tennison Road, South Norwood, although his association with the area lived on through Holmes himself, who lived at 221B Baker Street. Doyle chose this address carefully – there was then no 221B. Over 400 people write to Sherlock Holmes at this address each year, and they receive a courteous reply from the Abbey National, which now stands where 221B should be, opposite Baker Street Underground station: 'You will appreciate that Mr Holmes had to vacate his rooms and unfortunately we do not know his present whereabouts.'[15] Dedicated Holmesians point to 'the real house' further down Baker Street and near to George Street as being where 'He' lived. The chemist John Bell & Croyden, from which Holmes bought his cocaine, remains in Wigmore Street. The Sherlock Holmes pub is not in fact in Marylebone but at 10 Northumberland Street, the justification for this site being that the Northumberland Hotel once stood here, where Sir Henry Baskerville lived.

Some fictional characters who lived in or near Harley Street have included Professor Higgins of *Pygmalion* fame at 27A Wimpole Street and Sir Roderick Glossop – as Bertie Wooster puts it, 'he is always called a nerve specialist, because it sounds better, but everybody knows that he's a sort of janitor to the looney-bin' – at 6B Harley Street. His daughter Honoria is described by the hapless Bertie as 'One of those robust girls with the muscles of a welterweight and a laugh like a squadron of cavalry charging over a tin bridge. The sort of girl who reduces you to pulp with sixteen sets of tennis and a few rounds of golf, and then comes down to dinner as fresh as a daisy, expecting you to take an intelligent interest in Freud.'[16] She nearly but not quite takes Bertie with her to the altar.

Rather like Conan Doyle in his versatility, John Buchan was another man of action who lived in Marylebone and who has enjoyed much popular if not critical literary success. He lived at 76 Portland Place between 1912 and 1919, years in which he wrote *The Thirty-Nine Steps, Greenmantle* and other bestsellers, as well as being heavily involved in the Ministry of Information during the First World War. Buchan had begun his working life as a barrister, and his first book, published in 1905, has the distinctly unexciting title *The Law Relating to the Taxation of Foreign Income*.[17] In 1919 he and his wife moved out of London to a small village near Oxford where he turned out an adventure-book each year, wrote an excellent biography of Oliver Cromwell, became an MP and finished up as Governor-General of Canada under the title Viscount Tweedsmuir.

The twentieth century has seen little change in the style and architecture of Marylebone, although offices and businesses have to a large extent ousted private residents. The squares remain, such as the charming Manchester Square which from 1900 has housed the Wallace Collection, in Hertford House on the north side. Much of the collection's riches were accumulated in the nineteenth century by the 3rd Marquess of Hertford, who appears as the unpleasant Lord Steyne in Thackeray's *Vanity Fair*. Marylebone has continued to attract well-known writers, such as Arnold Bennett who lived for the last few months of his life close to Baker Street Underground at Chiltern Court, where he died in March 1931. It had not been a successful move, as the rumble of the trains underneath was very noticeable and Bennett had strained himself moving his thousands of books.[18] H. G. Wells, who had also once lived at Chiltern Court, resided at 13 Hanover Terrace, Regent's Park, from 1937 until his death in 1946. They were years spent writing his two-volume *Experiment in Autobiography*, a work which is both sour – 'For all my desire to be interested I have to confess that for most things and people I don't care a damn' – and moving in its description of his early life. The young C. P. Snow came to lunch – an occasion which was not a success because Wells was jealous when his female companion talked to Snow.[19] The earlier, vigorous Wells did show through at times – as when he leapt around during a bombing raid putting out incendiaries with a bucket of water.[20]

Today much of Marylebone is cold and impersonal, symbolised by the backs of the department stores such as D. H. Evans and Debenhams, but there are still several attractive little enclaves left, particularly in and near Marylebone High Street. For example, St Christopher's Place was once a slum but is now a smart shopping arcade. But perhaps Marylebone's greatest asset lies in the fact that Regent's Park is on its doorstep. Its Zoo has two important literary associations. The limerick-writer and artist Edward Lear's first job was drawing its parrots – a spell of employment which resulted in his first book, *Illustrations of the Family of Psittacidae, or Parrots*, in 1832.[21] And in 1935 another animal was immortalised in a sketchbook: Allen Lane sent a young artist here to draw a penguin, and the unwitting bird ended up on the cover of all Penguin books.[22]

Mayfair

16

The word 'Mayfair' conjures up images of smart shops, glamorous nightclubs and elegant people, yet it is only in the last 200 years that the area has become fashionable and prosperous. For hundreds of years, up to the end of the eighteenth century, the district was notorious for its proximity to Tyburn, London's main execution site from the twelfth century until 1783. The gallows stood at the top of what is now Edgware Road, near Marble Arch, and the site is marked by a plaque set into a traffic island.

With such a record of violent death it is not surprising that Tyburn entered deep into popular consciousness, so that, for example, the phrase 'to go west', still used to describe something as broken or finished, referred not to young men off to seek fame and fortune but rather to the three-hour cart-ride from Newgate prison through Holborn to this then isolated spot – a journey often made through a gauntlet of jeering crowds. The name of one of Tyburn's hangmen, Jack Ketch, was a familiar bogeyman to generations of children.[1] And sure enough Tyburn attracted the interest of several writers, who either visited it as observers or who killed off some of their characters here.

There was of course Samuel Pepys, who let no aspect of the human condition pass him by. He came to Tyburn on 21 January 1664 to see the end of the robber Turner:

... I got for a shilling to stand upon the wheel of a cart, in great pain, above an hour before the execution was done – he delaying the time by long discourses and prayers one after another, in hopes of a reprieve; but none came, and at last was flung off the lather in his cloak. A comely-looked man he was, and kept his countenance to the end – I was sorry to see him. It was believed there was at least twelve or fourteen thousand people in the street.

James Boswell, too, came to Tyburn on 4 May 1763, in this case to witness the end of a highwayman called Paul Lewis. It was a scene which threw him into 'a very deep melancholy', and for several nights afterwards he was 'so haunted with frightful imaginations that I durst not lie by myself', having to share a bed with a (male) friend.

As a magistrate Henry Fielding had a professional interest in Tyburn, but in fact he condemned its very existence: '... we sacrifice the lives of men, not for the reformation but for the diversion of the populace.'[2] The main protagonist of his novel *Jonathan Wild* (1743) finishes up on these gallows. Wild nonchalantly dismisses the prospect of his execution, saying: 'D—n me, it is only a dance without music.' Tyburn also spawned its own literature, known as the 'Last Confessions' and published from the 1620s. A 'ghost writer' would produce the autobiography of the condemned, who was then expected in the final few minutes he or she was standing beside the gallows to publicise it, the royalties going to the dead person's family or friends.[3] Not all of those involved in this gallows literature are gone and forgotten; in fact one of them is now a fully recognised member of the pantheon of 'English Literature'. Daniel Defoe supplemented his income by churning out several such works, naturally claiming that they were authentic. In his account of Jonathan Wild, the publicity claimed that the book was 'Not made up of fiction and fable, but taken from his own mouth, and collected from papers of his own writing'. Tyburn also featured prominently in the *Newgate Calendar*, a five-volume collection first published in 1773. The *Calendar* contained the supposed life-stories of prominent criminals, all of whom ended up at Tyburn. In the nineteenth century the *Calendar* was the basis for what Thackeray called 'the Newgate novel', a genre made famous by Harrison Ainsworth whose racy Victorian melodramas sold in hundreds of thousands of copies. For example, Ainsworth's *Jack Sheppard*, published in 1839, was about one of the thieves executed at Tyburn because of the treachery of Jonathan Wild.

The orgiastic proceedings at Tyburn – it has been estimated that a crowd of 200,000 spectators witnessed the departure of Wild[4] – ensured that there was no rush by developers to build in the area. The gallows stood in splendid isolation with Marylebone Fields to the north and Hyde Park to the south. The park had once been owned by the monks of Westminster Abbey but was acquired by Henry VIII in 1536 as a hunting park 'for his own disport and pastime'. He enclosed it with a fence in order to deter poachers, and a century later Charles I opened it to the public. Sold off in three lots for a total of £17,071 6s 8d by Parliament in 1652, it was opened up once more to the public by Charles II and was the scene of a weekly fashion parade on Sunday mornings.[5] When Pepys came here with his wife Elizabeth, he reported in his diary with a mixture of pride and jealousy that the Duke of York, later James II, 'did eye my wife mightily'. Hyde Park was also a notorious duelling site. John Wilkes, author, politician and libertine, fought here and was wounded. Just to the south of Hyde Park was the marshy and deserted swamp which is now Belgravia, enlivened only by the famous coaching inn called the Pillars of Hercules, where Henry Fielding's Squire Western stays when he comes to London in pursuit of his daughter Sophia and her lover Tom Jones.

After 1660 and the Restoration of Charles II, several returning royalist exiles were rewarded for their loyalty by being granted land to the north of Piccadilly. Most notable was Lord Clarendon, the Lord Chancellor, to whom Charles gave thirty acres. Clarendon built himself a palatial mansion which cost him over £40,000, a sum twice as much as he expected. This extravagance fuelled claims that Clarendon was siphoning off money from the public purse. In 1667 he had once more to flee to exile in France and this time there was to be no return, but he did use his leisure to write an important history of the Civil War as well as an autobiography. In 1683 the diarist John Evelyn drove past Clarendon House with Clarendon's son as it was being demolished.[6] In one of the few personal touches which light up his writings, Evelyn notes that 'I turn'd my head the Contrary til the Coach was gon past it, least I might minister occasion of speaking it, which must needes have grieved his Lordship that in so short a time, their pomp was fallen . . .'.[7] None of the other mansions has survived, although the names of their former owners remain in such street-names as Albemarle, Dover, Sackville and Burlington.

In the late seventeenth and early eighteenth century Mayfair suffered from another blight in addition to nearby Tyburn, namely the fair held every May from the 1690s which gave the place its name. Whereas most fairs at least pretended to include some commercial purpose, this May fair was given over solely to the dedicated pursuit of pleasure and constituted a Bacchanalia which lasted a fortnight. The contemporary observer Ned Ward – a sort of smutty Samuel Pepys – came here and wrote of his visit: 'We now began to look about us, and take a view of the spectators, but could not, among the many thousands, find one man that appear'd above the degree of a gentleman's valet, nor one whore that could have the impudence to ask above sixpence for an hour of her cursed company.' Ward went on in ringing tones to berate the rascals and strumpets as being 'a scandal to the Creation, mere antidotes against lechery, and enemies to cleanliness'.[8]

However, in the course of the eighteenth century a long-drawn-out battle was waged between Mayfair's undoubted attractions – Hyde Park, Piccadilly, Green Park to the south – and its less salubrious aspects: Tyburn and May Fair. As the wealthy and influential moved in, so something had to give. The fair was ended in the 1730s and replaced by Shepherd Market. Tyburn was more rooted in its popular appeal, lasting until 1783 when the gallows were moved to Newgate prison. The new Mayfair residents acted quickly to obliterate traces of past associations. Tyburn Road was renamed Oxford Street and Tyburn Lane became Park Lane. They also did their best to fashion their own aristocratic 'ghetto', a process completed by the construction of Regent Street, which sealed off Mayfair to the east. Its architect John Nash stated quite bluntly in 1810 that the aim of Regent Street was to introduce 'a boundary and complete separation between the Streets and Squares occupied by the Nobility and Gentry, and the narrower Streets and meaner houses occupied by mechanics and the trading part of the community'.[9]

Mayfair was, and still is, owned by the Dukes of Westminster, whose family name is Grosvenor. Their wealth grew because of the high rents garnered from members of the nobility now finding themselves a 'des. res.' here in Mayfair. One of the first to arrive was Lord Chesterfield. After his marriage in 1734 he moved into 45 Grosvenor Square while waiting for his own residence, Chesterfield House in South Audley Street, to be completed. It was to number 45 that Samuel Johnson came to discuss the plan of his *Dictionary* with Chesterfield. The first meeting seems to have gone well but the second never took place. Johnson, having been kept waiting by his lordship, stomped off in anger. Chesterfield claimed later that the delay had been due to a misunderstanding. After Johnson's *Dictionary* was finally published in 1755, Chesterfield wrote two flattering notices, which did not prevent Johnson delivering a magisterial rebuke which he had clearly been storing up for some years: 'The notice, which you have been pleased to take of my Labours, had it been early, had been kind; but it has been delayed till I am indifferent and cannot enjoy it, till I am solitary and cannot impart it, till I am known and do not want it. . . .'[10] It was a response as effective in its own way as Johnson's mugging the mugger in Grosvenor Square who had stolen his handkerchief.

Chesterfield does not seem to have been unduly perturbed by Johnson's letter, often showing it around to his friends. He was a skilled correspondent himself, writing many letters to his illegitimate son, Philip Stanhope. These were published after Chesterfield's death in 1773. They consist of guidelines to behaviour, some of which suggest that he cannot always have been a particularly agreeable companion: 'There is nothing so illiberal and so illbred, as audible laughter . . . not to mention the disagreeable noise that it makes, and the shocking distortion of the face that it occasions.' As for his views on women, 'a man of sense only trifles with them, plays with them'. Chesterfield House itself was pulled down in 1934, and some flats of that name now stand on its former site.

Not every Mayfair resident was as affluent as Lord Chesterfield, and two writers in particular were often reduced to dire poverty. The first was Laurence Sterne, author of *Tristram Shandy* and *A Sentimental Journey*, who died at 41 Old Bond Street in March 1768. It was not a pleasant death; as he lay dying he saw the attendants rifling through his belongings. Worse, however, lay in store. Buried in a cemetery just to the west of today's Marble Arch, his corpse was whisked away by body-snatchers after only a few days and ended up on the dissecting-table of the Professor of Anatomy at Cambridge University.[11] When Richard Sheridan, author of the plays *The School for Scandal* and *The Rivals*, lived in Bruton Street in 1786 he dared not open the front door for fear of the army of creditors camped on the pavement outside.

Sterne and Sheridan were the exceptions to the rule of Mayfair prosperity, and by the early nineteenth century the area was virtually a self-sufficient entity. It boasted elegant gardens, squares such as Grosvenor, Berkeley and Hanover Squares, and its own churches, the most magnificent being St George's, Hanover Square. Here the composer George Frederick Handel, who set much of the verse of Milton and Pope to music, was a churchwarden for many years. St George's has always been a fashionable church in which to get married, and some of the literary figures who have trooped up its aisle have been Shelley and his first wife Harriet (in 1816 she drowned herself in the Serpentine), Benjamin Disraeli, George Eliot, John Galsworthy and John Buchan. St George's did not prove large enough for the expanding Mayfair population, and the attractive little Grosvenor Chapel was built in South Audley Street in 1730. It is still there, an additional asset being its charming little garden to the rear. Its recent literary connections have been with Sir John Betjeman, who often worshipped here, as did Rose Macaulay, who always called it 'my Chapel'. After the morning service Macaulay often went off for a swim in the Serpentine: 'After church I now go and bathe in the Serpentine often, the weather now [May 1951] being less frigid. It is lovely there in the mornings at nine; very empty, and smooth and green – and rather cool, of course.'[12]

Mayfair also had and still has its own exclusive bachelor-style residences, the chambers at Albany – it is regarded as lamentable ignorance to call it 'the' Albany or to refer to the rooms as 'flats'. The historian G. M. Macaulay lived there for several years after 1840, leading 'the sort of life to my taste – college life at the West End of London' and writing many of his histories while in residence.[13] Other literary figures who have enjoyed its collegiate existence have included Byron, Arnold Bennett, Allen Lane, J. B. Priestley and Graham Greene. The Victorian novelist Bulwer Lytton, immensely popular in his time but scarcely read today, also had chambers in Albany, writing once to his wife that he was alone with solitude. She turned up unexpectedly and found 'Solitude' dressed in white muslin and sitting on his knee.[14] Mayfair had and has its own publishers, too, and the firm of John

Murray has been at 50 Albemarle Street since 1812. The John Murray of those days published the poems of Byron, but also burnt the poet's autobiography in 1824 because of its supposed immorality.

Mayfair's rather smug, self-satisfied world is portrayed by Oscar Wilde in his only novel, *The Picture of Dorian Gray*, published in 1891. Aunt Agatha lives in Berkeley Square, Henry Wotton in Curzon Street, Lord Fermor at Albany and Dorian himself near Grosvenor Square. Most of Wilde's characters rarely leave Mayfair; if they do, as in the case of Aunt Agatha, it is to venture into the East End to brighten up the lives of its inhabitants with piano duets. Wilde knew Mayfair reasonably well, making a point of buying his buttonholes in the Burlington Arcade before strolling down Piccadilly to Chelsea to see his friend, the actress Lillie Langtry. It was a habit which W. S. Gilbert could not resist parodying in *Patience* (1881):

Though the Philistines may jostle, you will rank as an apostle in the
  high aesthetic band,
If you walk down Piccadilly with a poppy or a lily in your medieval
  hand.

Wilde always had lunch every day at exactly 1 o'clock at the Café Royal in Regent Street. He was also a member of the Albemarle Club at 13 Albemarle Street, and it was here that the events which led to his downfall were set in motion. On 18 February 1895 the Marquis of Queensberry, father of the Lord Alfred Douglas with whom Wilde had fallen in love, handed in a note to the porter calling Wilde a 'somdomite' (spelling was not the Marquis's strong point). Wilde decided to sue him, a fateful decision which eventually resulted in his own criminal prosecution.[15]

A sharper depiction of this brittle Mayfair society than Wilde's was sketched out by 'Saki' (Hector Hugh Munro) in *The Unbearable Bassington*. Like Orwell after him, Munro was once in the Burma military police. His portrayal of Mayfair society in the Edwardian Age is short and pungent. The plot centres around Francesca Bassington – 'Francesca prided herself on being able to see things from other people's points of view, which meant, as it usually does, that she could see her own point of view from various aspects' – and her wish to remain in Blue Street, Mayfair, and not leave 'her square mile of Mecca and go out into the wilderness of bricks and mortar'. She succeeds, but her son

Comus is estranged from her and dies in West Africa. Saki himself, best known for his short stories, was shot in the head and killed during the First World War.

Three well-known fictional characters have resided in Mayfair. Dorothy L. Sayers's Lord Peter Wimsey, for example, had his flat at 110 Piccadilly, overlooking Green Park. Margery Allingham's Albert Campion lives above a police station in Bottle Street, which was probably based on Vine Street. The Campion mystery novel *The Tiger in the Smoke* (1952) is one of the best books with a London background. Finally there is Bertie Wooster, who lived at 3A Berkeley Mansions, Berkeley Street, along with his 'gentleman's personal gentleman' Jeeves, who spends his time getting Bertie and his pals out of various scrapes. In *The Mating Season* (1949) Jeeves is described as 'a Mayfair consultant'. Bertie frequents the Drones Club, which was apparently based on Buck's in Clifford Street, and Jeeves the Junior Ganymede in Curzon Street.[16] Bertie's favourite aunt, Aunt Dahlia, lives nearby at 47 Charles Street. Bertie had unfortunate experiences in two of the roads which encircle Mayfair; he was once chased down Park Lane by his valet Bingley who was armed with a knife, and he also recalls that 'Many's the time, back in London, I've hurried along Piccadilly and felt the hot breath of the toucher [or borrower] on the back of my neck and heard his sharp, excited yapping as he closed in on me'.[17] Bertie's creator, P. G. Wodehouse, himself once lived in Mayfair, first at 23 Gilbert Street when he complained that it was difficult to concentrate on his writing because of the multitude of dinners and lunches he was expected to attend; and secondly at 17 Norfolk (now Dunraven) Street in the 1930s when his wife Ethel rented a sixteen-room apartment at a cost of £450 per month. As a present Ethel installed a smart and elegant library for 'Plum' to write in, but with a typically unassuming air he preferred to work upstairs in a small, cramped bedroom, his typewriter perched precariously on a wooden table. When Wodehouse found his wife's dinner-parties too noisy he strolled around Hyde Park.[18]

Today a Bertie Wooster would be unlikely to live in Mayfair. Between the wars business and commerce, particularly hotels, moved in and the private residents moved out. Most of the vast houses which once dotted the neighbourhood were demolished, and only Burlington House, home of the Royal Academy, and Crewe House in Curzon Street are reminders of past glories.

Crewe House was rebuilt by Sir John Soane at the end of the eighteenth century. During the First World War it was the headquarters of the ministry responsible for issuing anti-German propaganda. This organisation was headed by the newspaper proprietor Lord Northcliffe, and H. G. Wells was also on the staff.

One of the businesses situated in Mayfair was known to quite a few literary figures. The tutors Gabbitas Thring & Co. in Sackville Street specialised in finding teaching posts for young men just down from Oxford and Cambridge with poor degrees: Evelyn Waugh, Graham Greene and John Betjeman all made use of their services within a few years of each other. Waugh came here in 1926 and was sent off to a school on the Welsh coast. In his first novel, *Decline and Fall* (1928), Waugh depicts Paul Pennyfeather, sent down from Oxford for indecent behaviour, being interviewed by Mr Levy of Church & Gargoyle, 'scholastic agents'. Mr Levy tells Paul of a job at Llanabba Castle, the headmaster requiring someone 'to teach Classics and English to University Standard with subsidiary Mathematics, German and French. Experience essential; first-class games essential.'

'Might have been made for you,' said Mr Levy.
'But I don't know a word of German, I've had no experience, I've got no testimonials, and I can't play cricket.'
'It doesn't do to be too modest', said Mr Levy.

Paul gets the post, in the face of very little opposition, and his weird and wonderful adventures begin.

When Graham Greene was out of money in the 1920s he realised, as he puts it in his autobiography, *A Sort of Life*: 'It was Sackville Street or nothing. To the young men of my generation, down from the university without work, recourse to Sackville Street was like recourse to the pawnshop in earlier days.' He obtained a private tutoring job. As for John Betjeman, he was sent off to be cricketing master at a Buckinghamshire prep school, even though he barely knew one end of a cricket bat from the other. In his first match he duly collected a 'pair'.[19]

Although some of the character of Mayfair has been squeezed out by impersonal businesses and offices – and current plans propose the turning of St Mark's in North Audley Street into a hamburger restaurant and the demolition of the Georgian buildings in Lancashire Court and Horse Shoe Yard – pleasant neighbourhoods and buildings have survived. There is Shepherd

Market where Nicholas Jenkins, narrator of Anthony Powell's *A Dance to the Music of Time*, lived in the 1920s, surrounded by inhabitants 'many of them existing precariously on their bridge earnings, or hire of their bodies'[20] – the latter are still plying their trade here today. Another survivor is the bookshop in Curzon Street which was started by Heywood Hill in 1936 and where the novelist Nancy Mitford was an assistant between 1942 and 1945. The Burlington Arcade is certainly worth a visit – to window-shop if not to purchase any of its beautiful but expensive luxuries – as, too, is the Jesuit Church of the Immaculate Conception in Farm Street, where both Evelyn Waugh and Edith Sitwell were received into the Catholic Church.

Yet somehow Mayfair seems to lack the essential ingredient of people who actually live there, and it is with a sense of relief that the Sunday visitor chances upon the crowds milling around Speaker's Corner near Marble Arch. Despite its fame, or notoriety, Speaker's Corner makes little appearance in the annals of literary London. William Morris once delivered a fiery speech here about the necessity for socialism and was nearly thrown into the Serpentine by an angry crowd for his efforts,[21] while Siegfried Sassoon in *Memoirs of a Fox-hunting Man* (1928) notes of the main protagonist George Sherston: 'Socialists, for me, began and ended in Hyde Park, which was quite a harmless place for them to function in.'

But perhaps the strangest scene, and a wonderfully unlikely one with which to end a chapter on literary Mayfair, is that of Lenin and his wife Nadia Krupskaya often visiting Speaker's Corner when they were living in London in 1902–3:

> An atheist, standing among a group of curious listeners, proved there was no God. We were particularly keen on listening to one speaker of this kind. He spoke with an Irish accent, which was easier for us to understand. Nearby a Salvation Army officer uttered hysterical shouts in appeal to God Almighty, while a little farther on a shop-assistant was holding forth on the hours of servitude of assistants in the big stores.[22]

There is something rather amazing in the thought that the man who fifteen years later was to topple a regime and a ruling class far away in Russia learnt English, presumably with an Irish accent, only a few yards away from what was then the wealthiest part of London.

St James's
and Whitehall

The particular ambience of St James's derives from the wonderful mixture of power and style to be found here. Within its boundaries may be found Buckingham Palace, 10 Downing Street, the gentlemen's clubs along Pall Mall and the civil servants in Whitehall. Above all, it boasts the presence of St James's Park, for my money the finest of all the fine royal parks, ninety-three acres of greenery in the middle of one of the world's largest cities. Even with the traffic hurtling down the Mall it does not require much imagination to picture Charles II strolling here 300 years ago, exercising his spaniels, playing at a game of croquet called 'paille-maille' and chatting to his favourite mistress whom he had installed nearby. John Evelyn noted disapprovingly in his diary for 2 March 1671 that he was out walking with the king and heard 'a very familiar discourse' between Charles and 'Mrs Nellie as they cal'd an impudent Comedian, she looking out of her Garden on a Tarrace at the top of the Wall, and [Charles] standing on the greene Walke under it; I was heartily sorry at this scene'. Number 79 Pall Mall stands on the site of Nell Gwyn's house and carries a plaque.

St James's and Whitehall have had royal connections ever since Edward the Confessor in 1042 commanded that Westminster Palace should be built, ensuring that the monarch should be a convenient distance away from the ever-prying and demanding City of London. A thousand years ago Westminster was a small village surrounded by fields, its rural character indicated by the full name of the church which stands in Trafalgar Square, St Martin-in-the-Fields. Successive kings kept their royal falcons in the mews which was situated roughly where the National Gallery is now. In 1391, Richard II appointed Geoffrey Chaucer his 'Clerk of our Works at our Palace of Westminster, our Tower of London . . . and our Mews for falcons at Charing Cross'. That was not nearly the end of Chaucer's duties; he was also to look after

> our gardens, fish-ponds, mills and park enclosures pertaining to the said Palace, Tower, Castles, Manors, Lodges, and Mews, with powers (by self or deputy) to choose and take masons, carpenters and all and sundry other workmen and labourers who are needed for our works, wheresoever they can be found, within or without all liberties (Church fee alone excepted); and to set the same to labour at the said works, at our wages.[1]

Henry VIII was interested in the open fields as offering excellent hunting parks. He moved from the increasingly ramshackle Palace of Westminster into York Place, once occupied by Cardinal Wolsey. Wolsey had failed to obtain Henry a divorce from Catherine of Aragon and he fell from royal favour in 1529. Henry moved in, building a 'White Hall' for festive occasions; as Shakespeare warned in *Henry VIII*:

> *You must no more call it York Place. That's past;*
> *For since the Cardinal fell that title's lost.*
> *'Tis now the King's, and called Whitehall.*

Henry also ordered a new palace to be built, that of St James, of which only the Tudor gateway in Pall Mall survives today. When animal-loving James I succeeded to the throne he used the park just to the south of this new palace not for hunting but for storing his menagerie which included an 'ellefant', crocodiles and also an aviary – hence Birdcage Walk on the south side of St James's Park.[2] His son Charles I planned to rebuild Whitehall Palace, although the only work actually completed was Inigo Jones's Banqueting Hall of 1622. The sad irony here is that it was from the Banqueting Hall on 30 January 1649 that Charles stepped out to his execution, after a walk through St James's Park. One of the observers of this momentous event was the fifteen-year-old Samuel Pepys, still a pupil at St Paul's School. Oliver Cromwell moved into Whitehall Palace in Charles's place, being often visited by the poet John Milton who had been appointed his secretary. Charles II lived here after the Restoration in 1660, and the older and more powerful Samuel Pepys returned, noting that he once saw the underwear of one of the royal mistresses hanging out to dry – an act of voyeurism which clearly stirred his imagination: '. . . saw the finest smocks and linen petticoats of my Lady Castlemain – it did me good to look upon them.' Within thirty years, however, Whitehall Palace had come to an end; a fire of January 1698 led that other seventeenth-century diarist John Evelyn to write: 'White-hall utterly burnt to the ground, nothing but the walles and ruines left.'[3] Fortunately Evelyn was not quite accurate: Jones's Banqueting Hall remained.

By then, due largely to Charles II's influence, St James's had become the most fashionable area in London. Henry Jermyn laid out St James's Square, a residence so well patronised by the aristocracy that by the 1720s the square numbered among its residents six dukes and seven earls.[4] The Dukes of Buckingham had built themselves a large mansion called Buckingham House to the west of the park, and St James's Park itself is often referred to in the Restoration comedies of Wycherley and Congreve. As with Mayfair a few years later, St James's was to have its own church, namely Sir Christopher Wren's church of St James, Piccadilly, completed in 1684. Vanbrugh's play *The Relapse; or, Virtue in Danger* suggests that it was used as much for display as for worship:

> *Berintha.* Pray which church does your lordship most oblige with your presence?
> *Lord Foppington.* Oh! St James', madam: there's much the best company.
> *Amanda.* Is there good preaching too?
> *Lord Foppington.* Why, faith, madam, I can't tell. A man must have very little to do there that can give an account of the sermon.

Although badly bombed during the Blitz, St James's has been well restored, and one is amply repaid for visiting what Wren himself considered the model of a parish church. Fortunately the church authorities had removed the wonderful Grinling Gibbons

stone font, with its stem representing the Tree of Life and with
Adam and Eve to either side, before the bombing. At this font
both Lord Chesterfield of the *Letters* and William Blake were
baptised. St James's was also where Robert Graves was married in
1918 after several years' war service. As he recalls in his autobiography, *Good-bye to All That*, there were problems with his
feminist fiancée Nancy:

> Nancy had read the marriage-service for the first time that
> morning and had been horrified by it. She all but refused to go
> through the ceremony at all, though I had arranged for it to be
> modified and reduced to the shortest possible form. Another
> caricature scene to look back on: myself striding up the red
> carpet wearing field-boots, spurs, and sword; Nancy meeting
> me in a blue-check silk wedding dress, utterly furious; packed
> benches on either side of the church, full of relatives; aunts
> using handkerchiefs; the choir boys out of tune; Nancy sav-
> agely muttering the responses, myself shouting them out in a
> parade-ground voice.

Max Beerbohm and Wilfred Owen were among the congregation, while a man later to be famous as a conductor, Leopold
Stokowski, was the organist.[5] The marriage did not last.

Not the least of the attractions of St James, Piccadilly, is the
attractive Garden of Remembrance laid out to one side; this was
sponsored by Viscount Southwood, proprietor of the *Daily Herald*
and the man who built up the printing firm Odhams, in honour
of Londoners' bravery during the Blitz.

Apart from its own square and church, St James's also possessed its own clubs, the first of which was founded by an Italian
called Francis White in 1693 and is still in St James's Street. In the
eighteenth century White's was distinguished by the ability of its
members to gamble on virtually anything. The diarist, letter-
writer and man about London, Horace Walpole, recorded the
occasion when 'A man dropped down dead at the door [of
White's], was carried in and the club immediately made bets
whether he was dead or not. When they were going to bleed him,
the wagerers for his death interposed, and said it would affect the
fairness of the bet. . . .'[6] Every time Jonathan Swift passed
White's he shook his fist at it in anger at what he considered to be
its wasteful folly.[7] White's was soon followed by other clubs such
as Brooks's and Boodle's.

During the eighteenth century the centre of government came to be established in the vicinity. Some of the land to the west of Whitehall had been owned by Sir George Downing, once Samuel Pepys's boss. We do not know what Downing thought of Pepys, but we do know that Pepys wrote of Downing 'He is so stingy a fellow, I care not to see him'. Downing offered the land to the Crown on his death. In 1731, George II in turn offered 10 Downing Street to Sir Robert Walpole, the leading statesman of the day. Walpole refused the gift on a personal basis but said that he would occupy it in his office as First Lord of the Treasury, a convention which still holds true today. For a time Walpole lived here with his son Horace. In 1742 both Walpoles left Downing Street for 5 Arlington Street (at the back of the Ritz and marked by a plaque). Horace lived in Arlington Street for over thirty years; he was here in 1748 when he bought a small cottage in Twickenham overlooking the Thames which he gradually turned into the Gothic castle called Strawberry Hill. Inspired by this building Walpole wrote *The Castle of Otranto*, published in 1765 and the first Gothic melodrama, replete with the full paraphernalia of ghosts, storms, gloomy monasteries and menaced maidens. Strawberry Hill is now a teachers' training college.

Eighteenth-century Downing Street seems to have attracted aspiring writers. Tobias Smollett, later to produce *Humphry Clinker*, lived in the street for two years from 1744, trying to establish himself as a surgeon but being let down by his bad temper. Eighteen years after Smollett left, a young James Boswell took lodgings just across from 10 Downing Street: 'I took a lodging up two pair of stairs with the use of a handsome parlour all the forenoon, for which I agreed to pay forty guineas a year, but I took it for a fortnight first, by way of a trial.'[8] It was an arrangement which came to grief, both landlord and tenant ending up at Sir John Fielding's Bow Street magistrates' court after a fierce dispute over the rent. The lodgings have since been demolished.

Boswell knew the area well, especially its varied pleasures. In December 1762 he visited the Cockpit at St James's Park to witness the sport of cockfighting. The Cockpit was a circular room surrounded by rows of seats:

The cocks, nicely cut and dressed and armed with silver heels, are set down and fight with amazing bitterness and resolution. . . . The uproar and noise of betting is prodigious. A great deal of money made a very quick circulation from hand to hand. . . . I was sorry for the poor cocks. I looked round to see if any of the spectators pitied them when mangled and torn in a most cruel manner, but I could not observe the smallest relenting sign in any countenance.

Cockfighting was outlawed in the nineteenth century, although a reminder of the 'sport' is provided by the name of Cockspur Street which leads west off Trafalgar Square. Boswell also visited St James's Park because it was a notorious spot for picking up prostitutes. He came here in March 1763: 'She who submitted to my lusty embraces was a young Shropshire girl, only seventeen, very well-looked, her name Elizabeth Parker. Poor being, she has a sad time of it!'

St James's fashionableness was maintained during the nineteenth century, although some of its most important literary links have since been erased. It was at 8 St James's Street that Byron lived from 1808 until 1814 and where, after the publication of *Childe Harold*, he said: 'I awoke one morning and found myself famous'. Byron House now stands on its site. Also gone is 22 St James's Place where the banker Samuel Rogers lived from 1800 to his death in 1855. His drawing-room was frequented by all the most famous literary figures of the first half of the nineteenth century, such as Byron, Wordsworth and Sir Walter Scott. Some rather dismal modern flats occupy its position today.

Nevertheless enough survives to make up for these acts of destruction. There are Carlton Gardens and Carlton House Terrace, both built by John Nash, who also remodelled Buckingham Palace. Nash was often shoddy and slapdash in his work, but when it comes off such designs as the Carltons are splendid. He also recognised the merits of informality, laying out St James's Park in a less French and rigid style than it had been. Other delights of St James's are clubs like the Athenaeum which was founded in Waterloo Place in 1824. Its library is where Thackeray wrote many of his books and also where Anthony Trollope decided to kill off the memorable character of Mrs Proudie in his Barsetshire series. Trollope records in his autobiography that he was sitting quietly on his own when he overheard two clergymen criticising some of his literary creations, including Mrs Proudie: 'It was impossible for me not to hear their words, and almost impossible to hear them and be quiet. I got up, and standing between them, I acknowledged myself to be the culprit. "As to Mrs Proudie," I said, "I will go home and kill her before the week is over." And so I did.' Charles Dickens was also a member of the Athenaeum, elected in 1838 at the early age of twenty-six. It was on the club's steps that Dickens and Thackeray finally shook hands and made up after a quarrel arising out of a less than respectful article written by a friend of Dickens about a friend of Thackeray. The reconciliation occurred only a few months before Thackeray's death in December 1863. Just around the corner from the Athenaeum is the Reform Club. It was in the drawing-room here that Jules Verne's hero Phileas Fogg bet that he could travel around the world in eighty days. Henry James often stayed at the Reform, and a hole was bored in the door of his favourite room so that the valet could check before knocking so as not to disturb James if he was writing. The hole is still there.

The rather grubby area to the north-east of St James's was cleaned up in the early nineteenth century by the creation of Trafalgar Square with its focal point of Nelson's Column. Although much visited by tourists and visitors to London, Trafalgar Square has never been much loved by writers. Dickens in one of his pieces in *The Uncommercial Traveller* refers to its 'abortive ugliness', and William Morris in *News from Nowhere* envisaged the square in the future as a vast garden full of apricot trees – his dislike of it was no doubt influenced by 'Bloody Sunday' in November 1887 when a protest march was dispersed by the police and Morris received a crack on the head. Another writer with unhappy memories of Trafalgar Square was George Orwell, who slept out here in August 1931 on one of his 'tramping' expeditions: 'Some of the people I met on the square had been there without a break for six weeks, and did not seem much the worse, except that they are all fantastically dirty.'[9] Orwell found it almost impossible to sleep, and the next morning he shaved in the fountains and headed off towards Kent. Later he drew upon his experiences for his novel *A Clergyman's Daughter* (1935) in which Dorothy Hare, the rector's daughter from Suffolk who has lost her memory, sleeps out in Trafalgar Square for ten nights: 'There is a chorus of varying sound – groans, curses, bursts of laughter, and singing, and through them all the uncontrollable chattering of teeth.'

Two other notable institutions were introduced to Victorian St James's, one of which remains though the other has vanished.

The survivor is the London Library, founded by Thomas Carlyle in 1840 and for all but the first four years of its life at 14 St James's Square. The London Library, unlike the British Library in Bloomsbury, allows its members to borrow books and it possesses a friendly air often described as 'typically English' in the seemingly chaotic but ultimately successful way in which things get done. Part of the reason for its success lies in the continuity of staff: a past librarian called Mr Cox, for example, worked here for nearly seventy years between 1882 and 1951. Fictional members have included Dr Watson and James Bond, and amongst the factual have been George Eliot, H. G. Wells, E. M. Forster, Virginia Woolf and many other famous literary names.[10] Members are not supposed to mark the books in any way, yet Carlyle himself was notorious for his learned but also sometimes bad-tempered marginalia.

What has gone is the famous theatre called the St James's which, although opened in 1835, two years before Queen Victoria came to the throne, established itself in the late nineteenth century with the birth of the West End theatre. On 5 January 1895 it staged the première of Henry James's historical costume drama *Guy Domville*. James arrived at the end of the play and went on stage to take a curtain call, not realising that half the audience had spent much of the evening barracking play and actors. The torrent of abuse hurled at the unfortunate playwright surprised even the most veteran observers of English crowds.[11] *Guy Domville* was replaced by Oscar Wilde's *The Importance of Being Earnest*, and this time the première was an unqualified success. Wilde was present, as was nearly the Marquis of Queensberry, father of Wilde's lover Lord Alfred Douglas. Worried that the Marquis might disrupt the play, theatre staff were told to refuse him admittance, which they successfully managed to do, even though he tried to sneak in through the stage-door.[12] During Wilde's trial for 'acts of gross indecency with other male persons', *Importance* was still produced at the St James's but black strips were pasted over the author's name, thus sparing the audience embarrassment. The theatre was demolished in 1957 and a trip today to 23–4 King Street confirms that yet another modern office block is shortly to make its unwelcome bow where the playhouse once stood. The good news is that the four tableaux which once decorated the balconies and included images of Oscar Wilde, Sir Laurence Olivier and Vivien Leigh (the latter two starred here in a famous version of *Antony and Cleopatra*) are to be erected next door in Angel Court.[13]

Several Victorian prime ministers were rather more than just politicians. Benjamin Disraeli, for example, first made his name as a novelist, and on his departure from Downing Street in 1880 he accepted an advance of £10,000 to write a novel which he called *Endymion*. As for William Gladstone, the 'Grand Old Man' was still Prime Minister at the age of eighty-four. On the morning of his retirement in March 1894 he spent several hours translating the love-poems of Horace before setting off for Buckingham Palace, whose occupant herself kept a diary from the age of thirteen until her death at eighty-two in 1901. This constitutes perhaps the longest-kept such work in history. It amounted to over a hundred volumes, extracts from which were published as *Leaves from the Journal of Our Life in the Highlands* in 1868, *More Leaves* following in 1883. Queen Victoria was also an artist, and in the summer of 1846 Edward Lear came regularly to Buckingham Palace in order to give her lessons.

As government expenditure grew, so did the number of civil servants based in Whitehall and also the grand buildings which line both sides of the road. Several literary figures have worked within these buildings. T. E. Lawrence, for instance, was appointed by Winston Churchill in 1921 to be political adviser to the Middle Eastern Department at the Colonial Office. During the Second World War, Iris Murdoch was employed at the Treasury between 1940 and 1942, whilst John Betjeman and Richard Hughes were at the Admiralty. In fact Hughes, author of *A High Wind in Jamaica*, was awarded the OBE not for this novel but for his war work and in 1956 he published the decidedly non-fictional *The Administration of War Production*. Also at the Admiralty at the same time, based in room 39, was Ian Fleming who as personal assistant to the Director of Naval Intelligence rose to the rank of commander and later used some of his experiences for the character of Commander James Bond, '007'.[14] Since the war other civil servants who have established themselves as writers have included John le Carré, who was once in the Foreign Office, and the crime writer P. D. James, formerly of the Home Office.

There have been some excellent novels featuring the machinery of government. One of the first was Edgar Wallace's gripping *The Four Just Men* (1905) in which a group of conspirators set out to assassinate the Foreign Secretary, Sir Philip

Ramon. In 1964, C. P. Snow published *Corridors of Power*, a work which is highly topical today in that it concerns nuclear disarmament. Snow depicts in detail the minutiae of Whitehall power, the endless committee meetings, the subtle manoeuvring for position and the influence of senior civil servants. It is a theme explored most recently, and with rather more humour, in 'Yes, Minister' and 'Yes, Prime Minister', a series of television programmes and then books which have done much to expose the workings of government. The writers Anthony Jay and Jonathan Lynn have acknowledged their indebtedness to the *Crossman Diaries*, the first page of which supplied their title.[15]

With the Civil Service firmly installed in Whitehall and most of the private residents having left St James's the area inevitably appears rather impersonal, rather like the gentlemen's clubs which have no name-plate. The implication is that if you have to ask you shouldn't be there in the first place. Be that as it may, everyone has the right to enjoy the beauty of St James's Park.

St Paul's
and Its Environs

Amen Court, Ave Maria Lane, Dean's Court, Paternoster Row –
the street-names are enough to tell the pedestrian that he or she
is near to some major religious establishment. The baroque
cathedral of St Paul which we see today is Sir Christopher Wren's
masterpiece. It took over thirty years in the making and was paid
for by a tax levied on all coal entering the capital. Postwar tower
blocks and commercial offices mean that it does not dominate the
skyline as once it did and should, yet one can still imagine the
startling effect it must have had in the years from its completion
in 1710 until the 1950s.

The first cathedral on the site was started in the seventh century but was later destroyed by Viking invaders. The Norman St
Paul's took nearly 200 years to complete, and its size and
splendour established it as a focus for medieval London. The
bustle and vigour of city life have always flowed around it, and
sometimes through it. Much activity, for example, took place
around St Paul's Cross, which stood in the churchyard. Made of
timber and erected upon blocks of stone, the Cross was the scene
of early democratic debate about the governance of the City.
During the thirteenth century a statute laid down that 'if any
man of London neglects to attend at one of these three folkmotes,
he is to forfeit forty shillings to the King'. Thomas Carlyle once

183

described the Cross as having been 'a kind of *Times* newspaper', but it was just as much an early House of Commons and Speaker's Corner combined. Cardinal Wolsey twice burnt the works of Martin Luther here during the 1520s. St Paul's Cross was pulled down in 1643 in the course of the Civil War and not replaced. Its site is marked today by a modern column, built in 1910, with a statue of St Paul on top.

Just down the street from the cathedral is Cheapside. In the Middle Ages it was London's busiest thoroughfare, primarily because it was the City's main shopping centre. The names of the adjoining streets indicate the type of goods sold in each: Milk Street, Wood Street, Bread Street. There is also a Love Lane which branches off Wood Street; here London's medieval prostitutes gathered to ply their trade. Not surprisingly Cheapside was the venue for much medieval jollification, as Chaucer indicated in his unfinished 'The Cook's Tale' which was to have told the story of an apprentice called 'Revelling Perkin':

> For whan ther any ridyng was in Chepe,
> Out of the shoppe thider wolde he lepe –
> Til that he hadde al the sighte yseyn,
> And daunced wel, he wolde nat come ayeyn –
> And gadered him a meynee of his sort
> To hoppe and synge and maken swich disport. . . .

Chaucer's Perkin was most certainly a cockney, having been born within the sound of the Bow Bells, rung at St Mary-le-Bow on the south side of Cheapside.

Another important religious establishment, this time to the west of St Paul's, was the monastery of the Blackfriars, which had been founded on the bank of the Fleet river in the thirteenth century by the black-robed friars of the Order of St Dominic. Parliament met here on a number of occasions when Westminster Hall was out of use, including that session in 1529 when Sir Thomas More first made it clear that he would not countenance a divorce between Henry VIII and Catherine of Aragon. Blackfriars was dissolved in the 1530s; all that remains now is a small section of wall, visible in Ireland Yard. Part of the ruins housed a playhouse during the sixteenth century.[1] In 1597, James Burbage purchased a share in it, intending that his company from the Theatre in Shoreditch, soon to be transferred to the Globe in Southwark, should play here in the winter months when the audience was reluctant to visit what were then far-flung districts of London. He was unsuccessful, apparently because wealthy residents objected to the idea of a theatre in their neighbourhood. As a result Burbage's son had to let the playhouse to an altogether more respectable children's company. In 1642 the building was closed down by the Puritans. Today's Playhouse Yard marks its original site.

Quite apart from the fact that he had a part-share in the management of the Blackfriars theatre, William Shakespeare knew this district well, because from 1602 he lived in Silver Street, now subsumed into London Wall. Perhaps the nicest testament to Shakespeare lies inside what was once St Mary Aldermanbury. This church, on the north side of Love Lane, was shifted brick by brick to Fulton, Missouri, in 1965. The space left behind has now been turned into an attractive garden and it contains a memorial to John Heminge and Henry Condell, topped by a bust of Shakespeare. Heminge and Condell are hardly household names, but their contribution to the literary heritage of this country was invaluable. Both were Elizabethan actors and friends of Shakespeare, and after his death they collected his plays and published them in 1623 as the First Folio. Had they not done so, Shakespeare's works would have come down to us in incomplete form. The thirty-six plays were in one volume and cost twenty shillings. Acting companies were reluctant to allow their plays to be printed because they feared that publication would reduce the size of their audiences.

When Shakespeare lived in Silver Street he would have attended meetings of the Friday Street Club, which held gatherings at the Mermaid tavern in Bread Street, Cheapside. There he contested with Ben Jonson 'the battle of the wits'. Their near-contemporary Thomas Fuller records of these encounters that one playwright was like a 'Spanish galleon' and the other an 'English man-of-war': 'Master Jonson, like the former, was built far higher in learning; solid but slow in his performances. Shakespeare was the English man-of-war, lesser in bulk, but lighter in sailing, could turn with all tides, tack about, and take advantage of all winds, by the quickness of his wit and invention.'[2] John Keats wrote 'Lines on the Mermaid Tavern':

> *Souls of poets dead and gone,*
> *What Elysium have ye known,*

Happy field or mossy cavern,
Choicer than the Mermaid Tavern?

The Mermaid did not survive the Great Fire of 1666.

The bustle outside the cathedral was hardly less than that created by the variety of activities within. For a start everyone used the aisles as a convenient short cut to save having to walk around the churchyard. It did not matter a jot if one happened to be leading mules, horses or dogs, for they came, too. In 1554 the Common Council tried to forbid the carrying of food or the leading of animals through the cathedral, but to no avail. Fifty years later it was reported that the nave was used as 'a common passage and thoroughfare for all kinds of Burden bearing people as Colliers with sacks of coal'. Lawyers and prostitutes took up position behind specific pillars, and lotteries were held at the West Door in Elizabethan times in order to raise money for the government. The nave was a recognised sanctuary for debtors. There was even a 'Duke Humphrey's tomb' where the hungry and penniless gathered in the hope that a friend would bail them out – hence the phrase 'dining with Duke Humphrey' for being without funds.[3] The hubbub inside St Paul's has been described by contemporary writers. Thomas Dekker in *The Gull's Hornbook* of 1609 referred to 'Powle's Walk' as something of a seventeenth-century fashion show, with rival tailors fighting to display their latest creations to best advantage, and John Earle wrote of the continual noise of St Paul's 'like that of bees, a strange humming or buzz mixed with the sound of walking feet and wagging tongues; it is a kind of still roar or loud whisper. It is the great exchange of all discourse, and no business whatsoever but is here stirring and afoot. . . .'[4]

It was a turmoil with which John Donne, Dean of St Paul's from 1621 to 1631, had to contend. Donne's fiery sermons brought huge crowds both to the cathedral and to St Paul's Cross. Towards the end of his life he posed for a painting whilst wrapped in a shroud; after his death a white marble statue was produced modelled on the painting. It was one of the few items inside the cathedral which survived the Great Fire, falling through the floor into the crypt. Scorch marks can be seen around the base of the effigy, which can be seen today in the South Choir aisle.

Donne was fortunate not to see what the Puritans did to St Paul's during the English Civil War in the 1640s. The silver vessels were sold in order to make artillery, the restoration fund was plundered to pay the Parliament troops, shops were situated in the portico, ninepin bowling took place up and down the aisles, and 800 horses were stabled in the nave.[5]

In the Great Fire, St Paul's was almost completely razed to the ground. John Evelyn reported on 4 September: '. . . the stones of Paules flew like granados, the Lead melting downe the streetes in a streame, and the very pavements of them glowing with fiery rednesse, so as nor horse nor man was able to tread on them, and the demolitions had stopped all the passages, so as no help could be applied. . . .' John Dryden was pleased to see St Paul's destroyed.

> *The daring flames peep'd in, and saw from far*
> *The awful beauties of the sacred quire:*
> *But since it was profan'd by Civil war,*
> *Heaven thought it fit to have it purg'd by fire.*

Out of the ashes came Wren's St Paul's.

One group of people who suffered especially badly in the Fire of 1666 were the booksellers and publishers who had made St Paul's Churchyard the centre of London's book trade. In 1611 the Stationers' Company had moved to Ludgate Hill, which is the site of their present premises. The Company had been founded as a Brotherhood in 1403, and by 1557 the Stationers were powerful enough to be granted a royal charter. Any work published in this country until the late seventeenth century had to be passed by a court-appointed 'licenser' and afterwards checked by a warden of the Company. On payment of sixpence it was entered in a register. The book could then be sold in St Paul's Churchyard. On one occasion both licenser and warden slipped up and a Bible was passed which ordered 'Thou shalt commit adultery'. It was thereafter known as the 'Wicked Bible', and the Company was compelled to try to retrieve as many copies as possible.

Many of the booksellers in St Paul's Churchyard were also publishers. On 6 October 1645, John Milton's *Poems* was published at the Sign of the Prince's Arms. No one paid much attention to it as there was, after all, a Civil War going on. It was several years before the first edition sold out.[6] Milton had been born in 1608 at the Sign of the Spread Eagle – there were no house-numbers in London until the eighteenth century and hanging signs were the only means of identification – in Bread

Street, Cheapside. He was educated at St Paul's School, just down the road from his home, but seems to have picked up more when studying on his own. The sadistic master of St Paul's was apparently subject to 'whipping fits'. After attending Cambridge University, Milton returned to the Spread Eagle, where he lived until 1631. Later in his life, following the publication of *Paradise Lost*, sightseers came to the Spread Eagle, possibly the first ever London literary pilgrimage.

Another old boy of St Paul's School in the early seventeenth century was Samuel Pepys, who also went on to Cambridge University. Pepys later knew the churchyard well – his bookseller, Joshua Kirton, was based here. Sadly, Kirton lost everything in the Fire. After 1666 several booksellers moved further west, including Pepys's new bookseller, Mr Martin, who set up at Temple Bar in Fleet Street. Nevertheless the churchyard's link with the book trade was maintained by the number of publishers who established premises here. In 1719 a Mr John Taylor, based at the Sign of the Ship in Paternoster Row, brought out Daniel Defoe's *Robinson Crusoe*, which may be considered the first English novel. Five years later Taylor sold out to a Thomas Longman for the sum of £2282, and Longmans the publishers are still in existence. Until the Second World War, Paternoster Row was almost synonymous with publishing, although it is almost impossible to believe today as one walks around the ghastly modern buildings constructed over the badly bombed area. The only plaque in the vicinity is to John Newbery, a friend of Oliver Goldsmith who called him 'the philanthropic bookseller of St Paul's Churchyard' and portrayed him as Dr Primrose in *The Vicar of Wakefield*. Newbery was a man of great energy; Dr Johnson once satirised him as Jack Whirler: 'When he enters a house his first declaration is that he cannot sit down, and so short are his visits that he seldom appears to have come for any other reason but to say he must go.' Newbery began in St Paul's Churchyard at the Sign of the Bible and Sun, selling not just books but also patent medicines and fever powders. In 1744 he began to produce short volumes called Nursery Classics, which were the first children's books. Well illustrated and costing sixpence each, Newbery's most famous publications were *Little Goody Two-Shoes* and *Mother Goose*. He died here above the shop in 1767. It is revealing that the plaque to Newbery should have needed the Pennsylvania Library Association to erect it.

To the north of St Paul's, just by today's Barbican, was Grub Street, a small and dingy thoroughfare. Samuel Johnson in his *Dictionary* (1754) referred to it as 'a street near Moorfields, much inhabited by writers of small histories, dictionaries, and temporary poems; whence any mean production is called Grub Street'; and a Victorian critic thought that Grub Street had been responsible for 'a class of writing which was neither exalted nor pure'.[7] In other words, Grub Street was an early 'Street of Shame', a mixture of *Private Eye*, the *Sun* and the *News of the World*. The Grub Street hacks catered for the growing readership of the eighteenth century, turning out a flood of material on every conceivable subject. In his *Dunciad*, completed in 1743, Pope lashed the Grub Street writers, as did Swift and most other 'respectable' authors of the century, but there is no indication that their attacks had any effect whatsoever on sales. By the early nineteenth century the Grub Street writers, most of them in any case anonymous or writing under false names, had dispersed, and the street was renamed Milton Street – somewhat ironically in view of the fact that Milton was the very opposite of a typical Grub Street writer.[8]

Just as St Paul's was often used for a multiplicity of purposes, so, too, was the Guildhall. It was the meeting-place of the Corporation of the City of London, which wielded immense power; it was where state lotteries were drawn between 1694 and 1826; and it was also a court. Lady Jane Grey was tried at the Guildhall in the sixteenth century, as was a very different and fictional lady of the eighteenth century called Fanny Hill. It was the venue, too, for Bardell v. Pickwick in Dickens's *Pickwick Papers*. Several windows in the Guildhall have literary associations. In the North Window of the Old Library the three upper-centre lights deal with the introduction of printing to England. William Caxton can be seen showing his works to Edward IV, while his foreman, de Worde, is pulling a proof. Also present are Richard Pynson, later to be Henry VIII's printer; Bishop Coverdale, the translator of the Bible into English; John Milton and John Stow. In the crypt, which dates from 1411, the modern stained-glass windows contain the figures of Chaucer, Caxton, More, Wren and Pepys.

Not far from the Guildhall was Newgate, which was London's main prison from the thirteenth century. Its conditions were appalling; many inmates died of gaol fever and until as late as 1714 pigs could be kept inside the walls by the inmates.[9]

Amongst Newgate's occupants have been the playwright Christopher Marlowe, William Cobbett, Ben Jonson, John Gay's highwayman Captain Macheath and also Daniel Defoe, who described how Moll Flanders was born and nearly died here. One visitor to Newgate in May 1763 was James Boswell, who wrote of the cells as 'surely most dismal places': 'All this afternoon I felt myself more melancholy, Newgate being upon my mind like a black cloud.'[10]

Although the prison was demolished during the Peasants' Revolt of 1381 and again during the Gordon Riots of 1780, it was rebuilt each time. During the nineteenth century Newgate's claim to a dubious fame rested on the public executions which took place outside its walls. Originally they had been held at Tyburn, but in the 1780s the residents of now fashionable Mayfair managed to have the site changed. Crowds of up to 30,000 people would gather outside Newgate, often taking up their positions the night before. The cry of 'Hats off!' was a token not of the spectators' respect to the dead or dying but of the desire to witness every detail without obstruction. Dickens's *Oliver Twist* (1837–9) conveys the scene graphically:

> A great multitude had already assembled, the windows were filled with people, smoking and playing cards to beguile the time, the crowds were pushing, quarrelling, joking. Everything told of life and animation, but one dark cluster of objects in the centre of all – the black stage, the cross-beam, the rope and all the hideous apparatus of death.

In 1902, Newgate was demolished for good and replaced on the site by today's Old Bailey, the country's leading criminal court. A whipping-post and two interior doors from Newgate are in the Museum of London.

The Old Bailey had originally stood alongside Newgate prison, and it was there that Oscar Wilde was prosecuted in May 1895; it is described in Dickens's *A Tale of Two Cities* and Richard Hughes's *A High Wind in Jamaica*. After the move to its present site Compton Mackenzie was prosecuted there for his book *Greek Memories*, published in 1932. In disclosing details about the disastrous Dardanelles campaign of 1915 with which he had been involved he was considered to have infringed the Official Secrets Act. October to November 1960 saw the famous *Lady Chatterley's Lover* trial, after which the publishers, Penguin, were found not guilty of publishing an obscene article. Of the fictional characters portrayed here, the most famous is John Mortimer's barrister Rumpole.

Close to Newgate prison was Christ's Hospital, along with St Paul's this area's other major school. The boys of Christ's were always known as 'Bluecoats' because of the colour of their uniform. At the end of the eighteenth century this school attracted three remarkable pupils: Samuel Taylor Coleridge, Charles Lamb and Leigh Hunt. None of them enjoyed his stay here; all were horrified by the frequency of the beatings administered. Lamb, in one of the essays of Elia about Christ's Hospital, wrote of the master who 'would sometimes, with ironic deference, send to borrow a rod of the Under Master, and then, with sardonic grin, observe to one of the upper boys "how neat and fresh the twigs looked"'. The sickly Coleridge spent much of his time in the Christ's Hospital sick ward. There is a bust of Lamb at the back of St Sepulchre's church in Giltspur Street which carries an inscription calling him 'perhaps the most loved name in English literature'.

Several of Coleridge's and Lamb's contemporaries also knew the neighbourhood around St Paul's. Wordsworth, for instance, wrote 'The Reverie of Poor Susan', the country girl passing the end of Wood Street who hears a thrush singing in a tree, which reminds her of her past rural life. The tree is still there in the churchyard of what was once St Peter in Chepe, a church destroyed in the Great Fire. Soon after Wordsworth walked down Wood Street the young Charles Dickens followed, for the Cross Keys inn was where he was deposited as a boy when his family left Chatham for Dover. It was also where Pip in *Great Expectations* arrived after his journey from Rochester, returning later in the book to meet the beautiful and haughty Estella. Wood Street has changed much since Dickens's day and has little to commend it other than Wordsworth's tree and the Wood Street compter, which is still in a little backyard on the east side. Now used as a store by a wine merchant, the compter, set up in 1555, was used mainly for the incarceration of debtors. Fastidious Brisk in Ben Jonson's *Every Man Out of his Humour* (1599) is a prisoner here: 'O, master Fastidious, what a pity is it to see so sweet a man as you are in so sour a place!' The compter was closed down at the end of the eighteenth century.

'O Cheapside! Cheapside!' said I, as I advanced up that mighty thoroughfare, 'truly thou art a wonderful place for hurry, noise, and riches! Men talk of the bazaars of the East – I have never seen them – but I dare say that, compared to thee, they are poor places, silent places, abounding with empty boxes . . . a place of wonder and astonishment! – and, were it right and fitting to wish that anything should endure for ever, I would say prosperity to Cheapside, throughout all ages – may it be the world's resort for merchandise, world without end.'

George Borrow wrote these lines in *Lavengro*, published in 1851. His world without end was to last less than thirty years. With the rise of the West End and its department stores in the second half of the nineteenth century, Cheapside quickly lost its ancient role as the capital's retail centre. Schools such as St Paul's and Christ's moved out of the City, and businesses moved in. One of the largest of these was the Post Office, whose buildings then were on the east side of St Martin-le-Grand. An early employee here was Anthony Trollope, who also lived nearby.[11] He was paid £90 a year but was continually in debt, plagued by visits from his tailor demanding payment and by a girlfriend's mother demanding that he should marry her daughter. After four years of dissipation Trollope finally had a nervous breakdown in 1841. On his recovery he was sent to Ireland, a posting which proved the making of him in that it introduced him both to his future wife and to the sport of hunting, an activity which occupied much of his leisure time. The most charming feature of this part of London is Postmen's Park, tucked away off Little Britain. Under the shelter are memorials to the 'heroic self-sacrifice' of ordinary people who lost their lives trying to save those of others. Today the main post office is in King Edward Street.

The area around St Paul's was badly bombed during the Second World War, although the cathedral emerged practically un-scathed. Churches, company halls, shops were all destroyed. Whole areas, particularly around the Barbican, were razed to the ground. In particular the attempt by the Germans on 29 December 1940 to start 'a second Fire of London' led to the destruction of many publishers' offices and warehouses near St Paul's. Some 5 million volumes were lost; 25,000 books in the Guildhall Library were destroyed. The most evocative descriptions of this wasteland are in Rose Macaulay's novel *The World My Wilderness*

(1950) which tells of a young French girl, brought up in the Resistance, who lives with her father and stepmother in the Adelphi but finds the ruins of the City more friendly than grim, postwar London. Barbary and her stepbrother Raoul are out exploring one day when they discover this ruined, wild world:

> The children stood still, gazing down on a wilderness of little streets, caves and cellars, the foundations of a wrecked merchant city, grown over by green and golden fennel and ragwort, coltsfoot, purple loosestrife, rosebay willow herb, bracken, bramble and tall nettles, among which rabbits burrowed and wild cats crept and hens laid eggs.

It is all a far cry from today's drab Barbican which now stands there. Barbary and Raoul set up a base in a bombed house, explore the smashed church of St Giles, Cripplegate, and store their shoplifted goods in the derelict Barbers' Hall, until Barbary is badly injured in a fall. With its almost obsessive topographical detail, Macaulay's novel shows a world which has now been covered up and replaced — by what? Faceless modern offices which are thought suitable for Londoners of the twentieth century but which Londoners of the previous nineteen centuries would simply not have endured. Here, around St Paul's, one would give almost anything to wipe out the last hundred years and return to the atmosphere familiar to Chaucer, Pepys, Milton and Johnson.

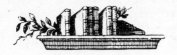

Shoreditch
and Finsbury

Ever since it was opened in 1761 the City Road has been one of London's most featureless thoroughfares. Built as the extension of the New Road (our Marylebone, Euston and Pentonville Roads), it formed in effect the first 'North Circular', allowing traffic to bypass crowded central London and yet still reach the City. Traffic pounds along it day and night, intent only on getting somewhere else as fast as possible. Surely there is little here for the London literary pilgrim? Wrong: on the west side of City Road just down from Old Street is the burial-ground called Bunhill Fields, which offers a sort of alternative or nonconformist 'Poets' Corner'. Here, within fifty yards of each other, lie the graves of John Bunyan, Daniel Defoe and William Blake, as well as that of Dr Daniel Williams, founder of one of the capital's largest and oldest libraries.

The name 'Bunhill' comes from the words Bones Hill, and the cemetery, then well out in the fields of Finsbury away from the City, was intended for the victims of the plague of 1665.[1] It was never used for this purpose, nor was it ever consecrated, prompting the nonconformists to use it as their own site. The last of the 120,000 bodies here was interred in 1854. Badly bombed in the Second World War, the northern section is now a pleasant garden. However, it is the graves in the southern end which provide the real reason for coming to Bunhill Fields. First of all there is that of John Bunyan who, although he spent most of his life in Bedford, including those years in Bedford gaol during which he wrote *The Pilgrim's Progress*, visited London on a preaching trip in 1688. The forty-mile journey had been made in teeming rain, and Bunyan, who was staying with his friend Mr Strudwick, a grocer in nearby Snow Hill, caught a chill and died.[2] His body was brought here. The tomb shows Bunyan reclining on the top, displaying the new nose which replaced the one knocked off by bomb shrapnel during the Blitz. The join can just be made out. On one side of the tomb is a panel depicting Christian from *The Pilgrim's Progress* with the burden on his back, leaning wearily on his staff; on the other side the burden has fallen away. Although Bunyan will always be associated with *The Pilgrim's Progress* and its gallery of human types who remain ever present – Mr Faintheart, Mr Facing-both-Ways, Lady Feigning, Mr Worldly-Wiseman – Bunyan wrote nearly sixty other books, including a spiritual autobiography called *Grace Abounding* which sold over 100,000 copies in his lifetime.[3]

To the north of Bunyan's grave is an obelisk marking the remains of Daniel Defoe. He was born in 1660 in Fore Street near the Barbican and must therefore as a young boy have played in the very London streets which Samuel Pepys was describing in his diary. The plague caused Daniel's father to shut up his family in the quarters above their tallow chandler's shop near the church of St Giles, Cripplegate. The family name was in fact 'Foe'; the 'De' was added later by Daniel when he began to aspire to political influence and he thought the name Foe unsuitable. From 1709, Defoe lived in Church Street in rural Stoke Newington; not in quiet enjoyment but engaged in frantic literary labour, turning out biographies, novels, pamphlets and histories.[4] In 1722 alone, at the then ripe old age of sixty-two, he produced 3000 pages of print and all in longhand. His first and most famous novel, *Robinson Crusoe*, was published in 1719 and was followed by, amongst many others, *Moll Flanders*, *Roxana* and the quasi-documentary *A Journal of the Plague Year*. As with John Bunyan, Defoe's nonconformist background gave his writings a distinctive bite and edge. In his poem *The True-Born Englishman*, for example, he pointed out that we English were 'a mongrel race':

We have been Europe's sink, the jakes where she
Voids all her offal outcast progeny.[5]

In his pamphlets Defoe can be found advocating education for women, a police force, a London University, quasi-Keynesian proposals for the government to stimulate the economy in order to provide jobs, and better street-lighting. That Defoe was so far in advance of his time is shown by his novels *Moll Flanders* and *Roxana*, both of which are presented from the heroine's point of view with perception and sympathy. His writings are clear and direct:

> If any man were to ask me what I would suppose to be a perfect style or language, I would answer that in which a man speaking to five hundred people, of all common and various capacities, idiots and lunatics excepted, should be understood by them all, and in the same sense which the speaker intended to be understood.[6]

Surely this is an approach which could profitably be adopted by many politicians, historians and academics.

The last few months of Defoe's life are shrouded in mystery. In 1730, aged seventy, he suddenly fled his Stoke Newington home – its site is our Defoe Road – and lived incognito in a little City byway called Ropemaker's Alley. Here he died in April 1731. He was buried in Bunhill Fields cemetery, even though no one was sure who he was – the gravedigger called him 'Mr Dubowe' on the stone, a sad end to a most successful and versatile career. The present obelisk was erected in 1870 by the *Christian Monitor* newspaper through funds gathered from 'the boys and girls of England'.

Five yards from Defoe a stone marks the graves of William Blake and his wife Catherine, although the exact spot of their burial in Bunhill Fields is not known. Like Defoe, Blake did not restrict his talents to a single field but made his name both as a poet and a painter. The mystical qualities of his work led many Victorians to dismiss him as insane, and it is only in the last hundred years that his reputation has been established. Nowadays his poem 'Jerusalem', which begins 'And did those feet in ancient time', is familiar as a hymn to thousands of people who have never heard of Blake.

To the east of Blake's stone, and in a part of the cemetery which is usually locked but will be opened by the park-keepers on request, lies the tomb of Dr Daniel Williams, the leading dissenter of the early eighteenth century. Williams was fortunate or shrewd enough to marry twice into money, and he used his wives' wealth to build up a substantial private library of 6000 theological volumes. He died in 1716 (and was the subject of a short biography by Defoe); in his immensely detailed forty-five-page will he directed that his library should be made open to all. The Dr Williams Library was first opened nearby in Cripplegate in 1729. It is now in Gordon Square, Bloomsbury, and is the largest library in Britain specialising in religious literature.[7]

Also buried in Bunhill Fields are a son and a son-in-law of Oliver Cromwell and various Puritan ministers whose tombstones bear some marvellous inscriptions. We learn, for instance, of John Owen, Vice-Chancellor of Oxford University under the Commonwealth, that 'The Arminian, Socinian, and Popish errors, those hydras whose contaminated breath and deadly poison infested the Church, he, with more than herculean labour, repulsed, vanquished, and destroyed'; his body 'crushed under the weight of intense and unremitting studies . . . became an incommodious mansion for the vigorous exertion of the spirit in the service of its God' – that is, he died.[8]

The fields of Finsbury and Hoxton lay well outside the boundary of the City of London and therefore outside the jurisdiction of the stern and puritanical City Fathers – a factor which was of paramount importance to a certain actor named James Burbage. The leader of the Earl of Leicester's Men, a troupe of strolling players, in 1576 Burbage decided to forsake the rigours of life on the road for the certainties of a permanent base. After borrowing £100 from his wealthy brother-in-law, a grocer called John Brayne, Burbage built the country's first ever theatre, called 'The Theatre'. It was tacked on to the back of a tavern called the George. The next year a rival playhouse called the Curtain was put up nearby. Over the next twenty years these two theatres were the home of Elizabethan drama, putting on the plays of Shakespeare and Ben Jonson amongst others. Shakespeare was a member of Burbage's troupe and lived in the actors' colony to the south of the two playhouses. In 1598, after a row with the ground landlord over the terms of the renewal of the lease, the Theatre was dismantled and its timbers moved across the river and used in a new building called the Globe.[9] The Curtain remained open until the early seventeenth century. Nothing remains today of either theatre, but a plaque on the side of 86–8

Curtain Road roughly indicates the former location of the Theatre.

A few hundred yards away in Fortune Street another plaque informs pedestrians that 'Good Master Alleyn's Fortune Theatre stood on a site near here in 1600'. Edward Alleyn spent the large sum of £550 on this playhouse, which took its name from the statue of the Goddess of Fortune that stood over its entrance. The Fortune was renowned for its special effects. An observer of 1620 recalls visiting a performance of Marlowe's *Doctor Faustus* here and seeing: 'Shagg-hayred Deuills runne roaring ouer the Stage with Squibs in their mouthes, while Drummers make Thunder in the Tyring-house, and the twelue-penny Hirelings make artificiall Lightning in the Heauens.'[10] Alleyn was so successful with the Fortune that he was able to use the profits to build Dulwich Art Gallery and a school today known as Dulwich College (since attended by the writers P. G. Wodehouse, C. S. Forester, Dennis Wheatley and Raymond Chandler). The Fortune was closed down in 1642 and demolished a few years later.

With three important theatres in the neighbourhood, Shoreditch became the actors' quarter of London. The church of St Leonard, standing at the foot of the Kingsland Road, was the first actors' church, a title now given to St Paul's, Covent Garden. Here at St Leonard's were buried James Burbage, Will Somers, formerly court jester to Henry VIII, and Richard Tarleton, Shakespeare's first fool. St Leonard's also contains a plaque erected in 1913 by the London Shakespeare League to commemorate 'the players, musicians, and other men of the theatre who are buried within the precincts of this Church'. The list includes the name of Gabriel Spencer, the actor killed fighting a duel in Hoxton Fields in 1598 with an up-and-coming playwright called Ben Jonson. No one knows the cause of the quarrel, although both men were notoriously short-tempered. Spencer was a few years younger than Jonson, he fought with a rapier ten inches longer, and yet despite managing to wound his opponent in the arm it was Jonson who killed Spencer. Jonson was immediately arrested and put in Newgate gaol. At his trial the jurors delivered a verdict that 'the aforesaid Benjamin Johnson feloniously and wilfully slew and killed the aforesaid Gabriel Spencer at Shoreditch aforesaid' – that is, murder. Tyburn beckoned to Jonson, but there was a way out. For a first offence, a guilty party could plead 'benefit of clergy', a ruse enabling literate people to secure church protection. Jonson was branded on the thumb of his left hand, so that he could not plead benefit of clergy a second time.[11] Jonson's experiences did not prevent him placing much of the action of his play *Every Man in His Humour* in Hoxton Fields. The fields themselves were swallowed up by the huge expansion of London northwards in the nineteenth century. The only reminder of this part of once rural Hoxton is the name of Bowling Green Lane, which leads off Hoxton Square.

This area of Finsbury and Shoreditch to the north of Moorgate, the seventh and last of the City gates, with its marshy, damp fields or moor, was of more interest to the young people of London who used it as a recreation ground than to builders and developers. London's first historian, William Fitzstephen, writing at the end of the twelfth century, noted that

> When the great Fen of Moor which waters the walls of the city towards the north is hard frozen, the youth in great numbers go to divert themselves on the ice. . . . They place certain bones – the leg bones of animals – under the soles of their feet, by tying them round their ankles. And then, taking a pole shod with iron into their hands, they push themselves forward by striking it against the ice, and are carried on with a velocity equal to the flight of a bird, or a bolt discharged from a cross-bow.

Nearly 500 years later Samuel Pepys recorded on 28 June 1661: 'Went to Moorfields, and there walked and stood and saw the wrestling, which I never saw much of before, between the north and west country men.' This account suggests that Moorfields was a kind of early Wembley Stadium, hosting the country's sporting events.

The year after Pepys's visit a famous literary figure, John Milton, moved to the district, into 125 Artillery (now Bunhill) Row, a road which takes its name from the HAC (Honourable Artillery Company), the military body which has been here since 1642. By then, although blind, Milton was hard at work on *Paradise Lost*, which like his *Poems* was published to very little public or critical interest – the first edition of just 1300 copies took two years to sell out.[12] Number 125 Artillery Row was only a two-room house, and much of Milton's private library had had to be sold off before the move here. At least there was the consolation of Hoxton Fields a few hundred yards to the north in which Milton's third wife took him for long walks. In September 1666, Milton would have heard the thousands of refugees fleeing the Great Fire and passing his door on the way to Hoxton Fields where they camped out. Milton died in Artillery Row in November 1674 and was buried beside his father in St Giles, Cripplegate, the same church in which the young Daniel Foe had been baptised a few years before. A stone in the aisle marks Milton's grave, although quite how much of his remains are in fact underneath is debatable since in the late eighteenth century his body was dug up by fortune-hunters and bits sold off as relics.[13] Number 125 Bunhill Row is now covered by characterless modern buildings.

By the early eighteenth century the Moorfields were being built on and over – today the garden in the centre of Finsbury Circus is all that survives of the area's ancient greenery. In 1739, John Wesley took over a former gun foundry near to Old Street and not far from his old school, Charterhouse, which he had attended between 1714 and 1720, displaying even while a student a fierce determination.[14] Obeying his father's instructions, and despite his schoolfellows' ridicule, the young Wesley used to run around the playground three times each morning in order to keep fit. Wesley's preaching at the gun foundry often attracted crowds of up to 10,000 people, and his success enabled him to build New Chapel in 1778, living close to it in a house which is now a museum. Wesley was best known for his open-air preaching, but his literary labours were also prodigious, as one historian has pointed out:

> From then [1733] until his death in March 1791 Wesley and his brother Charles issued some 450 literary works, which passed through about 2,000 editions. These averaged 2,000 copies each, so that during their lifetimes they published over four million items, not to speak of millions more administrative documents: class-tickets, class-lists, band-tickets, advertisements, book-catalogues, publishing proposals, preaching-plans, itineraries, circular letters, only scattered examples of which have survived – a grand total of at least ten million printed items.[15]

In addition, John Wesley kept a journal for over fifty years. From 1778 this Wesleyan tide of printing was carried out at the New Chapel. Wesley's grave lies at the back of the chapel in a quiet little garden.

Wesley's New Chapel also sold Methodist literature, but members of the public who wanted a wider range of material still came to Finsbury in order to use 'The Temple of the Muses'. This bookshop was situated in the south-east corner of Finsbury Square and was founded by James Lackington in 1778, the same year in which the New Chapel opened its doors for the first time. Lackington had come to London from the West Country five years before, initially running a bookstall which doubled as a shoemaker's shop. He then borrowed £5 from 'Mr Wesley's people' and concentrated exclusively on bookselling. The Temple of the Muses had an enormous frontage of 140 feet and a dome on which a flag flew whenever Mr Lackington was present. Inside, the middle of the shop contained a large circular counter – Lackington once won a bet that a coach and four could be driven around it – with 'lounging rooms' upstairs. The galleries became increasingly shabby the higher the potential customer went. Lackington was perhaps London's first modern bookseller and was well aware of the benefits of publicity: he once offered to pay for the erection of a statue outside in Finsbury Square as long as it was of himself! He also issued the first ever catalogues, the first being issued in 1779 and listing 12,000 books, all of which were described by Lackington himself. It is a nice thought that perhaps one of the Temple's browsers was the young John Keats, who was born in 1795 at the Swan and Hoops stable in Finsbury Pavement, only a few hundred yards away, where his father was the ostler. Sadly the Temple of the Muses was burnt down early in the nineteenth century, and no plaque or memorial of any kind remains behind to liven up our dull Finsbury Square, although there is a Lackington Street nearby.[16]

By the early nineteenth century the continuing expansion of London led to the rapid development of Finsbury and Shoreditch. The population of Shoreditch doubled from 1800 to 1830 and then doubled again in the next thirty years. The district became run-down and poverty-stricken, the City Road full of pawnshops; hence the nursery rhyme:

> *Up and down the City Road,*
> *In and out the Eagle,*
> *That's the way the money goes,*
> *Pop goes the weasel.*

The Eagle was a famous pleasure resort along the City Road, and popping or pawning the weasel or silver plate was often the consequence of an evening's revels here. One group of fictional characters who knew the road's pawnshops were Dickens's Micawber family, who lived at Windsor Terrace, City Road. Mr Micawber directs David Copperfield to this out-of-the-way spot:

> Under the impression . . . that you might have some difficulty in penetrating the arcana of the Modern Babylon in the direction of the City Road – in short that you might lose yourself – I shall be happy to call this evening and instal you in the knowledge of the nearest way.

David arrives to find that

> The centre of the street-door was perfectly covered with a great brass plate, on which was engraved 'Mrs Micawber's Boarding Establishment for Young Ladies' but I never found that any young lady had ever been to school there; or that any young lady ever came, or proposed to come; or that the least preparation was ever made to receive any young lady. The only visitors I ever saw or heard of were creditors. They used to come at all hours, and some of them were quite ferocious.

Almost immediately David is called upon to dispose of the Micawbers' more portable articles of property at various stalls in the City Road. For once, something does fail to turn up, and the Micawbers leave Windsor Terrace bound for the King's Bench debtors' prison. At least Windsor Terrace still stands and, what is more, the road at its north end has been renamed Micawber Street.

Dickens also wrote a factual account of one of Shoreditch's most popular Victorian institutions, the Britannia Theatre, which stood on the west side of Hoxton Street. Run by Sam and then Sara Lane for nearly sixty years until Sara's death in 1899, 'the Brit' held nearly 5000 spectators – substantially more than the theatres at Covent Garden and Drury Lane – and was famed for its annual pantomimes and its exciting melodramas. Dickens described the Brit in both *Sketches by Boz* and *The Uncommercial Traveller*. In the latter piece he praised the theatre's lighting, ventilation, the general decorum of the audience and also the moral qualities of the plays themselves:

> Throughout the evening, I was pleased to observe Virtue quite as triumphant as she usually is out of doors, and indeed I

thought rather more so. We all agreed (for the time) that honesty was the best policy, and we were as hard as iron upon Vice, and we wouldn't hear of Villainy getting on in the world – no, not on any consideration whatever.

In the early years of this century the Brit became a cinema until it was destroyed by German bombing in 1940. A trip to 188 Hoxton Street today reveals modern flats but not a single reminder of one of London's best-loved theatres.[17]

One reason for the success of the Brit was that it offered a warmth and gaiety absent from the lives of many who lived in Victorian Shoreditch. A census of Hoxton – a part of Shoreditch – in 1881 revealed that its 6463 houses contained 57,954 people, that is, nine people living in each house, the dwellings themselves often being no more than small tenement buildings. Charles Booth in his monumental seventeen-volume *Life and Labour of the People of London* published at the end of the nineteenth century, referred to Hoxton as the leading criminal quarter in England. This criminality was particularly rife in 'the Old Nichol', the streets wedged between Hackney Road and Bethnal Green Road. It was this neighbourhood which Arthur Morrison called 'the Jago' and wrote about in his novel *A Child of the Jago* (1896).

Morrison had been born and brought up in the East End, and he also conducted firsthand research into the district, as he wrote in the preface to the third edition of the book:

It was my fate to encounter a place in Shoreditch, where children were born and reared in circumstances which gave them no reasonable chance of living decent lives: where they were born fore-damned to a criminal or semi-criminal career. It was my experience to learn the ways of this place, to know its inhabitants, to talk with them, eat, drink, and work with them.

Morrison combined this research with the ability to create living characters, so that the novel is much more than a social document. It is sad – the Perrott family are slowly dragged down by the influence of the Jago, and at the end the father Josh is hanged for the murder of a crooked receiver of stolen goods and little Dicky is stabbed in a street-fight – but the book lacks the cloying sentimentality of many nineteenth-century novels. In the same year that *A Child of the Jago* was published, the Nichol was cleared by the new London County Council and replaced by Arnold Circus, which still stands with its small garden and bandstand surrounded by what now seem rather grim blocks of flats.

Today Finsbury is crammed full of commercial businesses and featureless office blocks which are far removed from the stuff of literature. Only Bunhill Fields and Wesley's House and Museum offer a respite from the monotony. On the other side of Old Street, however, there is more of interest, in particular the attractive Hoxton Square. At 64B High Street is Hoxton Hall, opened in 1863 as a music-hall. Now a community centre, Hoxton Hall has retained its two balconies and intimate friendly atmosphere redolent of its origins.[18] But it is the excellent Geffrye Museum of Furniture in Kingsland Road, housed in early-eighteenth-century almshouses, which offers a glimpse of once rural Shoreditch, a pleasant neighbourhood to which Samuel Pepys returned in May 1667 for the first time since his boyhood:

> . . . and so my wife and I away and by coach to Islington, it being a fine day, and thence to Sir G. Whitmore's house, where we light and walked over the fields to Kingsland and back again, a walk I think I have not taken these twenty years but puts me in mind of my boy's time, when I boarded at Kingsland and used to shoot with my bow and arrows in these fields. A very pretty place it is. . . .

The fields have gone, but in the little garden beside the Geffrye Museum only the dullest of imaginations will not be able to conjure up pictures of the little Samuel Pepys hard at play, with the same enthusiasm and energy that he displayed throughout his life.

Soho
and Leicester Square

'Untidy, full of Greeks, Ishmaelites, cats, Italians, tomatoes, restaurants, organs, coloured stuffs, queer names . . . it dwells remote from the British body politic.' John Galsworthy's description in *The Forsyte Saga* of Soho at the end of the nineteenth century brings out the wonderful variety of this central London district. Here, in the space of a few yards, one can be accosted by a streetwalker, pass several peepshows and yet also shop in Great Windmill Street at the House of Floris, confectioners to HM Queen Elizabeth the Queen Mother.

For many people Soho is identified with sex and the seedy little shops which are present in virtually every street, and for some this reaction means that the other pleasures of Soho remain unknown. In P. D. James's *Unnatural Causes* (1967) Inspector Adam Dalgleish visits the area:

> Passing through the strip clubs, the grubby basement stairs, the silhouettes of bored girls against the upstairs window blinds, Dalgleish thought that a daily walk through these ugly streets could drive any man into a monastery, less from sexual disgust than from an intolerable ennui with the sameness, the joylessness of lust.

Twenty years after P. D. James's novel Westminster Council are now making determined attempts to close most of the sex shops, and, if they are successful, Soho may once again become one of the most sought-after addresses in London. Much of its charm derives from the fact that it retains its traditional street-pattern. Most of the streets date from the seventeenth or early eighteenth century, and a surprising number of old buildings remain. The two new roads, Shaftesbury Avenue and Charing Cross Road, were constructed in the 1880s. The narrowness of the old thoroughfares means that pedestrians have to keep a vigilant eye on the traffic, but the unexpected delights of encountering the tiny Meard and Peter Streets or the bustling Berwick Street market are more than adequate compensation.

Until the seventeenth century the area was little more than fields and countryside. Henry VIII once hunted here, and the name 'So-Ho' derives from the call used to draw off the hounds. Like Leicester Fields further to the south, the vicinity was ideal for duels such as that described by Thackeray in his historical novel *Henry Esmond*. After the Restoration in 1660 several noblemen began to build themselves large houses in the neighbourhood, the most palatial being that of the Duke of Monmouth, which occupied the south side of Soho Square. It was from here that Monmouth departed in 1685 on his attempted rebellion against his uncle James II, an uprising which proved fatal to him – he was executed on Tower Hill – and almost fatal to the man who later became one of England's greatest writers, Daniel Defoe. The strongly Protestant Defoe rode down from London to the West Country in order to join the Duke's revolt. He was present at the battle of Sedgemoor, but luckily for him the battle was fought in a dense fog and Defoe was able to slip away before the end, thus being spared the justice dispensed by Judge Jeffreys at the 'Bloody Assizes'.[1] The Monmouth rising was well portrayed by Sir Arthur Conan Doyle in his novel *Micah Clarke*.

Despite Monmouth's downfall Soho remained a fashionable area, particularly around Soho Square – then called King Square, after Charles II, whose statue stands in the garden. The diarist John Evelyn and his family wintered in 'the great Square' in 1689–90,[2] and as late as 1715 five lords still owned mansions in the neighbourhood.[3] But Soho was too near to the City to retain its fashionableness for long, and the aristocracy began to drift further west. None of their houses survives, apart from the House of St Barnabas which stands at the top of Greek Street. Built in the 1740s, it still contains some beautiful plasterwork, a fine decorated ceiling in the council chamber and a 'crinoline' staircase for the benefit of the ladies. Now a house of charity for distressed women in London, the little garden contains a bench commemorating the late Joyce Grenfell, a benefactor of St Barnabas. The house and chapel are open to visitors on Wednesday afternoons and Thursday mornings. It is a visit not to be missed.

Other than the House of St Barnabas, Soho's grand buildings were split up into multiple dwellings, ideal for two groups of people who could only afford cheap residences. The first were the waves of immigrants who have often made Soho their home. Evidence of one nationality is clear in the name 'Greek Street'. Two other groups still have churches in Soho Square: there is a French Protestant church on the north side, while the Roman Catholic St Patrick's was built for the Irish community.

From the eighteenth century the second group, artists and writers, seems to have been drawn irresistibly to the area, intrigued perhaps by its raffish air and cosmopolitan society. In 1764, Casanova stayed in Greek Street, a period of his life when he was beset by money troubles. Casanova, along with Mao Tse-Tung one of the world's unlikeliest former librarians, was later to publish an extremely boring twelve-volume autobiography called *Mémoires* in which his leapings into and out of bed soon take on 'the joylessness of lust' which Adam Dalgleish would have recognised. More interesting is the fact that, while Casanova was in Greek Street, Samuel Johnson started 'The Club' at the Turk's Head only a few houses away. Johnson was an inveterate frequenter of taverns – nothing, he said, 'has yet been contrived by man, by which so much happiness is produced as by a good tavern or inn' – and The Club seems to have met every Monday evening at 7 o'clock primarily to hear him talk. Edmund Burke and Oliver Goldsmith were amongst the original members, while David Garrick and James Boswell were admitted later. After a few years The Club moved from the Turk's Head in Greek Street to the Turk's Head at 9 Gerrard Street, the same street in which the poet John Dryden had lived for the last years of his life. Sadly, nothing remains of either Turk's Head.[4]

Even if Soho Square had lost its noble tenants, many of them returned in the 1760s and 1770s in order to visit the assembly rooms opened by a Mrs Cornelys on the east side of the square. Formerly a Viennese opera singer and one of Casanova's conquests (so he said), Mrs Cornelys offered the sort of entertainment normally put on at Ranelagh and Vauxhall pleasure gardens, but with the added attraction that, since the festivities took place inside, the English climate was not a factor. Horace Walpole attended a masque here in 1770, and Laurence Sterne, author of *Tristram Shandy*, was also a visitor. Fanny Burney went in 1770, but was disappointed not so much by the décor of the place as by the fact that the rest of London was there, too, and the assembly rooms were dreadfully overcrowded. Dickens in *Barnaby Rudge* sends Emma to Mrs Cornelys's. Unfortunately for Mrs Cornelys, a host of imitators soon sprang up, and she responded to the competition by presenting ever more risqué entertainment. Eventually she was indicted for keeping 'a disorderly house' and ended up in prison. Her assembly rooms were closed and then demolished. Mrs Cornelys enjoyed mixed fortunes on her release but still died penniless in the Fleet prison in 1797, a woman of spirit and courage who deserves to be much better known.[5]

Charles Dickens set much of his historical novel *A Tale of Two Cities* in the Soho of the 1780s, remarking upon its 'country airs'. A plane tree in the garden of the House of St Barnabas is pointed out as 'Dickens's Tree', as is an old mulberry tree – the sole survivor of those planted by the French Huguenots 300 years ago. Among other writers who actually resided in Soho at the turn of the eighteenth century was William Blake, born in 1757 in Marshall Street. His birthplace is now covered by an ugly modern office block, but at least it is called William Blake House. He later set up a printshop at 28 Poland Street with his brother before starting up on his own at 27 Broad Street in 1784. Thomas De Quincey ran away from school at seventeen and lived on his own in the derelict 61 Greek Street, serenaded by 'the noise of the rats'. He was later taken ill in Oxford Street and helped into Soho Square to recover by a street prostitute called Ann who was to befriend him. De Quincey later returned to Oxford Street, and it was from the chemist then at number 173 that he first began to buy opium, a step which resulted in *Confessions of an Opium Eater*, published in 1822. By this time Shelley had passed briefly through Soho, living at 15 Poland Street in 1811 after he had been sent down from Oxford for his part in the publication of a pamphlet called *The Necessity of Atheism.*

Another Soho resident who offended Victorian sensibilities was William Hazlitt. Although now not as well known as the others, Hazlitt was an excellent and outspoken critic. His pugnacious writings on almost every subject punctured many an inflated reputation. The generous John Keats called Hazlitt 'your only good damner, and if ever I am damn'd – damn me if I shouldn't like him to damn me'. Contrast this with the attitude of crabby old Wordsworth, who wrote to a friend: 'The miscreant Hazlitt continues, so I have heard, to abuse Southey, Coleridge and myself in *The Examiner* [Hazlitt's journal]. I hope you do not associate with the fellow, he is not a proper person to be admitted into respectable society.' Hazlitt once fell heavily in love with his landlady's daughter, a girl called Sarah Walker, and being Hazlitt the book he wrote about his feelings, *Liber Amoris*, lacked nothing in frankness. It was on account of this work that the Victorians quietly ignored the rest of Hazlitt's writings: Robert Louis Stevenson, for example, gave up his plan to write a biography of Hazlitt after he had read *Liber Amoris*.[6] Hazlitt died at 6 Frith Street in 1830, his end apparently hastened by excessive tea-drinking. Charles Lamb was there at his deathbed, and Hazlitt's last words were 'Well, I have had a happy life'. He was buried at St Anne's, Soho, and his tombstone is still visible beneath the tower.

In fact this tower is all that remains of the seventeenth-century church, possibly built by Sir Christopher Wren, intended for Soho's growing population. As the district expanded, so did the number of corpses requiring disposal. After 10,000 of them had been buried in the churchyard a halt had to be called. This explains why the garden is several feet higher than the street-level. The church was bombed in 1940 and only the tower, which is in any case a later addition, survived. In 1976, Sir John Betjeman launched an appeal with these words:

> High up in the air two barrels interlock
> To form the faces of this famous clock.
> Reduced to drawing-room size this clock would be
> A Paris ornament of 1803.
> Let's make it go again, let London know
> That life and heart and hope are in Soho.

The clock is now going again. Dorothy L. Sayers, the detective novelist, was a churchwarden at St Anne's, and when she died in December 1957 her ashes were scattered underneath the tower.[7] One other notable literary figure associated with St Anne's is David Williams, buried here in 1816. Clergyman and historian, Williams was the founder of the Royal Literary Fund set up to help 'Distressed Talents', and many writers have had cause to be grateful to him.

In the Victorian period both Soho and Leicester Square deteriorated rapidly. By 1851 there was an average of 327 inhabitants living on each acre of Soho, and such overcrowding formed a natural breeding-ground for cholera.[8] Michael Sadleir in his well-researched novel about Victorian London, *Fanny by Gaslight*, called Leicester Square 'London's most . . . dissipated district', and John Fowles in *The French Lieutenant's Woman* mentions the enormous number of prostitutes who made themselves available nearby along the Haymarket and in neighbouring streets. The cheapness of the district brought in a fresh group of immigrants – in this case the political refugees exiled from their own countries. The most famous of them all, Karl Marx, lived with his wife Jenny, maidservant Helene Demuth and three children in a two-room flat at 28 Dean Street between 1850 and 1856 (the GLC plaque gives a wrong date). Three more of the Marxes' children died here, and on one occasion the penniless Karl was reduced to begging money from acquaintances in order to pay for a coffin.[9] The British Museum was conveniently near, 'where I am most often from 9 in the morning until 7 in the evening', working on what was to become the three-volume *Das Kapital*, a work much known but little read. In 1856 a family legacy and extra financial help from their ever-faithful friend Engels enabled the family to move away to the more salubrious Kentish Town. Ironically in view of the Marx family's poverty, 28 Dean Street is currently occupied by a very expensive Italian restaurant. The political refugees have now gone, but the atmosphere of Soho at this time, with its perpetual gloom and poverty, has been captured for us by Joseph Conrad in *The Secret Agent* (1907).

Not all of Victorian Soho was dingy and tatty. The unpleasant and wealthy uncle Ralph Nickleby in Dickens's novel lives in Golden Square. The gardens of this square contain a statue of George II in incongruous Roman toga, 'the guardian genius of a little wilderness of shrubs'. The shrubs have gone: the garden was dug up in the Second World War and used as an air-raid shelter.

Mr Jaggers in *Great Expectations* lives in Gerrard Street, his house remarkable above all for its dirty windows.

By the late nineteenth century the district was beginning to establish a reputation for something other than its poverty and overcrowding. The growth of the eating-out habit led to an upsurge in the number of restaurants, and Soho became famous for its food. Most of these establishments set up then have long since shut down, but one remains. Kettner's, founded in 1868 by a French chef of that name, is still in Romilly Street and continues to serve food with a style and elegance which explain why it was Oscar Wilde's favourite restaurant.

As for Leicester Square, its reputation centred on the provision of live entertainment, especially its music-halls. The most famous was the Empire, opened in 1887 and much patronised by vigorous young men about town, attracted as much by the young women parading inside as by the entertainment on stage. In the 1890s a Mrs Ormiston Chant led a campaign for the erection of screens in order to shut off the offending walkways from the bar. The opposition to this move was led by a young man from Sandhurst who was later to become this century's best-selling historian and much else besides, Winston Churchill. One Saturday night a crowd demolished the screens, and in *My Early Life* Churchill describes making his maiden public speech amid the debris before 'we all sallied out into the Square brandishing fragments of wood and canvas as trophies or symbols. It reminded me of the death of Julius Caesar when the conspirators rushed forth into the streets waving the bloody daggers with which they had slain the tyrant. I thought also of the taking of the Bastille' – evidence at any early stage of Churchill's lively historical imagination. Unfortunately for Churchill and his friends, the barricades at the Empire were later rebuilt in brick. Two years before Churchill pulled down the screens Thomas Hardy also went to the Empire, but he complained not about the prostitutes in the auditorium but rather about the physical condition of the girls on stage: 'The dancing-girls are nearly all skeletons. One can see drawn lines and puckers in their young flesh. They should be penned and fattened for a month to round out their beauty.'[10]

Apart from the Empire there were also several playhouses built along Shaftesbury Avenue and Charing Cross Road, and the architect Frank Matcham designed the sumptuous Hippodrome in 1900, followed by the London Palladium in 1910. By this time the gardens in the middle of the square bore the statue of William Shakespeare, who in fact had no known connection with this area. A small bust of him – minus the hand lost during the Blitz – also looks out over Carnaby Street, from the corner of the Shakespeare's Head pub. In 1981, Charlie Chaplin was added to Leicester Square's statuary. Ever since the interwar period Leicester Square's music-halls have been cinemas.

Apart from Winston Churchill, another young man enjoyed living it up in Leicester Square, namely Bertie Wooster, who made a point of pinching a policeman's helmet every Boat Race night. Unfortunately in P. G. Wodehouse's *The Code of the Woosters*, owing to an excess of drink, Bertie forgot to give the necessary forward push to eject the policeman first, and he was 'pinched'. Bertie also came to the Alhambra music-hall in Leicester Square to listen to Ben Bloom and his Sixteen Baltimore Buddies, an experience which leads him in *Thank You, Jeeves* to take up the banjo with such cacophonous results that Jeeves temporarily resigns.

Soho and Leicester Square were also famous for their bookshops, as they had been ever since the Victorian age when Lamb, Macaulay and Gladstone were among the many who delved into the secondhand stalls in Wardour Street.[11] In this century the bookshops have catered for every taste, from the revolutionary to the recherché. Henderson's 'Bomb Shop' in Charing Cross Road, for example, was stuffed full of socialist and anarchist literature and run by a father and son who both sported huge red ties. Foyle's is perhaps the district's most famous bookshop – here Noël Coward came across and purchased several old bound volumes of the *Illustrated London News*, using them as the inspiration for his very successful musical *Cavalcade* in 1931.[12] Michael in David Lodge's *How Far Can You Go?* seems to have spent much of his student days in the 1950s loitering around outside bookshops offering more salacious material. This kind of bookshop was far removed from the decent respectability of the now world-renowned Marks & Co., which was situated at 84 Charing Cross Road, as everyone who has read Helene Hanff's book of that name will know. By the time Miss Hanff made it to London in 1971 Frank Doel, her correspondent for over twenty years, was dead, and the shop itself had closed down. Miss Hanff describes Charing Cross Road as 'a narrow, honky-tonky street, choked with traffic, lined with second-hand bookshops'. Fifteen years on, the traffic is still too obviously there, but the bookshops have been much reduced in number. Some of the decline in reading can no doubt be traced back to an invention which was pioneered in Soho: in January 1926, John Logie Baird gave the first public demonstration of television in the attic of 22 Frith Street. Also in decline has been Carnaby Street, which although still there is only a shadow of its former 'swinging' self. Novels yet to be written about the 1960s will struggle to convey its former vitality and energy. The Café Royal in Regent Street has also changed dramatically, so much so that its habituées of the past, such as Oscar Wilde and Compton Mackenzie, would barely recognise it. Cambridge Circus – 'The Circus' of John le Carré novels – has been redesigned.

Yet Soho goes on. Chinese immigrants have taken the place of the Greeks, French and Irish before them, and the street-signs around Lisle Street and Gerrard Street are now bilingual. The Chinese keep themselves to themselves, which makes Timothy Mo's excellent novel *Sour Sweet* (1982) all the more of an eye-opener, with its portrait of English life as seen through foreign eyes. Chen works in the Ho Ho, a Chinese restaurant off Gerrard Street:

> The waiters often held impromptu discussions, when the boss was on another floor, about the various idiosyncrasies of their hosts and patrons, the English. Among these eccentricities was the strange and widespread habit of not paying bills, a practice so prevalent as to arouse suspicions it was a national sport and which involved even the most respectable-looking of customers. Loud and rowdy behaviour was more comprehensible, including fencing with chopsticks and wearing inverted rice-bowls on the head like brittle skull-caps, writing odd things on the lavatory walls, and mixing the food on their plates in a disgusting way before putting soya sauce on everything.

Apart from the Chinese restaurants, Soho also contains many other well-known eating-places such as the Gay Hussar and L'Escargot; pubs such as the Coach and Horses, made famous by Jeffrey Bernard in his 'Low Life' articles in the *Spectator*; and clubs like Groucho's, much patronised by writers. As John Galsworthy wrote, Soho may be 'untidy', but that is its charm. Long may its teeming variety defy neat conventions and categories and the 'high life' meet the 'low life'.

Southwark
and Bankside

Bifil that in that seson on a day,
In Southwerk at the Tabard as I lay
Redy to wenden on my pilgrymage
To Caunterbury with ful devout corage,
At nyght was come into that hostelrye
Wel nyne and twenty in a compaignye,
Of sondry folk, by aventure yfalle
In felawshipe, and pilgrimes were they alle,
That toward Caunterbury wolden ryde. . . .

Chaucer's twenty-nine pilgrims set out from the Tabard inn, which stood on the east side of Borough High Street. Accompanied by the Tabard's host, Harry Baily, the pilgrims agree to tell two stories each on their way to Becket's shrine at Canterbury and two more on the journey back. The prize for the best story was to have been a free supper at the Tabard, but Chaucer never finished the work. However, in the figures of the Miller, the Prioress, the Knight, the Wife of Bath and the rest of the company, Chaucer's pilgrims provide not just a vivid and exciting picture of England in the fourteenth century but a portrait of human nature recognisable to the twentieth century and all the ages between. As the seventeenth-century poet John

215

Dryden exclaimed of *The Canterbury Tales*, 'Here is God's plenty!' The Chaucer window in nearby Southwark Cathedral depicts the pilgrims setting off on their journey.

One of the notable things about Chaucer's pilgrims is that, despite widely differing backgrounds, they all mingle together in the fellowship of tavern life, just as in Langland's contemporary poem *Piers Plowman* harlots, hermits, tinkers and hangmen drink together. Borough High Street was chockfull of taverns and inns, catering for the hordes of travellers who made their way up the Old Kent Road and then the Borough High Street itself on their way to London Bridge, which for centuries was the only permanent crossing over the Thames. Chaucer tells us that not the least of Southwark's attractions was its renowned ale:

> *The nappy strong ale of South worke*
> *Keep many a gossip from the Kirke [church].*

The bulk of London's residential quarter was on the north side of the river, but by the Middle Ages there was a substantial settlement in Southwark, where much of the land was owned by the Bishops of Winchester. The evidence of their piety remains with Southwark Cathedral, now tucked away between London Bridge and Borough Market, as well as being overlooked by a railway line. Originally founded in 1106 as St Mary Overie (or over the water), it contains the effigy of another famous fourteenth-century writer, John Gower. Shown dressed in contemporary costume, Gower's head rests on his three most famous books and his dog lies at his feet. Gower's *Confessio Amantis* is, like *The Canterbury Tales*, a patchwork of individual stories, in this case 141 of them. Gower's substantial contribution to the rebuilding of the cathedral in 1400 was rewarded by this large memorial.[1]

Of the less than holy activities carried on in this area with the tacit approval of the bishops, nothing now remains. There were 'stews' or brothels on Bankside here from the twelfth century. Most of the girls were imported from France and Holland, being referred to as 'Winchester geese' because of the bishops' ownership of the land. The bishops also ran their own private prison or 'Clink' which was just beside the Thames. The cells were always damp and extremely unhealthy. The Clink prison was destroyed during the Gordon Riots in 1780 and not rebuilt, although memory of it lives on in the name Clink Street and our expression 'to be in the clink'. The Bishops' Palace has also been demolished, the only surviving fragment being a charming fourteenth-century Rose Window which is hidden away amongst tall office blocks. The tiny Cardinal's Cap Alley was once notorious for its brothels.

The inns and brothels were only some of the various amusements which made Southwark the entertainment centre of London until the seventeenth century. On 28 July 1598 the City authorities sent a letter to the Privy Council which condemned 'the common exercise of stage plays' containing

> nothing but profane fables, lascivious matters, cozening devices, and scurrilous behaviours, which are so set forth as that they move wholly to invitation and not to the avoiding of those faults and vices which they represent. Among other inconveniences it is not the least that they give opportunity to the refuse sort of evil-disposed and ungodly people that are within and about this city to assemble themselves and to make their matches for all their lewd and ungodly practices. . . .[2]

The City authorities failed, but the players were always careful to locate themselves outside the jurisdiction of the City Fathers. The first two London theatres were in Shoreditch, the most famous being the Theatre, which was set up by James Burbage in 1576. By 1598, however, friction between the company and the ground landlord led the actors to take apart their wooden building, transport it over London Bridge, and to use the timber to form the seats of the new playhouse they called the Globe and which opened in the spring of 1599. It was not the first such building in this neighbourhood, as the Rose theatre had opened in 1587, and the Bear Gardens just down the street had been in business since about 1550.

Bankside was an ideal spot for the players, particularly since Henry VIII had closed down the brothels in 1546, thereby allowing the theatres room to expand their buildings. The fame of the Globe of course derives largely from Shakespeare's involvement with it, many of his tragedies being first performed here with James Burbage's son Richard in the leading parts. In June 1613 this first Globe was burnt down during a performance of Shakespeare's *Henry VIII*; fortunately for history, Sir Henry Wotton was an eyewitness to the disaster. There had been a scene in which the king arrives at Cardinal Wolsey's home:

. . . certain chambers [cannons] being shot off at his entry, some of the paper, or other stuff, wherewith one of them was stopped, did light on the thatch, where being thought at first but an idle smoke, and their eyes more attentive to the show, it kindled inwardly, and ran round like a train, consuming within less than an hour the whole house to the very grounds . . . nothing did perish but wood and straw, and a few forsaken cloaks; only one man had his breeches set on fire, that would perhaps have broiled him, if he had not by the benefit of a provident wit put it out with bottle ale.[3]

The Globe was rebuilt on a much grander scale, some contemporaries estimating that it could hold 3000 spectators. As at all the public playhouses, the audiences were volatile, lively and excitable. In 1602 hundreds of spectators turned up at the Swan (which had been built near today's Hopton Street) for a play called *England's Joy*. In fact they were the victims of a hoax perpetrated by a Richard Venner, who fled with the takings, although he was later caught. No matter: the frustrated audience 'revenged themselves upon the han(g)ings, curtains, chairs and stools, walls and whatever came in their way'.[4] The Globe, like most of London's theatres, fell a victim to the Civil War – London was controlled by the Parliament forces, who quickly closed down the playhouses, fearing that they might be used as mouthpieces for Royalist propaganda. It is commemorated by a large bronze memorial on a wall in Park Street near Southwark Bridge, while the Rose is remembered in the name Rose Alley. The Bear Garden Museum nearby, now being transformed into the Bankside Museum, deals with the history of the area and its theatres, and there is a statue of Shakespeare in Southwark Cathedral together with a Shakespeare Window. Sam Wanamaker, the American producer and actor, is in the throes of building a replica of the Globe just to the west of Emerson Street.

One of the first Shakespeare plays performed at the Globe was *Henry VI, Part Two*, which covers along with much else the rebellion led by Jack Cade in 1450. Cade and an army of several thousand men marched on London in June 1450, demanding the redress of several grievances. He established his headquarters at the White Hart in Borough High Street and effectively held the capital for several days until the authorities rallied their troops and a ferocious battle on London Bridge led to his defeat. Cade was captured and then quartered. In *Henry VI*, Shakespeare, never very sympathetic to rebels, portrays Cade as a ruffian and his followers as a rabble or, in the words of Stafford, 'rebellious hinds'. In fact, as the chronicler Hall pointed out, when Cade was stationed at the White Hart in Southwark he prohibited 'to all men murder, rape or robbery; by which colour he allured to him all the hartes of the common people'. Cade's rebellion should be as well known as that of Wat Tyler sixty-nine years before.[5]

The bustle and vigour of Southwark life was reflected in both the Borough Market, held out in the throughfare until the 1750s when it was moved off the road to where the market buildings now stand south of the Cathedral, and in Southwark Fair. This annual event was held every September from the middle of the fifteenth century. Like the market it was held in Borough High Street, and the congestion, traffic jams and subsequent bad temper generated must have been quite a sight. Samuel Pepys saw a puppet show at the fair in 1668 featuring Dick Whittington, while John Evelyn reported in his diary that a booth was temporarily suppressed in 1693 because an earthquake in Jamaica 'being prophanely and Ludicrously represented in a puppet play or some such lewd pass-time in the Faire at Southwarke, caused the Queene to put-downe and abolish that idle and vicious mock-shew'.[6] The most vivid portrayal of the fair was provided by William Hogarth in his painting 'Southwark Fair' of 1733. The fair finally came to an end in 1762.

At the time Hogarth executed his painting a new institution had only recently opened in Southwark. This was Guy's Hospital, which had begun to admit patients from 1725. The founder of the hospital, Thomas Guy, the son of a Thames lighterman, had been born in the neighbourhood in 1645. He was apprenticed to a bookseller before setting up his own business, and made a fortune from the sale of Bibles and the publications of the Oxford University Press. He was also one of the very few investors who made money out of the South Sea Bubble – for example, his near-namesake, the poet and dramatist John Gay, lost nearly everything he owned. Having become a governor of the nearby St Thomas's Hospital, which had grown out of the cathedral, Guy decided in 1722 to found another such institution. On his death in 1724 he left over £200,000 in order to complete the building of the new hospital, and a statue of its benefactor stands in the forecourt.[7] Literary alumni of Guy's have included the poet John

Keats, who began his medical studies here in October 1815, becoming a 'dresser' the next year; and C. S. Forester, famous for the Hornblower adventure series. In his autobiography, *Long before Forty*, Forester recalls his unsuccessful attempts to pass the hospital examination in 'Bones': 'I would far sooner start to learn the features, tastes, habits and past history of every one of the seven million inhabitants of London than all the intricate details of the four hundred bones of the human skeleton.' He left Guy's to become a gigolo and then a writer.

Apart from the Clink, Southwark was infamous for other prisons such as the Marshalsea and the King's Bench, which for centuries fronted the east side of Borough High Street just down from the busy inns. Both have held several literary figures, fictional and otherwise. An early inmate of the King's Bench was Daniel Defoe, incarcerated for a week for writing politically suspect pamphlets. In the early eighteenth century Edmund Curll, publisher of obscene books such as *The Nun in Her Smock*, was put here for selling pornography. In 1758 the King's Bench moved further westwards, to what is now Scovell Road. An early resident was the novelist Tobias Smollett, gaoled for three months and fined £100 for libelling an admiral. Smollett used his enforced leisure to finish off his novel *Sir Launcelot Greaves*, published in the 1760s. Two other inmates of the King's Bench in 1826 were Jeremiah Lear, the bankrupt father of painter and writer Edward Lear, and the political pamphleteer William Hone. Although little-known today, Hone was a famous anti-establishment figure in the early nineteenth century: in 1817 alone he was three times tried at the Guildhall for blasphemy and three times acquitted. In the 1820s he produced the *Every Day Book*, the *Table Book* and the *Year Book*, works which recorded in great detail the sayings and folklore of everyday life. One admirer was Charles Lamb, who wrote:

> *By every sort of taste your work is graced;*
> *Vast stores of modern anecdote we find,*
> *With good old story quaintly interlaced –*
> *The theme as various as the reader's mind. . . .*
> *Rags, relics, witches, ghosts, fiends, crown your page;*
> *Our fathers' mummeries we well-pleased behold. . . .*[8]

Friends paid off Hone's debts, and he was released from the King's Bench. Dickens's charming but feckless Mr Micawber, always confident that something would turn up, was another inmate of this prison. The King's Bench was demolished in 1880, and its site is now covered by the Scovell Estate.

As for the Marshalsea, Ben Jonson was imprisoned here for two months in 1597 because of his co-authorship of the play *The Isle of Dogs*. This was supposedly seditious, but no copy of it has survived to allow us to judge. With him was imprisoned the actor Gabriel Spencer, whom Jonson was to kill in the following year in a duel. Within eighteen months of his release Jonson was back in the Marshalsea, this time because of unpaid debts. In the early nineteenth century the Marshalsea was moved further south down Borough High Street, and it was here that Dickens knew it well. His family moved in here in the early 1820s, as a result of his father's bankruptcy, leaving young Charles to live on his own in nearby Lant Street. His landlord and landlady were later re-created as Mr and Mrs Garland in *The Old Curiosity Shop*. In his novel *Little Dorrit*, published between 1855 and 1857, Dickens sets much of the action in and around the Marshalsea. In the preface to the 1857 edition of the novel, Dickens describes returning to the area and searching for the prison in which Little Dorrit lived: 'I found the outer front courtyard, often mentioned here, metamorphosed into a butter shop; and then I almost gave up every brick of the gaol for lost.' However, 'The smallest boy I ever conversed with, carrying the largest baby I ever saw, offered a supernaturally intelligent explanation of the locality in its old uses', permitting the author to locate the old paving-stones, a narrow yard and some walls which 'stand among the crowding ghosts of many miserable years'. Close at hand is the church of St George the Martyr, rebuilt in 1736 and popularly known as 'Little Dorrit's church'. Little Dorrit was christened here and once slept in the portico when she returned late one night and was unable to get inside. A modern window in the church contains a small picture of Little Dorrit. The Marshalsea was shut down in 1842, although one of its iron grilles can still be seen at Dickens House in Bloomsbury. A search today for the Marshalsea discloses a tall brick wall which was once a part of the prison; it stands beside the John Harvard Library, close to the Local Studies Library.

The King's Bench and the Marshalsea were not all Southwark's prisons. Further to the south of Borough High Street was the small Horsemonger Gaol. The journalist Leigh Hunt was imprisoned here between 1813 and 1815 for calling the Prince

Regent 'a fat Adonis of fifty'. He was also fined £500. Hunt was often visited by Lord Byron, and in his reminiscences Hunt gives a fine picture of the poet and his often captivating personality. In November 1849, Charles Dickens witnessed the hanging outside the Horsemonger Gaol of Mr and Mrs Manning, two convicted murderers. He wrote about the event, and more particularly the ghoulish behaviour of the onlookers, in a letter to *The Times* which played a part in fomenting the gradual revulsion against public executions. This prison was pulled down in 1880, and Newington Recreation Ground stands on its site.

The figure of Charles Dickens is in fact inseparable from Southwark, quite apart from the many streets near Lant Street renamed after people from his novels. In his first novel, *Pickwick Papers*, he provided a description of the half-dozen Southwark coaching inns: 'Great, rambling, queer, old places they are, with galleries, and passages, and staircases, wide enough and antiquated enough to furnish materials for a hundred ghost stories.' And there in the courtyard of the White Hart is Sam Weller, complete with a striped waistcoat, bright red handkerchief round his neck and a white hat, cleaning boots:

'Number twenty-two wants his boots.'
'Ask number twenty-two, whether he'll have 'em now, or wait till he gets 'em,' was the reply.

Sam meets Mr Pickwick, is engaged as his manservant and immediately offers a refreshing counterpoint to the bumbling pomposity of his master. The character of Sam Weller proved vital to Dickens's career. The first three numbers of *Pickwick Papers* had sold less than 400 copies a month, and the young twenty-four-year-old author was told by his publishers that the serialisation might have to be stopped on the grounds of inadequate sales. Sam appeared in the fourth issue, and sales soared to 40,000 copies. The name of the writer – although he was still then being published as 'Boz' – was made.[9]

If Dickens had been writing only a few years later, he would have had to find somewhere else for Sam Weller and Mr Pickwick to meet. In 1836 the first railway station in London was opened at London Bridge, just behind St Thomas's Hospital. The coming of the railway spelled the end for the stagecoach, and after several hundred years the inns and taverns at the top of Borough High Street closed down. Jack Cade's and Sam Weller's

White Hart is today no more than a small alley, as is Chaucer's Tabard, while the Queen's Head, once run by the Harvard family, has vanished completely. In 1637, John Harvard had emigrated from Southwark to North America, where he founded Harvard University. There is a Harvard Chapel in Southwark Cathedral, and the library off Borough High Street is also named in his honour. The sole survivor of these old inns today is the George, the only galleried public house, although now only one of its original three galleries survives. Even this inn had to be rebuilt after Southwark's own 'Great Fire' in 1676, during which 500 buildings were razed to the ground. St Thomas's Hospital was finally forced to move in 1871, after fresh extensions were added to London Bridge station.

In the course of the nineteenth century Southwark, along with much of South London, was industrialised, a process which transformed parts of the district into squalid slums – when John Keats lived in St Thomas Street in 1815 he called the neighbourhood 'a beastly place in dirt, turnings and windings'. One of the worst areas lay to the east of Southwark, on the edge of the river, and went by the name of Jacob's Island. Here, in *Oliver Twist*, Bill Sikes meets his end in 'the filthiest, the strangest, the most extraordinary of the many localities that are hidden in London, wholly unknown, even by name, to the great mass of its inhabitants . . . in such a neighbourhood, beyond Dockhead, in the Borough of Southwark, stands Jacob's Island'. Warehouses sprang up all around Southwark Cathedral, turning the little streets into paths through deep canyons, certainly not to be negotiated at night. Today, of course, after the depopulation resulting from the Second World War and the bombing, together with the move away from the traditional leather and hop trades, the riverside has become very fashionable: a search for Jacob's Island today leads not to slums but to flats costing £300,000.

Whether or not you are looking for a place to live, Southwark does offer a splendid walk along the river between London Bridge and Blackfriars Bridge, a stroll which is steeped in literary history because of the Shakespearean playhouses which once stood here. Stop at the Anchor pub for a drink. The Anchor was built between 1770 and 1775, although there have been more recent additions, and stands partly on the site of the Globe. This little inn was close to the home and also the brewery owned by Mr and Mrs Thrale, good friends of Dr Samuel Johnson, who often came to stay with them. In May 1773 a dinner given by Mr Thrale at his Bankside house saw a guest-list which included Johnson, the artist Sir Joshua Reynolds, the actor David Garrick, the writer Oliver Goldsmith and the politician Edmund Burke. Both the brewery and the Thrales' home have been demolished, but the Anchor remains. Apparently it was one of Johnson's favourite watering-holes and, as is so often the case, the good doctor was quite right.[10]

22

The Temple
and Fleet Street

Opposite the Law Courts is a charming timber-framed building which dates back in part to the seventeenth century. This is the home of the Wig and Pen Club, whose emblems belong to the traditional activities of the Temple and Fleet Street – the law and the press. Although many of the newspapers have now left the area, it will be some years before the phrase 'Fleet Street', used as a convenient label to refer to the press, will die out.

The link with printing began in 1500 when Wynkyn de Worde, once apprenticed to William Caxton, moved the printing press which his master had left him from the Sign of the Red Pale in Westminster to the Sign of the Sun on the south side of Fleet Street, opposite Shoe Lane. He had realised the commercial possibilities of being situated on the busy highway of Fleet Street, which joined the City to Westminster. De Worde was soon only one of several printers in the neighbourhood; his rival Richard Pynson, for example, had his press near to St Dunstan in the West. De Worde's small cheap volumes on subjects ranging from sermons and etiquette to medicines for horses did indeed prove popular, and in his thirty-five years in Fleet Street he produced at least 600 titles.

When de Worde died in 1535 he was buried at St Bride's Church, the beginning of the tradition which has led to it being called 'the printers' cathedral'. In the crypt there is an excellent display, commemorating the newspaper proprietor Lord Beaverbrook, which gives a detailed account of Fleet Street's history. Also in the crypt can be seen some of the Roman finds uncovered after the bombing during the Second World War, such as a tessellated pavement. The other exhibition relevant to the history of 'the print' can be seen nearby in the Printer's Devil pub halfway up Fetter Lane – the 'printer's devil' was the name given to the errand boy or apprentice.

By walking under Sir Christopher Wren's gateway which arches over Middle Temple Lane, the pedestrian leaves the roar of Fleet Street for the tranquillity of the Temple, one of whose greatest attractions is the gardens which stretch south down to the Embankment. William Shakespeare set one of his most famous scenes here: in *Henry VI* a dispute between the York and Lancaster factions which had started in the Temple Hall comes to a head outside in the gardens:

> Plantagenet *Let him that is a true-born gentleman*
> *And stands upon the honour of his birth,*
> *If he suppose that I have pleaded truth,*
> *From off this brier pluck a white rose with me.*
> Somerset *Let him that is no coward nor no flatterer,*
> *But dare maintain the party of the truth,*
> *Pluck a red rose from off this thorn with me.*
> Warwick *I love no colours, and without all colour*
> *Of base insinuating flattery*
> *I pluck this white rose with Plantagenet.*
> Suffolk *I pluck this red rose with young Somerset,*
> *And say withal I think he held the right. . . .*
> Warwick *. . . I prophesy: this brawl today,*
> *Grown to this faction in the Temple garden,*
> *Shall send, between the red rose and the white,*
> *A thousand souls to death and deadly night.*

Thus begin the 'Wars of the Roses'.

The land here had once been owned by the Knights Templars, an order founded in 1118 in order to protect pilgrims journeying to the Holy Land. In 1185 the Templars consecrated the round Temple church. Although badly damaged during the Blitz, the Temple church has now been restored and still contains several of the original knights' effigies and also what Charles Lamb called 'the grotesque Gothic heads' that 'gape' and 'grin' between the arches in the oldest, round part of the church.[1] The heads are thought to represent souls in heaven and in hell. In the fourteenth century the Knights Hospitallers took over the land but they were in turn suppressed by Henry VIII, after which the land passed to the Crown. However, in 1608, James I granted a charter to the Benchers of the Inner Temple and the Middle Temple, and the lawyers have been here ever since. A condition of the grant is that they maintain the Temple church.

One of the many ironies of London's history is that, at the very time that the lawyers were moving into the Temple, a few hundred yards away scores of criminals, highwaymen and vagrants were also moving into their new home, which they called Alsatia, after the 'no man's land' that then lay between France and the German states. Originally the site of the Whitefriars monastery which had also been put down during the Reformation in the 1530s, the land still retained certain rights of sanctuary whereby wrongdoers there were for a time exempt from arrest and imprisonment. Just about every crook in London spent time in Alsatia, but so also did Daniel Defoe who in 1692 went bust to the then considerable tune of £17,000 and fled here to escape his creditors, one of whom was his mother-in-law whom he had defrauded with tales of a new scent made out of cats! Defoe was here for a month until he escaped to Bristol, where he negotiated a settlement.[2]

There is a graphic description of Alsatia in Sir Walter Scott's novel *The Fortunes of Nigel* (1822), set in the early seventeenth century:

> The wailing of children, the scolding of their mothers, the miserable exhibition of ragged linens hung from the windows to dry, spoke the wants and distresses of the wretched inhabitants; while the sounds of complaint were mocked and overwhelmed in the riotous shouts, oaths, and profane songs and boisterous laughter that issued from the alehouses and taverns which, as the signs indicated, were equal in number to all the other houses; and, that the full character of the place might be evident, several faded, tinselled and painted females looked boldly at the strangers from their open lattices, or more modestly seemed busied with the cracked flower-pots, filled

with mignonette and rosemary, which were disposed in front of the windows to the great risk of the passengers.

In 1697 troops were sent in to clear Alsatia. Its location is indicated by today's Whitefriars Street and the evocatively named Hanging Sword Alley. The fourteenth-century crypt of the original monastery is underneath the old *News of the World* building.

The existence of Alsatia ensured that Fleet Street was not considered a particularly desirable address in the sixteenth or seventeenth century, especially when the squalid character of the area was compounded by the River Fleet itself which flowed down the line of Farringdon Road and Farringdon Street. The Fleet rose in Hampstead and Highgate and made its way towards the Thames via King's Cross. By the time it reached Fleet Street it was carrying the detritus of the city, which was catalogued with a certain horrific relish by the *Tatler* in 1710:

> *Sweepings from butchers' stalls, dung, guts and blood,*
> *Drowned puppies, shaking sprats, all drenched in mud,*
> *Dead cats, and turnip tops, come tumbling down the flood.*[3]

It is not surprising that this distasteful area was the site for the notorious Fleet prison, which dated from Norman times. The main cause of the widespread abuses which went on inside was that the warden had unlimited powers to do as he wished, fining the wealthy, failing to feed the poor, inflicting whatever punishments he chose. The Begging Grate which looked on to the street was for many prisoners their only chance of obtaining food. Two of English literature's most famous characters endured spells here in the Fleet prison: Sir John Falstaff and Mr Samuel Pickwick. At the end of *Henry IV, Part Two* the Chief Justice orders:

> *Go, carry Sir John Falstaff to the Fleet.*
> *Take all his company along with him.*

As for Mr Pickwick, he is here because he refuses to pay the costs and damages which have been awarded to Mrs Bardell at the conclusion of the breach-of-promise case. Pickwick asks one of the other inmates if he is likely to be visited by any of his friends; the man's savage response points up the horrors of the Fleet:

'Friends!' interposed the man, in a voice which rattled in his throat. 'If I lay dead at the bottom of the deepest mine in the world, tight screwed down and soldered in my coffin, rotting in the dark and filthy ditch that drags its slime along beneath the foundations of this prison, I could not be more forgotten or unheeded than I am here. I am a dead man – dead to society, without the pity they bestow on those whose souls have passed to judgement. Friends to see *me*! My God! I have sunk from the prime of life into old age in this place, and there is not one to raise his hand above my bed, when I lie dead upon it, and say "It is a blessing he is gone!"'

Thackeray's journalist Shandon in *Pendennis* is another fictional character who ends up in the Fleet, as does his rogue Barry Lyndon, an inmate for nineteen years before dying of delirium tremens.

However, more than enough real people spent time in this prison. The Puritan William Prynne wrote a pamphlet called *Histrio-mastix* in 1632 which was taken to have libelled Charles I and his queen; he was sentenced to 'perpetual imprisonment' in the Fleet, to have his pamphlet burnt before his face as he stood in the pillory, and to be 'branded on the forehead, have his nose slit and his ears cropped'. Another Puritan, John Lilburne, was sentenced for his writings 'to be whipped through the street from the prison' to Whitehall, and 'to be laid alone with irons on his hands and legs in the wards of the Fleet'. William Hogarth's father Richard was here for a time, as was the writer John Cleland. Imprisoned for debt from November 1748 until March 1749, he took the opportunity to write *Memoirs of a Woman of Pleasure*, better known under the title of *Fanny Hill*. Charting the progress of a relatively innocent country girl into a London courtesan, Cleland treats the frequent sex scenes with a lively exuberance rather than the joyless tedium which is typical of such publications. His publisher earned £10,000 from *Fanny Hill*; Cleland himself less than £25. The book remained 'an underground classic' until it was republished in 1963.[4]

If the Fleet prison was not brutal enough, then interested individuals could always visit the Bridewell, situated on the other side of the river. Originally a royal palace, Edward VI gave it to the City as a convenient place in which to incarcerate homeless children and 'immoral' women. Rebuilt after the Great Fire, members of the public were permitted for a fee to watch the women being flogged, a practice which continued until 1791. At the end of the seventeenth century the London observer Ned Ward argued unsuccessfully that it was 'a shameful indecency for a woman to expose her naked body to the sight of man and boys, as if it was design'd rather to feast the eyes of the spectators, or stir up the appetites of lascivious persons, than to correct vice or reform manners'.[5] Both the Fleet prison and the Bridewell were demolished in the middle of the nineteenth century, their only legacy being the names of Fleet Lane and Bridewell Place. There is also a stone face of Edward VI over the entrance to the Scottish Assurance building which now stands on the site of the Bridewell. As for the Fleet river itself, it was covered over in the middle of the eighteenth century. However, if one stands on the pedestrian walkway underneath Blackfriars Bridge at low tide, the conduit which is then visible carries the dregs of the river into the Thames.

Another former inmate of the Fleet prison was the poet John Donne, who was sent there for marrying a young girl without her guardian's permission. He recovered from this mishap and eventually in 1626 was appointed the vicar of another of Fleet Street's longstanding churches, St Dunstan in the West. One of his congregation was Izaak Walton, author of *The Compleat Angler* (1653) and also one of the first English biographers, who lived nearby. Walton lived in Fleet Street in the 1660s and it is therefore likely that he was a member of the congregation at St Dunstan's on 18 August 1667; so, too, was Samuel Pepys:

... where I hear an able sermon from the minister of the place. And stood by a pretty, modest maid, whom I did labour to take by the hand and the body; but she would not, but got further and further from me, and at last I could perceive her to take pins out of her pocket to prick me if I should touch her again; which seeing, I did forbear, and was glad I did espy her design. And then I fell to gaze upon another pretty maid in a pew close to me, and she on me; and I did go about to take her by the hand, which she suffered a little and then withdrew. So the sermon ended and the church broke up, and my amours ended also; and so took coach and home. . . .

The St Dunstan's familiar to Pepys was rebuilt in 1830 a little to the north of the original site in order to allow the widening of Fleet Street. Its porch contains a bust of John Donne and there is also a tablet to Izaak Walton.

Samuel Pepys knew Fleet Street well: he had been born in Salisbury Court beside St Bride's church in February 1633. His father was a tailor and the family had their own pew in St Bride's, where Pepys was himself baptised. As a boy Pepys was sent to St Paul's School, which was just up Ludgate Hill, and he also served in his father's shop – something which in later, exalted life he was never in a hurry to recall. The Fleet Street which Pepys knew as a young man was destroyed during the Great Fire of 1666, the only survivor being 'Prince Henry's Room' at 17 Fleet Street. Appropriately enough, it now contains the Samuel Pepys Exhibition, a small collection of Pepysiana which was opened in 1975. Prince Henry's Room is open every weekday afternoon.

The Great Fire also wiped out the numerous taverns which had dotted Fleet Street, amongst them the Devil tavern which had stood almost opposite St Dunstan's. Here Ben Jonson had started the Apollo Club in 1624, and he would hold forth to his fellow-members while seated on a raised seat underneath a bust of Apollo. After the Fire the Devil was rebuilt, and then demolished again in 1787. Its whereabouts are marked by a plaque. Fleet Street's most famous pub, the Cheshire Cheese, was completed in 1666 as the first new building in the neighbourhood after the Fire, supposedly for the benefit of the workmen toiling away in the area.

Also after the Fire several publishers and booksellers moved away from St Paul's Churchyard to new premises in Fleet Street. One of the most famous of these newcomers was Jacob Tonson, who for twenty years published the works of the poet and critic John Dryden. Tonson was not always very fast in paying his authors, and on one occasion Dryden fired off a wounding personal description of Tonson:

> *With leering looks, bull-faced and freckled fair,*
> *With two left legs and Judas-coloured hair*
> *And frowzy pores that taint the ambient air.*

Surely no writer today would dare to talk about his publisher in such terms![6]

The year before Samuel Pepys died in 1703 he might well have read a copy of London's first daily newspaper, the *Daily Courant*, which was published on Ludgate Hill on 11 March 1702. The final paragraph read: 'This Courant (as the Title shews) will be Publish'd Daily; being design'd to give all the Material News as soon as every Post arrives: and is confin'd to half the Compass [size], to save the Publick at least half the Impertinences, of ordinary News-Papers.' The *Daily Courant* lasted until 1735.[7] Of all the many eighteenth-century newspapers which followed in the wake of the *Courant*, only one has survived. In 1785 the first copies of the *Universal Daily Register* were printed at Printing House Square, near Blackfriars, claiming to be 'the faithful recorder of every species of intelligence'. Three years later its name was changed to *The Times* and the paper was produced from Printing House Square for 189 years.

If one grubs under the railway bridge on the east side of Ludgate Circus one can find a tablet commemorating the existence of the *Daily Courant*. Similarly, if the literary enthusiast walks around the churchyard of St Bride's, he or she will find at the east end a number of worn and faded tombstones. One of them is that of Samuel Richardson, a young printer who had set himself up nearby in Salisbury Square in 1724. Apart from his printing work Richardson also began to make some extra money by helping illiterate lovers write suitably affectionate letters to their girlfriends.[8] From this service Richardson went on to compose letters to imaginary readers full of advice on how best to conduct oneself in life. One collection was entitled *Letters Written to and for Particular Friends on the Most Important Occasions, directing not only the requisite style and form to be observed in writing familiar letters, but how to think and act justly and prudently in the common concerns of human life*. As this title suggests, Richardson may have been well intentioned but he was also rather a killjoy. Over one-third of his *Apprentice's Vade Mecum* is devoted to the iniquities and vices of the theatre. Richardson went on to write a full-length novel in this epistolary style, and some have acclaimed *Pamela*, published in November 1740, as the first English novel. In three very long volumes the story unfolds of the master's attempt to seduce the maidservant Pamela. He fails, and eventually has to marry her in order to get what he wants. Richardson went on to write *Clarissa Harlowe*, issued in 1749. Both novels were extremely popular, but today they are read primarily for their historical interest. Richardson's printing career also prospered. In 1754 he was elected Master of the Stationers' Company and the next year he greatly expanded his Salisbury Square premises. When he died in 1761 he was buried in St Bride's. The main body of this church was blown apart during the Blitz, but at least Richardson's tombstone survived.

Defoe and Richardson have both been called the father of the English novel. A third candidate is Henry Fielding, who began his writing career by attacking Richardson with a parody called *Shamela* in which the female character is not, unlike Pamela, of pure and unblemished virtue but rather of a free and easy nature. Richardson never forgave him for this work. Fielding, like his rival, knew the neighbourhood well. He had begun his literary career as a dramatist, but after the Stage Licensing Act of 1737 introduced a rigorous form of theatre censorship Fielding decided to find a new profession. Accordingly he entered the Middle Temple in November 1737, and with typical energy completed the seven-year course in three years, being called to the Bar in 1740.[9] At the same time he was also editing a thrice-weekly magazine called the *Champion* and had a sick wife and two children to look after. He lived on the north side of Fleet Street where today's Law Courts now stand.

Fielding's legal career was never very successful, and *Shamela* was no doubt a useful way of supplementing his income. In 1742 he followed it with *Joseph Andrews*, which began as another parody of Richardson but fortunately branched off on its own, taking young Joseph and his mentor Parson Adams on an odyssey around mid-eighteenth-century England. Fielding was later to move to Covent Garden and to produce *Tom Jones*.

Yet another famous literary resident in the 1740s was the man whose statue stands at the top of Fleet Street, Samuel Johnson. A friend of Richardson, Johnson much preferred his novels to Fielding's: 'Sir, there is as much difference between the two as between a man who knows how a watch is made and a man who can merely tell the hour on the dial-plate.'[10]

The first thing that anyone would remark upon when meeting Johnson for the first time was his unusual appearance. James Boswell was introduced to him on 16 May 1763:

Mr Johnson is a man of most dreadful appearance. He is a very big man, is troubled with sore eyes, the palsy, the king's evil. He is very slovenly in his dress and speaks with a most uncouth voice. Yet his great knowledge and strength of expression command vast respect and render him excellent company. He has great humour and is a worthy man. But his

dogmatical roughness of manners is disagreeable. I shall mark
what I remember of his conversation.[11]

Johnson's physical deformities had prevented him from making a
success of schoolmastering in his native Staffordshire and in 1737
he had travelled to London with another young man seeking
fame and fortune, David Garrick. His first years here were difficult, living in a series of run-down lodgings along with his wife
Tetty and eking out an existence by pieces of journalism and
contributions to the *Gentleman's Magazine*, published in Clerkenwell. In 1749 he moved to a house at 17 Gough Square. The
household consisted of the Johnsons, a blind woman called Anna
Williams, the black manservant Francis Barber and Hodge the
cat.

It was here that Johnson did the bulk of the work on his
Dictionary, 'by which the pronunciation of our language may be
fixed, and its attainment facilitated; by which its purity may be
preserved, its use ascertained, and its duration lengthened'.
Helped by a series of researchers who worked upstairs at Gough
Square at a salary of twenty-five shillings a week, Johnson finally
published the *Dictionary of the English Language* in 1755, costing
four guineas. It proved a success: there were five editions in
Johnson's lifetime alone. However, his achievement was clouded
by the death in 1752 of Tetty to whom Johnson, despite her drink
problems, had been much attached.

Apart from the *Dictionary*, Johnson also wrote a play called
Irene which Garrick staged at Drury Lane, and catalogued the
Harleian collection of manuscripts which were subsequently
given to the British Museum. These bursts of activity – and Johnson was a naturally lazy man – were fuelled by huge quantities of
tea. He described himself as 'a hardened and a shameless tea-
drinker, who has for many years diluted his meals with only the
infusion of this fascinating plant; whose kettle has scarcely time
to cool; who with tea amuses the evening, with tea solaces the
midnights, with tea welcomes the morning'.[12] It was as well for
Johnson that in 1710 a Mr Thomas Twining had set up a shop at
the far end of Fleet Street near St Clement Danes which sold tea.
Twining's is still there, with the figures of two Chinamen by its
entrance.

Johnson was a familiar bulk shambling up and down Fleet
Street, visiting its numerous pubs such as the Cheshire Cheese,

the Mitre, the Devil, and the Essex Head (now the Edgar Wallace) in Essex Street. He had his own pew at St Clement Danes, where a plaque still marks the pew's site upstairs. Above all, wherever Johnson went there was talk and yet more talk. He was fortunate in later life to have a Boswell to record some of the gems which he scattered around him. Despite leaving Gough Square in 1759, Johnson never lived far from Fleet Street. From 1765 until 1776 he lived at Johnson's Court (the site of the house is marked by a plaque) and then he moved to 8 Bolt Court, where he died in December 1784. He was buried in Westminster Abbey.

Of all Johnson's London residences only one has survived: luckily for us it is that at 17 Gough Square, now 'Dr Johnson's House' and open to the public. After Johnson's departure from it the house enjoyed mixed fortunes, being amongst other things used as a printer's and as a hotel. In 1911 the newspaper proprietor Lord Harmsworth stumbled across it when it was on the verge of collapse: 'At the time of my purchase of the house in April, 1911, it presented every appearance of squalor and decay. . . . It is doubtful whether in the whole of London there existed a more forlorn and dilapidated tenement.' Harmsworth made over the house to a trust, which runs it today, as well as building the curator's house just to the south of 17 Gough Square.[13] A visit is essential for anyone at all interested in literary London. Quite apart from the Johnson connection the house itself, which dates back to about 1700, has a fine twisting staircase and wonderfully creaking floorboards.

Not everyone has revered the memory of Dr Samuel Johnson; William Cobbett called him 'a teacher of moping and melancholy' and 'this time serving, mean, dastardly old pensioner'.[14] The adjective 'mean' seems particularly unfair. Johnson was always very generous to those he liked. Francis Barber, for example, was left an income of £70 a year in Johnson's will and many of his personal possessions. He was a good friend, too, to Oliver Goldsmith, the lively, gregarious Irishman who always lived on a financial tight-rope. Once employed by Samuel Richardson as a proof-reader in Salisbury Square, Goldsmith was living at 6 Wine Office Court in 1763, when matters had become so bad that his landlady appropriated his clothes, demanding either the payment of the £36 rent due or else marriage. Johnson came around to help and found that Goldsmith had just finished a novel called *The Vicar of Wakefield*. Johnson promptly went off and sold it for sixty guineas. For the last nine years of his life Goldsmith lived at 2 Brick Court on the second floor. At his death in 1774 he owed nearly £2000, which led Johnson to ask 'Was ever poet so trusted before?' He was buried on the north side of the Temple church, where his tombstone can still be seen. It bears the simple inscription 'Here Lies Oliver Goldsmith'. Another of Johnson's circle familiar with the Temple was Boswell himself, who entered the Inner Temple in 1786.

According to Sir John Hawkins, Johnson's first biographer, he often borrowed his friends' books: '. . . if ever they came back to those that lent them, were so defaced as to be scarce worth owning, and yet, some of the friends were glad to receive and entertain them as curiosities.' Charles Lamb in his *Essays of Elia* (1823) advised:

> Reader, if haply thou art blessed with a moderate collection, be shy of showing it; or if thy heart overfloweth to lend them, lend thy books; but let it be to such a one as S.T.C. [Samuel Taylor Coleridge] – he will return them (generally anticipating the time appointed) with usury; enriched with annotations tripling their value. I have had experience.

Lamb was one of the most devoted admirers of Fleet Street: 'The man must have a rare recipe for melancholy, who can be dull in Fleet Street.' He had been born at 2 Crown Office Row in 1775 and he spent his early years in and around the Temple where his father was a legal clerk. After various London residences Lamb lived at 4 Inner Temple Lane from 1809 until 1817 while he was still working in the City for the East India Company. It was a happy period for him: his fame as an essayist was beginning to spread, and his Wednesday evenings here were taken up entertaining literary friends such as William Hazlitt and Samuel Taylor Coleridge. Lamb moved away from the Temple to Covent Garden and then to Islington. Hare Court in the Temple, the dark courtyard which Lamb overlooked, is still there.

Nineteenth-century Fleet Street was at the very heart of literary London. The centre of the radical press, for example, was at number 162 on the west corner of Bouverie Street and Fleet Street where Richard Carlile had his shop 'The Temple of Reason'.[15] A hundred yards away was 12 Salisbury Square, the home of 'the Salisbury Square School', which was in effect the Victorian equivalent of Mills & Boon, supplying cheap, easy to read (and write) penny fiction.[16] It was controlled by Edward Lloyd, who issued works with titles like *Ada the Betrayed; or, The Murder at the Old Smithy* and in 1850 the first published story about Sweeney Todd, 'the Demon Barber of Fleet Street'. Lloyd also profited hugely from plagiarisms of Dickens's novels. Dickens had in fact started his writing career here in Fleet Street, 'stealthily one evening at twilight with fear and trembling, into a dark letter box in a dark office up a dark Court in Fleet Street' dropping off his first manuscript. He was twenty-one years old and the office in Johnson's Court belonged to the *Monthly Magazine*, subtitled 'The British Register of Literature, Sciences, and Belles Lettres'. A few days later the December 1833 issue carried his story 'A Dinner at Poplar Walk'.

Not surprisingly, Fleet Street often appears in Dickens's novels. In *David Copperfield* he writes of the plunge bath which is still tucked away in Strand Lane and also of the waxworks housed in what is now Prince Henry's Room. Pip in *Great Expectations* lives in the Temple with Herbert Pocket in rooms where the returned convict Magwitch reveals the source of Pip's wealth. In *A Tale of Two Cities* Dickens describes Tellson's Bank as being

> very small, very dark, very ugly, very incommodious. Tellson's was the triumphant perfection of inconvenience. After bursting open a door of idiotic obstinacy, with a weak rattle in its throat, you fell into Tellson's down two steps, and came to your senses in a miserable little shop with two little counters [lit] by the dingiest of windows which were always under a shower-bath of mud from Fleet Street, and which were made the dingier by their own iron bars proper, and the heavy shadow of Temple Bar.

Tellson's is in fact Child's Bank – still at 1 Fleet Street. As for Temple Bar, the gate that once marked the western boundary of the City, Dickens in *Bleak House* referred to it as 'That leaden-headed old obstruction, appropriate ornament for the threshold of a leaden-headed old corporation'; it was removed from Fleet Street in 1870 and now stands in a rather dilapidated condition in Theobalds Park, Hertfordshire, although there are proposals that it should be returned to London.

Outside St Dunstan in the West is a statue of Elizabeth I, thought to be the oldest statue in London. It was originally fixed to the Ludgate until all the City gates were demolished in the

1760s and the statue was removed here. In 1576, Elizabeth had opened the Middle Temple Hall and Shakespeare's *Twelfth Night* was performed here twenty-five years later. The other statue outside St Dunstan's is a bust of Lord Northcliffe, the man who more than any other individual created Fleet Street's identification with newspapers.

In 1890, Alfred Harmsworth, as he then was, founded the weekly comics *Chips* and *Comic Cuts*, and the success of both ventures brought home to him that with the spread of literacy and the growth of advertising a huge new public was available, if he could only produce a cheap and readable newspaper. In 1896, therefore, at the then enormous expense of half a million pounds, Harmsworth launched the *Daily Mail*, which cost only a halfpenny. Within four years the *Daily Mail* could boast a circulation of a million. Much of the paper's appeal was its full-blooded imperialism, but also important was its attention to women's interests. Lord Northcliffe, as he became in 1905, raised the status of journalism; Geoffrey Dawson, for many years the editor of *The Times*, considered that 'The best and most enduring monument of Northcliffe's life-work was the final demolition of Grub Street'.[17] The *Daily Mail* was soon followed by the *Daily Express* and the *Daily Mirror*.

Northcliffe ushered in the age of the press baron, men like himself who controlled vast publishing empires. He appears as Lord Tilbury in P. G. Wodehouse's *Heavy Weather* (1933):

> Sunshine pierced the haze that enveloped London. It came down Fleet Street, turned to the right, stopped at the premises of the Mammoth Publishing Company, and, entering through an upper window, beamed pleasantly upon Lord Tilbury, founder and proprietor of that vast factory of popular literature, as he sat reading the batch of weekly papers which his secretary had placed on the desk for his inspection. Among the secrets of this great man's success was the fact that he kept a personal eye on all the firm's products.

The personal eye was always that of highly egocentric tycoons. Evelyn Waugh once worked for the *Daily Express* and in his novel *Scoop* (1938) he gave a memorable portrait of Lord Copper of the Megalopolitan Newspaper Corporation who, amongst his other foibles, loves giving banquets at which his employees are compulsory participants:

He [Lord Copper] had bought them and bound them, hand
and foot, with consommé and cream of chicken, turbot and
saddle, duck and pêche melba; and afterwards, when the
cigars had been furtively pocketed and the brandy glasses filled
with the horrible brown compound for which Lord Copper
was paying two pounds a bottle, there came the golden hour
when he rose to speak at whatever length he liked and on
whatever subject, without fear of rivalry or interruption.

No newspaper could survive without the army of sellers who
actually distribute it to the public. One small boy who sold
newspapers in Ludgate Circus at the end of the nineteenth century was paid three shillings a week 'which I spent in dissipation
– ginger-beer, theatres and a succulent toffee called "Devona"'.[18]
The small boy was called Edgar Wallace and he grew up to
become the best-selling writer of the interwar period: one out of
every four novels sold in these years was written by Wallace.
After several years as a soldier in South Africa, Wallace worked in
London as a journalist for Lord Northcliffe – 'You felt that to
argue [with Northcliffe] was to invite the thunder-bolts of Jove'[19]
– but he was sacked for libelling a naval officer. With his usual
optimism and energy Wallace turned to novel-writing, and his
first effort, *The Four Just Men* (1905), is still one of the best thril-
lers ever written. From this point on Wallace simply churned out
the novels and plays, on one occasion writing an 80,000-word
book over a weekend and producing more than 150 volumes in
twenty-seven years.[20] Although some do betray signs of haste,
most of his works are still enjoyable reading today, and Wallace
remains a much under-rated writer. He went to Hollywood in
1931, desperately trying to earn money to pay off his gambling
debts, and there he wrote the screenplay for the film *King Kong*.
Wallace died suddenly in America in February 1932. There is a
pub in Essex Street named after him and a tablet to him on the
north-west corner of Ludgate Circus. The inscription ends: 'He
knew wealth and poverty yet had walked with kings and kept his
bearing, and his talents he gave lavishly to authorship but to Fleet
Street he gave his heart.'

Another literary phenomenon was created in this neighbourhood, namely what was called the 'sword and cloak school' of
fiction. It was born on 25 November 1893 when a young barrister, Anthony Hope Hawkins, was returning to his chambers in

the Temple when he suddenly thought up the idea for a novel. He proceeded to write two chapters a day, and finished the book within a month. Published as *The Prisoner of Zenda*, it proved to be one of the most popular novels of all time.[21] Anthony Hope, as this lawyer called himself, has been just one in the line of the Temple's successful writers, a tradition carried on by John Buchan and today by John Mortimer, creator of Rumpole. No doubt there are several more to come.

In J. M. Barrie's first novel, *When a Man's Single* (1888), an aspiring journalist called Rob comes to London for the first time and makes his way to Fleet Street: 'A certain awe came upon Rob as he went down Fleet Street on the one side, and up it on the other. He could not resist looking into the faces of the persons who passed him, and wondering if they edited *The Times*.' Nowadays of course the editor of *The Times* is to be found in Wapping High Street.

Tower Hill

Tower Hill is dominated by the Tower of London, that collection of buildings which today forms one of Britain's foremost tourist attractions, visited by over 2 million people each year. William Shakespeare thought that the Tower had been built by the Romans: in *Richard II* he referred to it as 'Julius Caesar's ill-created Tower' and in *Richard III* Buckingham is sure that the records bear out that Caesar was its architect. Shakespeare may have been confused by the existence of the Roman wall nearby, a large chunk of which can still be seen in Cooper's Row. In fact the Tower of London was built in 1078 on the orders of William the Conqueror, who was determined that London's citizens should be permanently and visibly aware of Norman military strength. Gundulf, then Bishop of Rochester, was responsible for carrying out William's command.

Very soon the Tower served a multitude of purposes, as the sixteenth-century London historian John Stow recorded in his *Survey of London*:

This tower is a citadell, to defend or commaund the Citie: a royall place for assemblies, and treaties. A Prison of estate, for the most daungerous offenders: the onely place of coynage for all England at this time: the armorie for warlike provision: the Treasurie of the ornaments and Jewels of the crowne, and

241

generall conserver of the most Recordes of the kings Courts of
justice at Westminster.

It is the Tower's associations with imprisonment and execution
which are probably strongest in the popular imagination. This is
the place where the two little princes were murdered in 1483 and
whose prisoners have included several wives of Henry VIII, the
future Elizabeth I, Sir Thomas More and Sir Walter Ralegh. The
last was held in the Bloody Tower for thirteen years by James I,
the king whose aviary gave rise to today's Birdcage Walk along
the south side of St James's Park and one of whose sons declared
of Ralegh's imprisonment that 'Only my father could keep such a
bird in a cage!' Ralegh took the opportunity of his imprisonment
to write *The History of the World*, the first volume of which was
published in 1614 and was a contemporary bestseller – far more
so, according to A. L. Rowse, than the plays of Shakespeare.[1]

Some of the Tower's inmates were executed on Tower Green,
others out on Tower Hill where the site of the scaffold is marked
by a memorial in Trinity Gardens. Too often these executions
were neither swift nor competent. In 1381 the Archbishop of
Canterbury, so one chronicler noted, was hacked about until
'being mangled with eight several strokes in the neck and head,
he fulfilled most worthy martyrdom'. As for the Duke of
Monmouth in 1685, his executioner John Ketch – who became
in the guise of 'Jack Ketch' a familiar bogyman to generations of
London children – was in gruesomely inefficient form. When five
strokes of the axe were not sufficient, he had to resort to his
knife. Not surprisingly, he was pensioned off the following year.
The most famous literary figure to end his life on Tower Hill was
Sir Thomas More, who seems to have been in characteristically
impish mood. On ascending the scaffold he remarked to the
lieutenant: 'I pray you, Master Lieutenant, see me safe up, and
for coming down let me shift for myself.' To the hesitant executioner More said: 'Pluck up thy spirits, man, and be not afraid to
do thine office: my neck is very short.'[2]

However, not every occupant of the Tower subsequently met a
violent death, certainly not Samuel Pepys, the man who was
twice a prisoner and yet who died happily in his bed aged
seventy. Pepys's presence dominates the area around Tower Hill.
Here he lived for many years after 1660, the year in which he was
appointed Clerk of Acts to the Navy Board and in which he

started his diary, thus ensuring that we are more familiar with the Pepys household than with almost any other in history. Pepys and his wife Elizabeth lived in a nine-room house in Seething Lane, and we know that they had a dog still not house-trained: 'Hence home where my wife and I had some high words upon my telling her that I would fling the dog which her brother gave her out at the window if he pissed the house any more.' Mr and Mrs Pepys regularly visited St Olave's church where the sermon was sometimes less than gripping: 'So up and to church, where Mr Mills preached; but I know not how, I slept most of the sermon.' And on 13 November 1664: 'This morning to church where mighty sport to hear the Clerk sing out of tune.' Pepys had a love–hate relationship with Mr Mills – at one stage he refers to him as 'a fat lazy priest'; however, several pages later in the diary the Millses are to be found dining with the Pepyses.[3]

It was from his home in Seething Lane that Pepys went to the theatre and the taverns, consorted with his girlfriends, worked long hours at the Navy Board and grew jealous over his wife's Italian dancing master. It was here, too, that he heard about the outbreak of the Great Fire in September 1666. He buried his wine and Parmesan cheese in a pit in the garden, carried his valuables to a friend's home in Bethnal Green and from the tower of All Hallows Barking watched the conflagration creep ever nearer his home: 'I up to the top of Barkeing steeple, and there saw the saddest sight of desolation that I ever saw. Everywhere great fires. Oyle cellars and brimstone and other things burning. I became afeared to stay there long; and therefore down again as fast as I could, the fire being spread as far as I could see it. . . .'

Another diarist of the 1660s, John Evelyn, was particularly afraid of what the Fire might do to Tower Hill because he knew that the White Tower was full of gunpowder and that its explosion 'would undoubtedly have not only beaten down and destroyed all the Bridge, but sunk and torn all the vessels in the river and rendered the demolition beyond all expression for several miles even about the country at many miles distance'. In fact the blaze spared the Tower, St Olave's and also Pepys's house in Seething Lane.

Pepys occasionally took his friends and guests to see the lions at the Tower and the Crown Jewels housed there. At the royal command he once conducted three searches in the fortress for the treasure supposedly buried in the Bell Tower by Oliver

Cromwell's lieutenant, but found nothing. It was ten years after he had finished writing his diary that Pepys was himself imprisoned in the Tower for suspected treasonable dealings with France. Charles II sent him a fat buck with which to feed his friends, while good, faithful John Evelyn came and dined in the Tower with him. He was released after six weeks. In 1690 he was back again, this time on the grounds of suspected Jacobitism. Again, he was released unharmed. By now Pepys had moved away from Seething Lane and he was a widower, his wife Elizabeth having died in November 1669. She had been buried at St Olave's, and Pepys was buried with her in the chancel after his own death on 26 May 1703.

Although Pepys's house has gone, as has the Navy Board, St Olave's church remains. It is approached under a gateway sur-mounted by a wonderful skull and crossbones and also some spikes to deter body-snatchers (Dickens in one of his essays called it 'the churchyard of Saint Ghastly Grim'), but once inside it has an especially intimate and friendly atmosphere. The main body of the church dates back to 1450, having survived the Great Fire and having been well restored after damage during the Second World War. High up in the sanctuary is a bust of Elizabeth Pepys, placed there by Samuel after her death so that he could gaze at her during another of Mr Mills's long sermons – fortunately it was moved away to safety at the start of the Second World War. The monument to Pepys himself covers the blocked doorway to the gallery which once contained the Navy Office pew on the south side of the church. Underneath is a memorial to H. B. Wheatley, author of several still useful books on London, who was the editor of the fullest version of the diary until the recent definitive edition by Robert Latham. There is a bust of Pepys in Seething Lane, and a plaque close by marks the site of the Navy Board, while the tower of All Hallows down the road is substan-tially that up which Pepys clambered on 5 September 1666.

A hundred and fifty years after Pepys took a party of friends to see the lions in the Tower the young Samuel Taylor Coleridge enjoyed his 'fifty-times repeated visit to the lions in the Tower'.[4] Ever since the twelfth century the Tower had been used as a royal menagerie. In 1319, for instance, Edward II 'commanded the Sheriffs of London to pay to the keepers of the King's Leopard in the Tower of London sixpence the day for the sustenance of the leopard, and three halfpence a day for diet of the said keeper'.

Ned Ward, a more scurrilous observer of London life than Pepys and who was writing from the 1690s onwards, remarks upon the potential danger of a visit: '. . . as a Madman will be apt to Salute you with a Bowl of Chamber-Lie, so will the Leopard, if you come near him, stare in your Face, and Piss upon you, his urine being as Hot as Aqua Fortis, and stinks worse than a Pole-cats.' The intrepid Ward also reports in *The London Spy* about the armour displayed on wooden dummies within the Tower. Apparently part of Henry VIII's figure was 'the Codpiece of that Great Prince, who never spar'd Woman in his Lust, nor Man in his Anger; and in it, to this Day remains this Vertue, that if any Married Woman, tho' she has for many Years been Barren, if she sticks a Pin in this Member-Case, the next time she uses proper means, let her think of the Tower Pin-Cushion, and she need not fear Conception'.[5] This seems a strange custom in view of Henry's poor record in producing male heirs. The animals, lions and all, were transferred to the new Regent's Park Zoo in 1834. The Royal Mint had been moved out over twenty years before to a fine building which overlooked the Tower. In the 1970s the Mint moved again, this time to Wales, and only the shell of the early-nineteenth-century building remains.

Pepys came to see the Crown Jewels just a few years before the infamous Captain Blood tried to steal them in 1671, being foiled only by the sudden and unexpected appearance of the deputy keeper's son. Surprisingly enough, Captain Blood was never punished. John Evelyn reflected that 'How he came to be pardoned and even received to favour, not only after this, but several other exploits almost as daring, both in Ireland and here, I could never come to understand. Some believed he became a spy of several parties. . . .'[6]

Such was the popular interest in the Tower that it became the first of the sights of London to have its own comprehensive guidebook, *An Historical Description of the Tower of London and Its Curiosities* being published in 1750. The extraordinary thing is that at this time the Tower still held political prisoners, despite the sightseers. John Wilkes, for example, was brought here in May 1763 because of his attack on the government in a newspaper which he edited. He was visited by Horace Walpole; James Boswell missed him: 'I walked up to the Tower in order to see Mr Wilkes come out. But he was gone.'[7]

After many of the Tower's original functions were transferred elsewhere during the course of the nineteenth century, it became above all a tourist attraction, helped by the enormous success of Harrison Ainsworth's novel of 1840 called *The Tower of London*. Ainsworth was adept at writing historical melodramas, using authentic topographical detail to support stories jammed full of dashing heroes, swooning women and assorted ghosts and giants. He did, however, research his subjects thoroughly. One night when writing *The Tower of London* he found himself unsure about some point, jumped into a hansom cab, roused the officials at the Tower (who cannot have been best pleased) and cleared up his query.[8] Not that the Tower's custodians needed any lessons on how best to exploit their public quarry: a small fire in 1841 led them to charge sixpence to see the ruins which they then sold off as charred relics.

Charles Dickens was another frequent visitor to the Tower, and it appears in some of his novels. In *Barnaby Rudge* Gordon is incarcerated here 'in a dreary room whose thick stone walls shut out the hum of life, and made a stillness which the records left by former prisoners . . . seemed to deepen and intensify . . .'. During the Gordon Riots of 1780 the insurgents had planned to break into the Tower and set free the lions. David Copperfield visits the Tower for relaxation, while Quilp in *The Old Curiosity Shop* lives on Tower Hill. There is now a Dickens Inn housed in a converted eighteenth-century warehouse at St Katharine's Dock. It was whilst walking across Tower Hill towards the end of the nineteenth century that the Polish seaman Joseph Conrad suddenly realised 'that I had done with the sea and that henceforth I had to be a writer'.

Today the massive building belonging to the Port of London Authority sits on the north side of Tower Hill, alongside the less imposing and yet more attractive Trinity House, the institution whose charter was drawn up by Samuel Pepys. St Katharine's Dock has been turned into a marina and tourist trap, while the renovated Ivory House which was built in 1850 now contains luxury flats and smart shops. Yet amongst all the razzmatazz aimed at the tourists who come to Tower Hill for the Tower the district possesses hidden charms such as the Crescent, some of whose eighteenth-century houses remain just behind Tower Hill Underground station, and also the moving memorials to the men of the merchant navy killed in both wars. But above all it has St Olave's and the imperishable connections with Samuel Pepys, the man whose infectious enjoyment of life has enriched the lives of so many others.

Westminster

In 1476 an English merchant called William Caxton returned to London after many years spent abroad, mainly in Bruges and Cologne. While on the Continent he had become familiar with the printing press recently pioneered by the German Johann Gutenberg, and he decided to set up his own press back in London. Caxton established it at 'The Sign of the Red Pale', hiring some land near the Chapter House from the monks of Westminster Abbey. Five years later he moved to the east end of Tothill Street. In his fifteen years in Westminster, Caxton produced nearly a hundred printed books, ranging from the poems and *The Canterbury Tales* of Chaucer to a version of *King Arthur* and also the very successful *The Game and Playe of Chess*.[1] Caxton often faced an uphill struggle to sell his books – although they were relatively cheap, his woodcut volumes were far less beautiful than the rival illuminated manuscripts, and in June 1483 his first patron, Earl Rivers, was beheaded for treason.[2] However, by the time of Caxton's death in 1491 the printing press had been firmly established in this country. He was buried in the church of St Margaret, Westminster, alongside his wife Maud, but unfortunately there are no signs of his tomb.[3] Today a stained-glass window in St Margaret's depicts him and nearby is Caxton Street.

Why did Caxton set up his press in Westminster? He shrewdly realised that Westminster at the time possessed two of London's three sources of power, namely the king at Westminster Hall and the church with its monks at Westminster Abbey. Moreover the Archbishop of Canterbury lived close by at Lambeth Palace. The third focus was the City. In other words Caxton wanted to be near his most influential readership.

Ever since Edward the Confessor the kings of England had been based in Westminster. William the Conqueror was crowned in the Abbey on Christmas Day, 1066, starting a tradition which has continued ever since. It was a convention which Shakespeare was able to make use of in one of his most famous scenes. At the end of *Henry IV, Part 2* the reprobate Prince Hal arrives to be transformed into the monarch Henry V. After the coronation he is confronted by his former friends outside the Abbey, above all by Sir John Falstaff with whom he has shared so many escapades. He repudiates him in a speech of shocking coldness:

> *I know thee not, old man. Fall to thy prayers.*
> *How ill white hairs become a fool and jester!*
> *I have long dreamed of such a kind of man,*
> *So surfeit-swelled, so old, and so profane. . . .*

The medieval monks of Westminster Abbey were always looking for extra ways of raising money. One method was to display various relics, usually of somewhat doubtful origin, in the hope that they would bring pilgrims and visitors bearing offerings to the Abbey. Chaucer in the Prologue to *The Canterbury Tales* is brutally frank about the Pardoner's little cache:

> *Ne was ther swich another pardoner.*
> *For in his male he hadde a pilwe-beer,*
> *Which that, he seyde, was Oure Ladye veyl:*
> *He seyde he hadde a gobet of the seyl*
> *That Seint Peter hadde, whan that he wente*
> *Upon the see, til Jhesu Crist hym hente.*
> *He hadde a croys of latoun ful of stones,*
> *And in a glas he hadde pigges bones.*[4]

Another way of making money was for the monks to put on show the effigies of the kings and queens which were traditionally carried in royal funeral processions. Pre-dating Madame Tussaud's by over 300 years, these waxworks were one of London's earliest tourist attractions. The ever-curious Samuel Pepys came with a party of friends in February 1669 and did show them all the tombs very finely, having one with us alone (there being other company this day to see the tombs, it being Shrove Tuesday); and here we did see, by particular favour, the body of Queen Katherine of Valois, and had her upper part of her body in my hands. And I did kiss her mouth, reflecting upon it that I did kiss a Queen, and that this was my birthday, 36 years old, that I did first kiss a Queen.

In later years the relics and waxworks became increasingly tatty – at one point Elizabeth I was clad in only a ruff.[5] The collection today is down in the Norman Undercroft which houses the Abbey Museum. The modern equivalent of the waxworks is Poets' Corner; and here, too, there were accusations that the Abbey authorities were more interested in material than in spiritual matters. In the nineteenth century Thomas Carlyle called the then Dean of Westminster Abbey a 'body-snatcher'. Some of the famous writers with plaques on the floor would probably be bewildered to see themselves remembered here: Dylan Thomas, for instance. Others were originally treated very shabbily by the Church; Byron, for example, has been given a plaque and yet on his death in 1824 the Dean had resolutely refused to let him be buried in the Abbey, so he now rests in Nottinghamshire.[6]

Poets' Corner represents the official face of English literature, but there are one or two stories which make it seem rather more human. Chaucer is here, but simply because he was the King's Clerk of the Works and not because of his writings. There is Ben Jonson, at his own suggestion buried standing up so that he would not take up too much room. Dickens's funeral in 1870 was a small affair attended by just fourteen mourners; the newspapers gave the names of thirteen of them, the other being the actress Ellen Ternan, for whom Dickens had separated from his wife.[7] Tennyson was buried along with the book of Shakespeare's poems he was reading at the time of his death. Samuel Johnson's memorial is obscured by chairs. Milton was buried at St Giles, Cripplegate; the testament to him here contains more on the benefactor who erected it than on the poet. Humour is provided by the eighteenth-century playwright John Gay who wrote the inscription on his monument (now up in the East Triforium) himself:

> *Life is a jest and all things show it,*
> *I thought so once and now I know it.*

If this had not been used, the authorities would have allowed Alexander Pope's alternative compliment to Gay's engaging naïvety: 'in wit a man, simplicity a child'.

There are a few memorials to women here. Apart from the plaques to Jane Austen and the Brontës, one can find the tomb of Aphra Behn, who in the late seventeenth century was the first professional female writer in England. Her play *Oroonoko; or, The History of the Royal Slave* (1668) is an attack on the slave trade. Another woman writer, whose effigy can be found reclining in the North Transept with her husband, is Margaret, Duchess of Newcastle, who was a prolific writer: 'This Duchess was a wise wittie and learned Lady, which her many Bookes do well testifie' – although it should be said that Pepys was not a fan of the Duchess's plays.

Westminster Abbey itself has often been admired by writers. James Boswell called it 'this magnificent and venerable temple',[8] and William Morris 'the most beautiful building in Europe'.[9] Oscar Wilde enjoyed many hours here absorbing the atmosphere, and when Trollope's Septimus Harding travels up to London in *The Warden* this is where he spends the afternoon. However, Charles Lamb in one of the *Last Essays of Elia* complains about the exorbitant fees charged here and at St Paul's for a tour: 'Shame these Sellers out of the Temple.'

Just beside Westminster Abbey is the church of St Margaret, Westminster, a building less cluttered and more intimate than the Abbey. Today's church is largely a creation of the sixteenth century, although it has later additions such as the modern stained-glass windows which have replaced those blown out during the Second World War. The windows at the west end were given in honour of Sir Walter Ralegh, who was beheaded in 1618 in front of the Palace of Westminster and may well have been buried in the chancel. A number of important literary figures have since been buried at St Margaret's. In 1665 the young Samuel Pepys married the even younger Elizabeth St Michel, she being all of fifteen years old. The next year John Milton was married here – another of the west windows is in his honour and shows the blind poet reciting his verse. In 1908, Winston Churchill married Clementine; she must have known from early on that both their lives would be dominated by politics – during the signing of the register the bridegroom and another witness, David Lloyd George, did nothing but talk about the current political situation.

Churchill's statue stands in Parliament Square, and although his literary fame will always rest on his histories – he received the Nobel Prize for Literature in 1953 – he also published a novel in 1900 called *Savrola*. In his autobiography *My Early Life* he declares: 'I have consistently urged my friends to abstain from reading it.' *Savrola* is in fact quite an entertaining adventure-story, set in a mythical European state run by a dictator who is challenged by the hero Savrola (Churchill in disguise!). For the book's obligatory love scene the inexperienced Churchill had to get advice from a fellow army officer.[10]

On the east side of Parliament Square are the Houses of Parliament, massive and imposing but less than 150 years old. Here stood Edward the Confessor's Palace of Westminster until a devastating fire in 1834 destroyed all but Westminster Hall and the crypt of St Stephen. From early times parliamentary accounts had been kept on splints of notched elm. By the 1830s this system was obsolete, and it was suggested that the mass of accumulated splints should be given away to the poor as firewood. But as Charles Dickens put it: 'They never had been useful, and official routine required that they never should be, and so the order went forth that they were to be privately and confidentially burnt.'[11] They were stuffed into a stove in the House of Lords, but the blaze which ensued raged out of control and the old Royal Palace was razed to the ground. The present building boasts 1100 rooms and over two miles of passages – those 'corridors of power' depicted in C. P. Snow's novel of that title. Westminster Hall was for hundreds of years, until 1882, a law court, full of lawyers touting for business. However, as a character in William Wycherley's play *The Plain Dealer* of 1676 remarked: 'Why, you need not be afraid of this place; for a man without money needs no more fear a crowd of lawyers than a crowd of pick-pockets.' Stalls and shops added to the Hall's already considerable noise.

Above all, of course, the Houses of Parliament are the Commons and the Lords, and here the literary associations are many and varied. MPs with a literary bent have included Samuel Pepys, John Wilkes, Benjamin Disraeli, William Gladstone, Winston Churchill and John Buchan, as well as modern writers such as Jeffrey Archer who have been able to make full use of their parliamentary experiences in their books. Lord Byron was a member of the House of Lords and distinguished himself by delivering some fiery speeches on poverty during the Napoleonic wars, while Baron (C. P.) Snow of Leicester was the Labour government's spokesman on technology between 1964 and 1966. During the constitutional crisis of 1910–11 the Liberal government of Asquith threatened to create hundreds of new peers in order to give themselves a majority in the House of Lords. The proposed list of new peers included the names of Thomas Hardy and H. G. Wells – the Conservative peers were so horrified at the prospect of the latter in particular joining their ranks that they backed down and passed the controversial legislation. Neither Hardy nor Wells ever became a peer.

Some writers have come to Parliament to hand in petitions, as did Daniel Defoe. Some were visitors; James Boswell's comments on his trip of March 1763 suggest that Parliament has always been the scene of much rowdy behaviour: 'My respect for it was greatly abated by seeing that it was such a tumultuous scene.' William Morris's respect for it was even less: in *News from Nowhere* he portrayed it in the future as the site of a dung-market.

Some of the people who have worked here in a role other than that of MP have included Samuel Johnson, who in the 1740s was employed by several magazines in composing parliamentary speeches from the notes brought to him by the doorkeepers. As it was then illegal to report MPs' deliberations it was necessary to print the debates as though they had taken place in the Senate House of Lilliput. In the late eighteenth century the printer Luke Hansard was the first person to report the proceedings in full, although his son had to win a court case to ensure that this continued. Samuel Richardson, the eighteenth-century novelist, was once the printer to the House of Commons, while Charles Dickens worked here between 1831 and 1836 as a parliamentary shorthand reporter. He was later invited to represent the constituency of Reading as an MP, but decided against the offer on the grounds that he would wield more influence as a writer.[12] For ten years, from 1904, the librarian of the House of Lords was Edmund Gosse, author of the fine autobiography *Father and Son* which records his battles with his zealot of a father.

Erskine Childers was a clerk at the House of Commons between 1895 and 1910. For his holidays he went on yachting trips in the North Sea, and it was on one of these expeditions that he thought up the plot for his thrilling novel about a planned

German invasion, *The Riddle of the Sands* (1903). During the First World War, Childers worked for the intelligence department; after it he was a member of the army fighting for an independent Irish republic. In 1922 he was captured by the British army, court-martialled and shot.

With Westminster Abbey, St Margaret's and the Houses of Parliament, the area seems full of venerable establishments, but there is yet a fourth, namely Westminster School. Originally an offshoot of the Abbey, the school was refounded by Elizabeth I in 1560, and its cloistered buildings still occupy one side of Dean's Yard. Its list of pupils is important to any literary history, and among the many writers who spent their youth there are poets and playwrights like Ben Jonson, John Dryden and A. A. Milne, the philosopher John Locke and the historian Edward Gibbon. Among the school's catalogue of the great and the good can be found the name of John Cleland, author of *Fanny Hill*. Robert Southey, future Poet Laureate, was expelled for an article he wrote for the magazine *The Flagellant*, criticising the widespread flogging which was administered;[13] the headmaster who expelled him, Dr Vincent, gave his name to Vincent Square. Henry Mayhew, author of the monumental *London Labour and the London Poor* published in the mid-nineteenth century, ran away from Westminster School in protest at the 'dead tongues' which he thought were educationally rammed down the boys' throats.[14]

In view of the eminence of the above establishments it is difficult to understand how for centuries Westminster also housed many of London's worst slums. The reason for its poverty was that, quite apart from its damp and unhealthy terrain, Westminster attracted hundreds of parasites and crooks who leeched off the Court when it was in residence at the Palace of Westminster. When it was not, they leeched off each other. A statute passed during the reign of Elizabeth I referred to the population gathered around Westminster Abbey as being 'for the most part without trade or mystery . . . many of them wholly given to vice and idleness'.[15] The situation was not helped by the refusal of the Dean and Chapter either to sell their lands or to grant long leases, thus ensuring that no property developer would build good-quality houses in Westminster.[16]

In the seventeenth century most of Westminster, other than the slum neighbourhoods and the Palace, Abbey and School, was still open countryside, as Pepys knew when he came to Tothill Fields with a girlfriend. A few years before, in 1652, John Milton moved to Petty France, taking up his residence in 'a pretty-garden house . . . opening into St James's Park'. During his eight years here Milton worked as Oliver Cromwell's secretary and started composing *Paradise Lost*. After the Restoration in 1660, Milton had to flee for his life. In later years other writers, including Jeremy Bentham and James and John Stuart Mill, lived near Milton's old home. When William Hazlitt lived in the house he erected a stone which read 'Sacred to Milton, the Prince of Poets'.[17] At the end of the nineteenth century the house was demolished and replaced by Queen Anne's Mansions, generally considered to have been one of the ugliest buildings in London. This in turn has now been replaced by the new Home Office building, one of central London's premier eyesores. The contrast between this featureless monstrosity and the elegant eighteenth-century Queen Anne's Gate just to the east of it does not show the twentieth century in a very good light.

The growth of Westminster's population in the eighteenth century prompted the building of a new church, St John's in Smith Square, one of whose early curates was Charles Churchill, a poet and satirist famous in his day but who dissipated his talents in an orgy of wine, women and song. When preaching he just read out his father's old sermons. The most famous comment on the design of St John's was made by Charles Dickens in *Our Mutual Friend*. He called it 'a very hideous church with four towers at the corners, generally resembling some petrified monster, frightful and gigantic, on its back with its legs in the air'. Erected on rather damp land, the four towers were included in the construction of the church in order to balance its weight. The church is now used as a concert-hall.

In the nineteenth century some of Westminster's slums were so bad that the district around Orchard Street, Pye Street and St Anne Street was known as 'the Devil's Acre'. Even smart-looking streets and alleys often housed nefarious activities. The pimp Alfred Taylor ran a male brothel at 13 Little College Street, a service frequented by Oscar Wilde amongst others.[18] Some determined efforts were made to wipe out some of the most squalid neighbourhoods; for instance, Victoria Street was constructed in the 1860s and 1870s so that it would pass through 'Devil's Acre'.[19] Over 5000 people were displaced. In their book on London published in 1872, Doré and Jerrold claimed that 'The light of heaven has been admitted through the pestilent dens, the foul byeways, the kens and fences of wicked Westminster'; although they did go on to warn that 'there are still terrible highways and passages round about the Abbey still'. Ironically one of the new institutions built along Victoria Street was the Roman Catholic Westminster Cathedral, a building which the novelist David Lodge has variously described as 'a huge and holy railway terminus' (in *How Far Can You Go?*) and 'the most blatantly phallic symbol on the London skyline' (in *The British Museum Is Falling Down*). More recent buildings include what is undoubtedly the ugliest modern creation in all of London – the three concrete slabs of the Department of the Environment in Marsham Street – and the comparatively more acceptable Queen Elizabeth II Conference Centre facing Westminster Abbey.

Yet despite the ceaseless traffic careering around Parliament Square and the feeling that both the Abbey and the Houses of Parliament represent very much London's official face, there is still something of a village atmosphere to parts of Westminster, especially in the neighbourhood surrounding Smith Square, which includes the beautiful early-eighteenth-century Barton, Cowley and Lord North Streets.

In *Mrs Dalloway*, Virginia Woolf's novel tracing the events in a single day leading up to a dinner-party, Clarissa Dalloway lives in this vicinity. Throughout, the action is punctuated by the noise from Westminster's most famous landmark, 'Big Ben':

> For having lived in Westminster – how many years now? over twenty, – one feels even in the midst of the traffic, or waking at night, Clarissa was positive, a particular hush, or solemnity; an indescribable pause; a suspense (but that might be her heart, affected, they said, by influenza) before Big Ben strikes. There! Out it boomed. First a warning, musical; then the hour, irrevocable.[20]

As for other literary associations, the wonderful baroque building of 1892 in Great Smith Street is the successor to the capital's first public library supported from the rates, which was opened on the other side of Great Smith Street in 1856.

Even in this little enclave, though, the developers are threatening 'modernisation' and, if so, all that will remain of old Westminster will be the small garden behind Little Dean's Yard, which is reputedly the country's oldest cultivated garden, dating back nearly a thousand years. It is pleasant to imagine that 500 years ago William Caxton, taking time off from his labours over the printing press, came here to stroll and relax.

Further Reading

THIS BRIEF ESSAY reviews the published material which might be of interest to anyone wanting to research further into 'Literary London'. Unless specified, the place of publication here and in the notes that follow is London. The date of publication refers to the edition I have used; in virtually every case this is the edition most easily obtainable.

A number of general books deal with the influence of place on literature in Britain but also contain sections or comments on London: John Freeman, *Literature and Locality* (1963); Dorothy Eagle and Hilary Carnell (eds), *The Oxford Literary Guide to the British Isles* (Oxford, 1977); Margaret Drabble, *A Writer's Britain* (1979); David Daiches, *Literary Landscapes of the British Isles* (1979); and Frank Morley, *Literary Britain* (1980). Particularly recommended is the book by Daiches because of its clear maps and gazetteer. Two useful books long out of print but obtainable through the larger libraries are A. St John Adcock, *The Booklover's London* (1913), and E. Beresford Chancellor, *The Literary Ghosts of London* (1933); Frank Swinnerton's *The Bookman's London* (1951) has been most helpful. Both Laurence Hutton, *Literary Landmarks of London* (1888), and William Kent, *London for the Literary Pilgrim* (1949), take a biographical approach. Rachel Hartley's pamphlet *A Literary Guide to the City* (1966) is a good introduction; while H. B. Bassett, *Literary Places In and Out of London* (1985), lists various literary addresses and places open to the public. G. G. Williams, *Guide to Literary London* (1973), is thorough and detailed but, I think, more of a catalogue to be consulted than a book to be read. A. H. Hedley (ed.), *London in Literature* (1921), prints relevant extracts – a volume to be supplemented by Hugh and Pauline Massingham (eds), *The London Anthology* (1950). The recent *Oxford Companion to English Literature* (Oxford, 1985), edited by Margaret Drabble, is invaluable for checking basic information.

As for the history of London generally, Ben Weinreb and Christopher Hibbert, *The London Encyclopaedia* (1983), is indispensable; scarcely less so, although harder to get hold of, are Walter Thornbury and Edward Walford, *Old and New London*, in six volumes (n.d.), and H. B. Wheatley and P. Cunningham, *London Past and Present* (1891), in three volumes. F. R. Banks, *The New Penguin Guide to London* (1986), is comprehensive; David Piper, *The Companion Guide to London* (1981), well written; and Felix Barker and Peter Jackson, *London: 2000 Years of a City and Its People* (1983), well illustrated. A good general history is Christopher Hibbert, *London: The Biography of a City* (1983). R. J. Mitchell and M. D. R. Leys, *A History of London Life* (1963), is an excellent introduction to the social history of the capital, although it is now a little out of date. For the local history of various areas, please see the notes to each chapter.

It is odd that none of the above books includes references or notes, and only four (Banks, Bassett, Hibbert and the *Oxford Guide*) have anything in the way of a reading list.

I have written this before (*The Map of London*, 1987, p. 106), and will probably do so again, but the best way to get to know parts of London is on foot. This physical exercise should then be supported by reading Pepys's diary and studying the paintings and engravings of William Hogarth.

Notes

Chapter 1: Around the Bank

1 Edgar Johnson, *Charles Dickens: His Tragedy and Triumph* (1977), pp. 155–7.
2 Anthony Trollope, *An Autobiography* (1950), p. 364.
3 Charles Lamb, 'The Superannuated Man', in *The Last Essays of Elia* (1833).
4 P. G. Wodehouse, 'Over Seventy', in *Wodehouse on Wodehouse* (1981), p. 266.
5 J. Ewing Ritchie, *East Anglia* (1893), p. 266.
6 P. R. Chalmers, *Kenneth Grahame* (1933), p. 113.
7 S. J. Kunitz and H. Haycraft, *Twentieth-Century Authors* (New York, 1942), p. 1191.
8 *Wodehouse on Wodehouse*, pp. 484–5.
9 John Pearson, *The Life of Ian Fleming* (1967), p. 83.
10 Johnson, *Charles Dickens*, p. 417.
11 Alexander Pope, 'To Lord Bathurst', in *Moral Essays* (1731–5).
12 *The Economist*, 15 November 1986.
13 Bonamy Dobrée in Allen Tate (ed.), *T. S. Eliot: The Man and His Work* (1967), p. 70.
14 In fact Smith had already suspected from the handwriting that the author of *Jane Eyre* was a woman: Winifred Gerin, *Charlotte Brontë* (1967), p. 364.
15 Washington Irving, 'The Boar's Head Tavern', in *The Sketch Book* (1821), p. 188.

Chapter 2: Bloomsbury

1 Hugh Meller, *St George's Bloomsbury* (1975), p. 1.
2 Edward Walford, *Old and New London*, Vol. 4 (n.d.), p. 482.
3 *Coram Foundation Guide* (n.d.), p. 8.
4 G. M. Trevelyan, *An Autobiography and Other Essays* (1945), p. 47.
5 *The Letters of Horace Walpole*, ed. Mrs Paget Toynbee, Vol. 3 (1903), p. 142.
6 J. Penn, *For Readers Only* (1936), p. 7.

7 Andrew Rothstein, *Lenin in Britain* (1970), p. 13.
8 Hesketh Pearson, *Bernard Shaw* (1961), p. 101.
9 Penn, *For Readers Only*, p. 102.
10 Rothstein, *Lenin in Britain*, pp. 28–30.
11 Ernest A. Payne, *A Venerable Dissenting Institution* (1979), p. 16.
12 Walford, *Old and New London*, Vol. 4, p. 564.
13 ibid., p. 542.
14 Anthony Trollope, *An Autobiography* (1950), p. 25.
15 William Kent, *London for the Literary Pilgrim* (1949), p. 227.
16 *The Letters of William Morris*, ed. Philip Henderson (1967), p. xxxix.
17 C. H. Hobday, 'Three-Deckers and Yellow-Backs', in *Our Time*, March 1947, p. 173; also the entry on Mudie in *The Dictionary of National Biography*, Vol. 39 (1894), p. 136.
18 Pamphlet issued by the church (n.d.).
19 James L. Brabazon, *Dorothy L. Sayers* (1981), p. 180.
20 Mary Wollstonecraft, *A Vindication of the Rights of Women*, ed. Mrs Henry Fawcett (1891), p. 29.
21 John Lehmann, *Holborn* (1970), p. 181.
22 Brabazon, *Dorothy L. Sayers*, pp. 86–7, 109.
23 Robert Sencourt, *T. S. Eliot: A Memoir* (1971), p. 138.

Chapter 3: Chelsea

1 Newspaper cuttings held in Reference Library, Chelsea, Vol. 8.
2 Edward Walford, *Old and New London*, Vol. 5 (n.d.), pp. 52 ff.
3 Information supplied by the British Federation of University Women.
4 Reginald Blunt, *By Chelsea Reach* (1921), pp. 97–139.
5 R. D. Altick, *The Shows of London* (Cambridge, Mass., 1978), pp. 17–19.
6 *The Royal Hospital* (1975).
7 Michael Millgate (ed.), *The Life and Work of Thomas Hardy* (1984), pp. 81, 109, 114, 127.
8 Hugh and Pauline Massingham (eds), *The London Anthology* (1950), p. 328.
9 Philippa Bernard, *Chelsea* (1983), p. 13.
10 William Kent, *London for the Literary Pilgrim* (1949), p. 208.
11 *Thomas Carlyle: Selected Writings*, ed. Alan Shelston (1971), p. 354.
12 *Jane Welsh Carlyle: A Selection of Her Letters*, ed. Trudy Bliss (1959), p. 206
13 *Reminiscences of Marx and Engels* (Moscow, n.d.), p. 238.
14 Bernard, *Chelsea*, p. 30.
15 Hesketh Pearson, *The Life of Oscar Wilde* (1960), p. 250.
16 Margaret Drabble, *Arnold Bennett* (1974), pp. 49, 51.

17 Frederic Raphael, *W. Somerset Maugham and His World* (1976), p. 34.
18 David A. Jasen, *P. G. Wodehouse: A Portrait of a Master* (New York, 1981), p. 25.
19 John Pearson, *The Life of Ian Fleming* (1967), pp. 240, 246.

Chapter 4: Clerkenwell and Smithfield

 1 William Hazlitt, *Lectures on the English Comic Writers* (1910), p. 123.
 2 Christopher Hibbert, *The Personal History of Samuel Johnson* (1984), p. 31.
 3 Arthur Crow, *The Clerks' Well* (1925).
 4 Alec Forshaw, *Smithfield Past and Present* (1980), p. 20.
 5 T. Winyard, *The Priory Church of Bartholomew the Great* (1970), pp. 1–2.
 6 Henry Morley, *Memoirs of Bartholomew Fair* (1973).
 7 Lionel Butler, *The Order of St John and the Peasants' Revolt of 1381* (1981).
 8 Christopher Edwards (ed.), *The London Theatre Guide, 1576–1642* (1979), p. 14.
 9 John Adlard, *In Sweet St James's Clerkenwell* (1984), pp. 11–13.
10 John Ashton, *Social Life in the Reign of Queen Anne* (1893), pp. 274–5.
11 Arthur Oswald, *The London Charterhouse Restored* (1959), p. 6.
12 Pieter Zwart, *Islington* (1973), p. 84.
13 Andrew Rothstein, *A House on Clerkenwell Green* (1983), p. 25.
14 *Letters of George Gissing to Members of His Family* (1927), letter to his sister, August 1887, p. 199.
15 Andrew Rothstein, 'William Morris at Clerkenwell', *The Times*, 11 April 1966.
16 *The Dictionary of National Biography, 1922–1930* (1937), p. 117.
17 Margaret Drabble, *Arnold Bennett* (1974), p. 277.

Chapter 5: Coming and Going

 1 Edward Walford, *Old and New London*, Vol. 3 (n.d.), pp. 287–9.
 2 J. J. Jusserand, *English Wayfaring Life in the Middle Ages* (1950), p. 25.
 3 David Piper, *The Companion Guide to London* (1981), p. 255.
 4 *The Diary of John Evelyn*, ed. John Bowle (Oxford, 1985), p. 310.
 5 *Boswell's London Journal, 1762–1763*, ed. F. A. Pottle (1950), pp. 154–5.

6 R. J. Mitchell and M. D. R. Leys, *A History of London Life* (1963), p. 147.
7 E. Beresford Chancellor, *The Literary Ghosts of London* (1933), p. 267.
8 William Kent, *London for the Literary Pilgrim* (1949), p. 54.
9 Diana Preston, 'Joseph Conrad', in *Port of London*, vol. 59, no. 4 (1984), p. 120.
10 *The Letters of William Morris*, ed. Philip Henderson (1967), p. 138 n.
11 Jerome K. Jerome, *My Life and Times* (1926), p. 103.
12 John Betjeman, 'London Railway Stations', in *First and Last Loves* (1969), p. 80.
13 Asa Briggs, *Marx in London* (1982), p. 55.
14 Cole Lesley, *The Life of Noël Coward* (1976), p. 2.
15 Frederic Raphael, *W. Somerset Maugham and His World* (1976), p. 14.
16 Constantine Fitzgibbon, *The Life of Dylan Thomas* (1965), p. 102.
17 Anthony Trollope, *An Autobiography* (1950), p. 103.
18 Morton Cohen, *Rider Haggard* (1968), p. 85.
19 Charles Wilson, *First with the News* (1985), p. 91.
20 J. E. Morpurgo, *Allen Lane: King Penguin* (1979), p. 80.
21 Derek Stanford, *John Betjeman* (1961), p. 73.

Chapter 6: Covent Garden and the Strand

1 James Boswell, *The Life of Samuel Johnson* (1791); A. St John Adcock, *The Booklover's London* (1913), p. 245; *London* (n.d.), p. 121.
2 R. C. Bald, *John Donne* (1970), p. 125.
3 Edmund Gosse, *The Life and Letters of John Donne*, Vol. 1 (1899), p. 103.
4 *The Diary of John Evelyn*, ed. John Bowle (Oxford, 1985), p. 182.
5 Edward Walford, *Old and New London*, Vol. 3 (n.d.), p. 258.
6 H. B. Wheatley and P. Cunningham, *London Past and Present*, Vol. 1 (1891), p. 462.
7 *Boswell's London Journal, 1762–1763*, ed. F. A. Pottle (1950), p. 259.
8 Pat Rogers, *Henry Fielding* (1979), p. 155.
9 Patrick Pringle, *Hue and Cry* (1955), pp. 77–90.
10 *Boswell's London Journal*, p. 254.
11 Walford, *Old and New London*, Vol. 3, p. 257.
12 *The Dictionary of National Biography*, Vol. 21 (1890), p. 24.
13 E. Beresford Chancellor, *The Literary Ghosts of London* (1933), p. 264.
14 Thomas Burke, *English Night-life* (1941), p. 94.
15 Leslie Shepard, *The Broadside Ballad* (Wakefield, 1978), p. 82.

16 Walford, *Old and New London*, Vol. 3, p. 237; ill-health prevented Dickens from attending the audition.
17 N. T. P. Murphy, *In Search of Blandings* (1986), p. xiv.
18 Kenneth Robinson, *Wilkie Collins* (1974), p. 197.
19 David Piper, *The Companion Guide to London* (1981), p. 28.
20 H. Barton Baker, *History of the London Stage* (1904), p. 129.
21 Rudyard Kipling, *Something of Myself* (1951), p. 80.
22 Lord Birkenhead, *Rudyard Kipling* (1978), p. 109.
23 Reginald Pound, *The Strand Magazine, 1891–1950* (1966), p. 43.
24 Michael Millgate (ed.), *The Life and Work of Thomas Hardy* (1984), p. 42.

Chapter 7: The East End

1 Thomas Burke, *Living in Bloomsbury* (1939), p. 87.
2 J. G. Birch, *Limehouse through Five Centuries* (1930), p. 144.
3 Hugh and Pauline Massingham (eds), *The London Anthology* (1925), p. 124.
4 G. G. Coulton, *Chaucer and His England* (1921), p. 93.
5 Marchette Chute, *Geoffrey Chaucer of England* (1962), p. 129.
6 Charles Poulsen, *English Rebels* (1984), p. 16.
7 Colm Kerrigan, *A History of Tower Hamlets* (1982), p. 31.
8 John Stow, *A Survey of London*, ed. C. L. Kingsford (1908), Vol. 1, p. 127.
9 For the rural East London of the eighteenth century, see the relevant maps in Andrew Davies, *The Map of London* (1987).
10 *East London Papers*, Vol. 6, no. 2 (1963), pp. 135–7.
11 Robert Barltrop, *Jack London* (1978), p. 80.
12 T. R. Fyvel, *George Orwell* (1983), pp. 33–4.
13 T. D. Critchley and P. D. James, *The Maul and the Pear Tree* (1971).
14 Donald Rumbelow, *The Complete Jack the Ripper* (1975), p. 23.
15 P. J. Keating's biographical study in the 1971 edition of *A Child of the Jago*, pp. 11–35.
16 Peter Haining, *Mystery!* (1977), p. 85; see also Julian Symons, *Bloody Murder* (1974), pp. 90–1.
17 Jean Liddiard, *Isaac Rosenberg: The Half Used Life* (1975), p. 40; reading out poems, p. 42.

Chapter 8: Fitzrovia

1 E. Beresford Chancellor, *London's Old Latin Quarter* (1930), p. 10.
2 V. S. Pritchett, *London Perceived* (1986), p. 147.

3 Edward Walford, *Old and New London*, Vol. 4 (n.d.), p. 461.
4 Anne Humphreys, *Travels into the Poor Man's Country* (1977), p. 181.
5 Nick Bailey, *Fitzrovia* (1981), p. 46.
6 Wilhelm Liebknecht, *Karl Marx* (1975), pp. 150–1.
7 *London Landmarks* (n.d.), p. 5.
8 Ivan Maisky, *Journey into the Past* (1962), pp. 35–9.
9 Jerome K. Jerome, *My Life and Times* (1926), p. 68.
10 H. G. Wells, *An Experiment in Autobiography*, Vol. 1 (1934), p. 315.
11 Constantine Fitzgibbon, *The Life of Dylan Thomas* (1965), p. 171;
    also Robert Hewison, *Under Siege* (1979), pp. 56 ff.
12 Julian Maclaren-Ross, *Memoirs of the Forties* (1984), p. 159.
13 *Selected Letters of Dylan Thomas*, ed. Constantine Fitzgibbon (1966),
    p. 153.
14 Paul Ferris, *Dylan Thomas* (1978), p. 145.
15 Alan Ross, introduction to Maclaren-Ross, *Memoirs of the Forties*,
    p. x; also 'Sohoitis' in ibid., p. 138.
16 Ian Rodger, *Radio Drama* (1982), p. 71.
17 W. E. Williams, *Allen Lane* (1973), pp. 46–7.
18 J. E. Morpurgo, *Allen Lane: King Penguin* (1979), pp. 111–13.
19 David Piper, *The Companion Guide to London* (1981), p. 235.
20 Elizabeth and Wayland Young, *London's Churches* (1986), p. 37.
21 R. L. Stevenson, *Memories and Portraits* (1925), pp. 214–15.

Chapter 9: Hampstead

1 Joseph Connolly, article in *The Times*, 30 October 1986.
2 C. Wade (ed.), *The Streets of Hampstead* (1972), p. 15.
3 Edward Thomas, *A Literary Pilgrim in England* (1980), p. 12.
4 William Addison, *English Spas* (1951), pp. 48–9.
5 History issued by Burgh House (n.d.).
6 M. C. Borer, *Hampstead and Highgate* (1976), p. 150.
7 Wilhelm Liebknecht, *Karl Marx* (1975), pp. 124–30.
8 Edward Walford, *Old and New London*, Vol. 5 (n.d.), p. 472.
9 William Kent, *London for the Literary Pilgrim* (1949), p. 23.
10 D. Barker, *Man of Principle* (1963), p. 234.
11 Material on Lawrence and his circle comes from the excellent
    pamphlet by Christopher Wade, *D. H. Lawrence and His Hampstead
    Circle* (1985).
12 Michael Holroyd, *Lytton Strachey*, Vol. 2 (1968), p. 179.
13 C. S. Forester, *Long before Forty* (1967), pp. 102–4.
14 Cole Lesley, *The Life of Noël Coward* (1976), p. 94.
15 *The Diaries of Evelyn Waugh*, ed. Michael Davie (1976), p. 185.
16 Introduction by Victoria Glendinning to the Virago reprint (1983)
    of Vita Sackville-West, *All Passion Spent*.
17 Ian Norrie (ed.), *Writers and Hampstead* (1987).

Chapter 10: Highgate

1 Edward Walford, *Old and New London*, Vol. 5 (n.d.), p. 390.
2 Laurence Hutton, *Literary Landmarks of London* (1888), p. 23.
3 William Howitt, *Homes and Haunts of the British Poets* (1894), p. 402.
4 Friends of Highgate Cemetery (1978), p. 2.
5 Richard Tames, *William Morris* (1972), p. 36.
6 Friends of Highgate Cemetery, *Highgate Cemetery*, p. 31.
7 John Betjeman, 'The Usher of Highgate Junior School', in R. March and Tambimuttu (eds), *T. S. Eliot* (1948), pp. 89–92.
8 Derek Stanford, *John Betjeman* (1961), p. 2.
9 R. P. Graves, *A. E. Housman* (1981), p. 68.

Chapter 11: Holborn and Lincoln's Inn

1 Walter Thornbury, *Old and New London*, Vol. 2 (n.d.), pp. 525–6.
2 R. C. Bald, *John Donne* (1970), p. 72.
3 R. Megarry, *An Introduction to Lincoln's Inn* (1971), p. 8.
4 Morton Cohen, *Rider Haggard* (1968), p. 219.
5 Edward Walford, *Old and New London*, Vol. 4 (n.d.), pp. 470–1.
6 Laurence Hutton, *Literary Landmarks of London* (1888), p. 4.
7 E. Beresford Chancellor, *The Literary Ghosts of London* (1933), p. 311.
8 William Kent, *London for the Literary Pilgrim* (1949), p. 153.
9 Penelope Fitzgerald's introduction to *The Novel on Blue Paper* (1982), p. x.
10 E. Beresford Chancellor, *Literary Diversions* (1925), p. 48; see also Charles G. Harper, *A Literary Man's London* (1926), pp. 11–20.
11 John Lehmann, *Holborn* (1970), p. 166.
12 Augustine Birrell, *William Hazlitt* (1902), p. 86.
13 G. G. Williams, *Guide to Literary London* (1973), p. 106.

Chapter 12: Islington

1 Keith Sugden, *History of Highbury* (1984), p. 15.
2 Lionel Butler, *The Order of St John and the Peasants' Revolt of 1381* (1981), p. 4.
3 John O'London, *London Stories* (1926), p. 126.
4 Dennis Arundel, *The Story of Sadler's Wells* (1965), p. 24.
5 Richard Findlater, *Joe Grimaldi* (Cambridge, 1978), p. 181.
6 The best edition of Grimaldi's *Memoirs* is that by Richard Findlater (1968).
7 Sugden, *History of Highbury*, p. 20.

8 Mary Cosh, *Barnsbury* (1981), p. 4.
9 Mary Cosh, *The New River* (1982), p. 1.
10 Charles Lamb, *The Essays of Elia* (n.d.), pp. 28–9.
11 William Kent, *London for the Literary Pilgrim* (1949), p. 125.
12 Angus Davidson, *Edward Lear* (1950), p. 136.
13 Kenneth Robinson, *Wilkie Collins* (1974), p. 33.
14 Cosh, *Barnsbury*, p. 5.
15 Elizabeth and Wayland Young, *London's Churches* (1986),
     pp. 187–8.
16 T. R. Fyvel, *George Orwell* (1983), p. 149.
17 George Woodcock, *The Crystal Spirit* (1967), p. 25.
18 John Lahr, *Prick Up Your Ears* (1980), pp. 95–6.
19 Tim Clark, 'Of Loot and Loos', *Time Out*, 15 April 1987.

Chapter 13: Kensington

1 *The Royal Borough of Kensington* (1933), p. 21.
2 *The Diary of John Evelyn*, ed. John Bowle (Oxford, 1985), p. 400.
3 Leigh Hunt, *The Old Court Suburb* (1902), Vol. 2, pp. 40, 42.
4 Edward Walford, *Old and New London*, Vol. 5 (n.d.), p. 166.
5 David A. Jasen, *P. G. Wodehouse: A Portrait of a Master* (New York,
     1981), p. 97.
6 William Kent, *London for the Literary Pilgrim* (1949), p. 142.
7 Hesketh Pearson, *Bernard Shaw* (1948), p. 304.
8 Laurence Hutton, *Literary Landmarks of London* (1888), p. 303.
9 Winifred Gerin, *Charlotte Brontë* (1967), p. 434.
10 Michael Millgate (ed.), *The Life and Work of Thomas Hardy* (1984),
     p. 219.
11 Hunt, *Old Court Suburb*, vol. 1, p. 17.
12 P. R. Chalmers, *Kenneth Grahame* (1931), pp. 121–3.
13 D. Felicitas Corrigan, *Siegfried Sassoon: Poet's Pilgrimage* (1973),
     p. 39.
14 Kent, *London for the Literary Pilgrim*, p. 69.
15 Peter Stansky, *William Morris* (1983), p. 41.
16 P. G. Wodehouse, *Thank You, Jeeves* (1975), p. 66.
17 H. G. Wells, *An Experiment in Autobiography*, Vol. 1 (1934), p. 207.
18 Richard Ellman, *James Joyce* (1976), p. 654.
19 Robert Sencourt, *T. S. Eliot: A Memoir* (1971), p. 130.

Chapter 14: Lambeth

1 Rosemary Nicholson, 'A Museum of Garden History', *Period Home*,
     vol. 4, no. 2 (1985), pp. 41–5.

2 R. D. Altick, *The Shows of London* (Cambridge, Mass., 1978), p. 11.
3 A. D. Nash, *Living in Lambeth, 1086–1914* (n.d.), p. 7.
4 Gordon Hueslin, *Lambeth Palace* (1974), pp. 8–9.
5 William Kent, *London for the Literary Pilgrim* (1949), p. 100.
6 Christina Hole, *English Sports and Pastimes* (1949), pp. 166–9.
7 Edward Walford, *Old and New London*, Vol. 6 (n.d.), p. 341.
8 J. S. Bratton and J. Traies, *Astley's Amphitheatre* (Cambridge, 1980), p. 15.
9 John Earl and John Stanton, *The Canterbury Hall and Theatre of Varieties* (Cambridge, 1982), pp. 37–8, 45–6.
10 John Booth, *The Old Vic, 1816–1916* (1917), p. 17.
11 Peter Roberts, *The Old Vic Story* (1976), p. 46.
12 Booth, *Old Vic*, p. 30.
13 Andrew Rothstein, *Lenin in Britain* (1970), p. 20.
14 Harcourt Williams (ed.), *Vic-Wells* (1938), p. 15.
15 P. G. Wodehouse, *Jeeves in the Offing* (1963), p. 37.
16 W. Somerset Maugham, *The Summing Up* (1938), p. 64.
17 Review of *Liza of Lambeth* in *The Times*, 28 December 1897.

Chapter 15: Marylebone

1 Oscar Sherwin, *Uncorking Old Sherry* (1960), pp. 81–3.
2 Elizabeth and Wayland Young, *London's Churches* (1986), p. 159.
3 Ronald Paulson, *Polite and Popular Art in the Age of Hogarth and Fielding* (Indiana, 1978), pp. 85–95.
4 Andrew Davies, *The Map of London* (1987), p. 12.
5 Edward Walford, *Old and New London*, Vol. 4 (n.d.), p. 435.
6 Thomas Burke, *English Night-life* (1941), p. 23.
7 E. Beresford Chancellor, *The Literary Ghosts of London* (1933), p. 220.
8 Leonard Cottrell, *Madame Tussaud* (1951).
9 Kenneth Robinson, *Wilkie Collins* (1974), pp. 136, 138.
10 Julian Symons, introduction to *The Woman in White* (1974), p. 11.
11 Robinson, *Wilkie Collins*, p. 195.
12 Percy Scholes (ed.), *The Oxford Companion to Music* (Oxford, 1970), p. 990.
13 Reginald Pound, *The Strand Magazine, 1891–1950* (1966), pp. 41–2.
14 Jerome K. Jerome, *My Life and Times* (1926), p. 104.
15 Peter Haining, *The Television Sherlock Holmes* (1986), p. 36.
16 P. G. Wodehouse, *Carry On, Jeeves* (1957), p. 125.
17 Janet Adam Smith, *John Buchan* (Oxford, 1985), p. 150.
18 Margaret Drabble, *Arnold Bennett* (1974), p. 345.
19 C. P. Snow, *Variety of Men* (1969), p. 59.
20 *The Dictionary of National Biography, 1941–1950* (1959), p. 948.

21 Angus Davidson, *Edward Lear* (1950), p. 22.
22 J. E. Morpurgo, *Allen Lane: King Penguin* (1979), pp. 88–9.

Chapter 16: Mayfair

1   Edward Walford, *Old and New London*, Vol. 5 (n.d.), p. 196.
2   M. D. George, *London Life in the Eighteenth Century* (1966), p. 20.
3   H. B. Wheatley and P. Cunningham, *London Past and Present*, Vol. 3 (1891), p. 418.
4   Christopher Hibbert, *The Road to Tyburn* (1957), p. 137.
5   Eric Dancy, *Hyde Park* (1937), p. 36.
6   M. C. Borer, *The Years of Grandeur* (1975), pp. 14–16.
7   *The Diary of John Evelyn*, ed. John Bowle (Oxford, 1985), p. 303.
8   Kenneth Fenwick (ed.), *The London Spy* (1955), p. 134.
9   Rodney Mace, *Trafalgar Square* (1976), p. 33.
10 Christopher Hibbert, *The Personal History of Samuel Johnson* (1984), pp. 92–3.
11 William Kent, *London for the Literary Pilgrim* (1949), p. 184.
12 Constance Babington Smith (ed.), *Letters to a Friend* (1961), p. 134.
13 E. Beresford Chancellor, *The Literary Ghosts of London* (1933), p. 286.
14 ibid., p. 303.
15 Hesketh Pearson, *The Life of Oscar Wilde* (1960), p. 277.
16 N. T. P. Murphy, *In Search of Blandings* (1986), pp. 72–83.
17 P. G. Wodehouse, *Carry On, Jeeves* (1957), p. 81.
18 David A. Jasen, *P. G. Wodehouse: A Portrait of a Master* (New York, 1981), p. 107.
19 Derek Stanford, *John Betjeman* (1961), p. 22.
20 Anthony Powell, *A Buyer's Market* (1967), p. 162.
21 *The Letters of William Morris*, ed. Philip Henderson (1967), p. 209.
22 Nadezhda Krupskaya, *Memories of Lenin* (1970), pp. 64–5.

Chapter 17: St James's and Whitehall

1   G. G. Coulton, *Chaucer and His England* (1921), pp. 60–1.
2   Hazel Thurston, *Royal Parks for the People* (1974), p. 36.
3   *The Diary of John Evelyn*, ed. John Bowle (Oxford, 1985), p. 403.
4   David Piper, *The Companion Guide to London* (1981), p. 72.
5   Martin Seymour-Smith, *Robert Graves* (1982), p. 62.
6   A. H. Phillips (ed.), *Georgian Scrapbook* (1949), p. 49.
7   Ben Weinreb and Christopher Hibbert (eds), *The London Encyclopaedia* (1983), p. 961.
8   *Boswell's London Journal, 1762–1763*, ed. F. A. Pottle (1950), p. 59.

9 *The Collected Essays, Journalism and Letters of George Orwell*, Vol. 1, *An Age Like This* (1970), pp. 75–7.
10 Miron Grindea (ed.), *The London Library* (1978), pp. 20–1, 64.
11 F. W. Dupee, *Henry James* (1951), pp. 171–2.
12 Hesketh Pearson, *The Life of Oscar Wilde* (1960), p. 277.
13 *The Standard*, 1 June 1987.
14 John Pearson, *The Life of Ian Fleming* (1967), p. 106.
15 Graham Turner, 'The Makers of Jim Hacker', in *Sunday Telegraph*, 11 January 1987.

Chapter 18: St Paul's and Its Environs

1 Alfred Harbage, *Shakespeare and the Rival Traditions* (Indiana, 1970), p. 40.
2 E. Beresford Chancellor, *The Literary Ghosts of London* (1933), pp. 44–5.
3 H. B. Wheatley and P. Cunningham, *London Past and Present*, Vol. 3 (1891), pp. 42–3.
4 Thomas Burke, *The Streets of London* (1941), pp. 26–8.
5 Walter Thornbury, *Old and New London*, Vol. 1 (n.d.), pp. 246–8.
6 A. N. Wilson, *The Life of John Milton* (1983), p. 154.
7 Laurence Hutton, *Literary Landmarks of London* (1888), p. 108.
8 Pat Rogers, *Grub Street* (1972).
9 Roy Porter, *English Society in the Eighteenth Century* (1982), p. 155.
10 *Boswell's London Journal, 1762–1763*, ed. F. A. Pottle (1950), pp. 245–6.
11 Anthony Trollope, *An Autobiography* (1950), pp. 51 ff.

Chapter 19: Shoreditch and Finsbury

1 A. W. Light, *Bunhill Fields* (1913).
2 Vera Brittain, *In the Steps of John Bunyan* (1950), pp. 386–91.
3 Annette T. Rubinstein, *The Great Tradition in English Literature* (New York, 1969), p. 189.
4 See the chapter 'The Reading Public and the Rise of the Novel', in Ian Watt, *The Rise of the Novel* (1972), pp. 38–65.
5 Christopher Hill, 'Robinson Crusoe', in *History Workshop*, no. 10 (Autumn 1980), p. 9.
6 Brian Fitzgerald, *Daniel Defoe* (1954), p. 202.
7 Stephen Kay Jones, *Dr Williams and His Library* (Cambridge, 1948).
8 City of London, *Bunhill Fields* (1981), p. 7.
9 M. C. Bradbrook, *Shakespeare the Craftsman* (Cambridge, 1979), pp. 38–9.

10 Christopher Edwards (ed.), *The London Theatre Guide, 1576–1642* (1979), p. 31.
11 Marchette Chute, *Ben Jonson of Westminster* (1962), p. 60.
12 A. N. Wilson, *The Life of John Milton* (Oxford, 1983), p. 242.
13 ibid., p. 259.
14 Laurence Hutton, *Literary Landmarks of London* (1888), p. 318.
15 Frank Barber, *John Wesley, London Publisher, 1733–1791* (1984).
16 E. Beresford Chancellor, *Literary Diversions* (1925), p. 51; and Victor Neuburg, *Popular Literature* (1977), pp. 200–2.
17 A. E. Wilson, *East End Entertainment* (1954), pp. 163–97; Clive Barker, 'The Audiences of the Britannia Theatre, Hoxton', in *Theatre Quarterly*, Vol. 34 (Summer 1979), pp. 27–41.
18 *Hoxton Hall: A Short History* (1977: available at the hall).

Chapter 20: Soho and Leicester Square

1 Brian Fitzgerald, *Daniel Defoe* (1954), pp. 58–61.
2 *The Diary of John Evelyn*, ed. John Bowle (Oxford, 1985), p. 376.
3 E. Beresford Chancellor, *The Romance of Soho* (1931), p. 48.
4 Christopher Hibbert, *The Personal History of Samuel Johnson* (1984), p. 79.
5 Chancellor, *Romance of Soho*, pp. 64–93.
6 Frank Swinnerton, introduction to P. P. Howe, *The Life of William Hazlitt* (1949), p. 13.
7 James L. Brabazon, *Dorothy L. Sayers* (1981), pp. 241, 272.
8 Ben Weinreb and Christopher Hibbert (eds), *The London Encyclopaedia* (1983), p. 792.
9 *Reminiscences of Marx and Engels* (Moscow, n.d.), p. 228.
10 Michael Millgate (ed.), *The Life and Work of Thomas Hardy* (1984), p. 265.
11 Chancellor, *Romance of Soho*, p. 136.
12 Cole Lesley, *The Life of Noël Coward* (1976), p. 158.

Chapter 21: Southwark and Bankside

1 W. Rendle, *Old Southwark and Its People* (1878), p. 181.
2 John Dover Wilson (ed.), *Life in Shakespeare's England* (1944), p. 230.
3 William Howitt, *Homes and Haunts of the British Poets* (1894), p. 32.
4 Christopher Edwards (ed.), *The London Theatre Guide, 1576–1642* (1979), p. 23.
5 Joseph Clayton, *The True Story of Jack Cade* (1909).
6 *The Diary of John Evelyn*, ed. John Bowle (Oxford, 1985), p. 389.

7 *The Dictionary of National Biography*, Vol. 24 (1890), pp. 390–2.
8 Edgell Rickword, *Literature in Society* (Manchester, 1978), p. 282.
9 Edgar Johnson, *Charles Dickens: His Tragedy and Triumph* (1977), pp. 98, 105.
10 W. Rendle and P. Norman, *The Inns of Old Southwark* (1888), p. 70.

Chapter 22: The Temple and Fleet Street

1 Charles Lamb, *The Essays of Elia* (n.d.), p. 162.
2 A. St John Adcock, *The Booklover's London* (1913), pp. 222–7.
3 Christopher Hibbert, *London: The Biography of a City* (1980), p. 74.
4 See the introduction by Peter Sabor to *Memoirs of a Woman of Pleasure* (Oxford, 1985), pp. 7–27.
5 Kenneth Fenwick (ed.), *The London Spy* (1955), p. 111.
6 See the exhibition in the crypt of St Bride's.
7 William Kent, *London for the Literary Pilgrim* (1949), p. 203.
8 Annette T. Rubinstein, *The Great Tradition in English Literature* (New York, 1969), pp. 295–6.
9 Pat Rogers, *Henry Fielding* (1979), p. 100.
10 Walter Thornbury, *Old and New London*, Vol. 1 (n.d.), pp. 145–6.
11 *Boswell's London Journal, 1762–1763*, ed. F. A. Pottle (1950), p. 254.
12 Christopher Hibbert, *The Personal History of Samuel Johnson* (1984), pp. 121–2.
13 *Dr Johnson's House* (1977), p. 11.
14 Cobbett once lived over Johnson's old rooms in Bolt Court. Daniel Green, *Great Cobbett* (Oxford, 1983), p. 442.
15 William Kent, *London for Heretics* (1932), pp. 33–4.
16 Thomas Frost, *Forty Years' Recollections* (1880), pp. 35 ff.; for Edward Lloyd, see Victor Neuburg, *Popular Literature* (1977), pp. 170–4.
17 *Dictionary of National Biography, 1922–1930* (1937), p. 403.
18 Edgar Wallace, *A Short Autobiography* (1929), p. 31.
19 ibid., p. 163.
20 Margaret Lane, *Edgar Wallace* (1964), pp. 226, 282.
21 C. Mallet, *Anthony Hope and His Books* (1935), pp. 73–4.

Chapter 23: Tower Hill

1 A. L. Rowse, *The Tower of London in the History of the Nation* (1972), p. 141.
2 William Roper, *The Life of Sir Thomas More* (1822), pp. 94–5.
3 For an excellent short version of the diary in one volume see *The Shorter Pepys*, ed. Robert Latham (1985).

4 Charles Lamb, *The Essays of Elia* (n.d.), p. 29.
5 R. D. Altick, *The Shows of London* (Cambridge, Mass., 1978), p. 88;
   and Kenneth Fenwick (ed.), *The London Spy* (1955), pp. 243–4.
6 *The Diary of John Evelyn*. ed. John Bowle (Oxford, 1985), p. 234.
7 *Boswell's London Journal, 1762–1763*, ed. F. A. Pottle (1950), p. 245.
8 Maurice Richardson, introduction to *Old St Paul's* (1968), p. 14.

Chapter 24: Westminster

1 Harry Golombek, *Chess: A History* (New York, 1976), pp. 64–5.
2 N. F. Blake, *Caxton and His World* (1969), pp. 90–1.
3 Walter Besant, *Westminster* (1925), p. 193.
4 From the translation by Nevill Coghill (1977).
5 R. D. Altick, *The Shows of London* (Cambridge, Mass., 1978), p. 91.
6 R. Noel, *Life of Lord Byron* (1890), p. 204.
7 William Kent, *London for the Literary Pilgrim* (1949), p. 83.
8 *Boswell's London Journal, 1762–1763*, ed. F. A. Pottle (1950), p. 263.
9 *The Letters of William Morris*, ed. Philip Henderson (1967), p. 368.
10 Henry Pelling, *Winston Churchill* (1974), p. 54.
11 Edward Walford, *Old and New London*, Vol. 3 (n.d.), p. 522.
12 Edgar Johnson, *Charles Dickens: His Tragedy and Triumph* (1977),
    p. 187.
13 C. C. Southey, *The Life and Correspondence of Robert Southey* (1849),
    pp. 161–2.
14 Anne Humphreys, *Travels into the Poor Man's Country* (1977), p. 12.
15 M. D. George, *London Life in the Eighteenth Century* (1966), p. 74.
16 Besant, *Westminster*, pp. 3–4.
17 William Howitt, *Homes and Haunts of the British Poets* (1894), p. 62.
18 Hesketh Pearson, *The Life of Oscar Wilde* (1960), p. 290.
19 Gustave Doré and Douglas Jerrold, *London* (1970), p. 99.
20 Virginia Woolf, *Mrs Dalloway* (1976), p. 6.

Index of People

Titles have been placed under their author's entry. Where known, the dates of authors have been given.

with Dickens in Covent Garden
and the Strand, 67; in Lincoln's
Inn Fields, 116; 'biography' of
Dickens, 116
Fowles, John *(1926–)*, 210; *The
French Lieutenant's Woman* and
Haymarket, 210
Foyle, William *(1885–1963)*:
buried in Highgate Cemetery,
108
Freud, Sigmund *(1856–1930)*:
lives in Hampstead, 100
Fuller, Thomas *(1608–61)*: on
Jonson and Shakespeare,
185

Galsworthy, John *(1867–1933)*,
32, 205, 214; dies in
Hampstead, 97; memorial in
Highgate Cemetery, 108;
married in Mayfair, 168; *The
Forsyte Saga*, 97, and Soho,
205
Gandhi, M. K. *(1869–1948)*, 13
Garrick, David *(1717–79)*, 34, 66,
207, 224, 234; acts at St John's
Gate, 36; and Covent Garden
Theatre, 65–6; lives in Covent
Garden and the Strand, 65
Gaskell, Mrs Elizabeth *(1810–65)*,
158; born in Chelsea, 30–1;
North and South and Harley
Street, 158
Gaskell, Rev., William, 30
Gaunt, John of, 59, 112
Gay, John *(1685–1732)*, 35, 62,
112, 115, 154; in Chelsea, 27;
on Tottenham Court Road
fields, 83; and South Sea
Bubble, 219; memorial in
Westminster Abbey, 250–1; *The
Beggar's Opera*, 35, and the road
to Tyburn, 112, and Macheath
in Newgate, 190; *Trivia; or, The
Art of Walking the Streets* and
football in Covent Garden, 62,
and dangers of Lincoln's Inn
Fields, 115
Geary, Stephen, 107

Gentleman's Magazine, 35–6, 84,
234
George I, 14
George II, 177
Gibbon, Edward *(1737–94)*, 254;
on Ranelagh, 27; lives in
Marylebone, 154; *The Decline
and Fall of the Roman Empire*,
154
Gibbons, Grinling: font in St
James's, Piccadilly, 175–6
Gibbons, Stella *(1902–)*: writing
Cold Comfort Farm on tube, 57
Gibbons, Dr William: house in
Hampstead, 93
Gilbert, W. S. *(1836–1911)*, 52, 68,
169; baptised at St Paul's,
Covent Garden, 68; marries at
St Mary Abbots, Kensington,
135; *Patience* and parody of
Wilde, 169
Gill, Thomas, 159
Gissing, George *(1857–1903)*, 44,
71; on the British Museum, 13;
The Nether World and
Clerkenwell, 43, and East End,
71; *New Grub Street* and the
British Museum, 13, and
Fitzrovia, 87; *The Private Papers
of Henry Ryecroft* and the British
Museum, 13, and Fitzrovia, 87
Gladstone, W. E. *(1809–98)*, 212,
252; at Lincoln's Inn, 114; at
10 Downing Street, 181
Goldsmith, Oliver *(1730–74)*, 34,
121, 124, 127, 133, 144, 188,
224; at St John's Gate, 35;
visits Islington, 120; works
near Fleet Street, 236; buried
near Temple church, 237; *A
Citizen of the World* and
Vauxhall, 144; *The Vicar of
Wakefield*, 133, 235–6, and
Ranelagh, 26–7, and John
Newbery, 188
Gollancz, Victor *(1893–1967)*, 100;
founds Left Book Club, 70
Gordon, Lord George, 145, 146,
246

Index of Places

Bloomsbury, 9–21; Strype on its healthiness, 9; 'The Field of Forty Footsteps', 9–10; the Foundling Hospital, 10–11; Sloane at Bloomsbury Place, 11; British Museum and British Library, 12–13; Dr Williams's Library, 13–14, 197; Gordon Rioters and Bloomsbury Square, 14; Disraeli in Bloomsbury Square, 14; Dickens House, 15–16; Hospital for Sick Children, 16–17; Working Man's College, 17; Mudie's Circulating Library, 17–18; University College, 18, 19; University Church of Christ the King, 18; Birkbeck College, 18; Senate House, 18–19; Bloomsbury Group, 19–21; Hogarth Press, 20; Dorothy L. Sayers in, 21; T. S. Eliot and, 21

British Museum, 9, 15, 20, 24, 109, 210; Sloane's collection, 11, 24; Montagu House, 12, 24; Reading Room, 12–13; Dickens at, 15

Carlyle's House, 28–30; Thomas and Jane Carlyle move to Chelsea, 28; Carlyle and noise, 28–9; death of Jane, 29

Charterhouse, 38, 40–1, 200; Thackeray's 'Slaughterhouse', 41; John Wesley in playground, 200

Cheapside, 184, 192; Chaucer's apprentice, 184; George Borrow on, 192

Chelsea, 2, 11, 22–33; mural in Town Hall, 22; Sir Thomas More in, 23–4; Crosby Hall, 24; Chelsea Old Church, 23, 25, 27, 30, 33; Sir Hans Sloane and the Manor of Chelsea, 24–5; Don Saltero's, 25; Chelsea Hospital, 25; Ranelagh Gardens, 25–7; Chelsea Bunhouse, 27; Monmouth House, 27; Carlyle's House, 28–9; Leigh Hunt in Chelsea, 29; Karl Marx in Chelsea, 29–30; St Luke's and Dickens, 30; Cheyne Walk, 30–1; Wilde in Tite Street, 31–2; Wilde's arrest at the Cadogan Hotel, 32; Arnold Bennett in Netherton Grove, 32; Royal Court Theatre, 32–3; Wodehouse in, 33; James, Eliot and Fleming in Carlyle Mansions, 33

The City, 1–8, 183–93, 241–7; Kenneth Grahame at the Bank of England, 1–3; Lamb and Mill at the East India Company, 2; P. G. Wodehouse in, 2–3; T. S. Eliot in, 2–3, 4; Dickens and Mr Beadnell, 4; Mr and Mrs Pooter at the Mansion House Ball, 4–5; Pope and Dickens on the Monument, 5; Dick Whittington and St Michael's, Paternoster Royal, 6; John Stow and St Andrew Undershaft, 6; Pepys nearly mugged by St Dunstan-in-the-East, 7; T. S. Eliot and St

London
Behold he

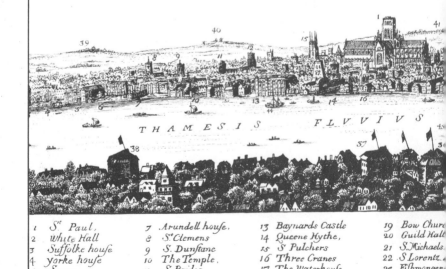

1	St. Paul.	7	Arundell house.	13	Baynards Castle	19	Bow Churc
2	White Hall	8	St. Clemens	14	Queene Hythe,	20	Guild Hall
3	Suffolke house	9	S. Dunstane	15	S Pulchers	21	S. Michaels.
4	Yorke house	10	The Temple.	16	Three Cranes	22	S Lorentz.
5	Savoy	11	S. Brides	17	The Waterhouse	23	Fishmongers
6	Somerset house	12	S. Andrew,	18	The Stillyarde	24	The Old Su